D0314511

[for other titles and publications please see back of book]

THE MESSIAH

THE MESSIAH

THE
MESSIAH

The Apostolic Foundation of the Christian Church
Volume Three

JOHN METCALFE

JOHN METCALFE PUBLISHING TRUST
Tylers Green Chapel · Penn · Buckinghamshire

John Metcalfe Publishing Trust
Penn, Buckinghamshire

—

First published 1978
Reprinted 1980

—

Copyright John Metcalfe Publishing Trust, 1978
All rights reserved

—

ISBN 0 9502515 8 5

—

Printed by M. & A. Thomson Litho Ltd.
East Kilbride
by arrangement with HM Repros
Glasgow

—

Price £2.45

J. M. P. T.

FOREWORD
by
Christian Puritz

FOREWORD

John Metcalfe has outstanding gifts as an exponent of scripture and as a preacher of the word, and these are abundantly evident in this his latest book. Equally evident are the fruits of many years of arduous study, earnest prayer with strong crying and tears, and spiritual exercise in the word of God, arising from a vital regeneration out of a completely irreligious state, a clear call to the work of the ministry, an overwhelming sense of helpless need to be taught of God what that gospel was that the apostles preached and the early saints believed, and a determination as much as in him lay to preach that gospel faithfully in his own day, as a servant of Jesus Christ. Many and deep have been his soul exercises also about the confused and chaotic state of the church, and her failure to answer to that which was in the beginning.

These exercises, and a steadfast pursuit of righteousness respecting them, have given rise to many sore and prolonged afflictions, both spiritual and providential — most heartbreaking of all, the refusal over decades of the church at large to hear and to face the issues — but have resulted also in a remarkable degree of entrance into and understanding of the mind of Christ as expressed in the scriptures; so that Mr. Metcalfe's approach is both thoroughly intelligent and truly spiritual, and *The Messiah* is marked by rare perceptiveness, insight into the heart of the doctrine, and unction.

The book deals with Matthew's portrayal of Jesus Christ as the Messiah, and of the kingdom of heaven which he came to bring in. A powerful introduction contrasts this spiritual kingdom with the external magnificence of the Old Testament ritual, and conveys the distinctive emphasis of Matthew's account. Indeed, one of the most valuable features of the book is the treatment where appropriate of the differences between the gospels. For instance, the contrasting genealogies and the different accounts of the birth of Jesus, in Matthew and Luke, are considered with great care and with real spiritual insight, so refreshingly unlike the explanations commonly accepted today. The thoughtful reader, who may have been perplexed by such differences and is not content just to ignore them, will find this very helpful indeed, both enlightening and spiritually edifying.

Throughout the book the truth is brought to bear on the situation of today, for the opening of the word of God is never an academic exercise. Some will no doubt be offended at the great plainness of speech with which this is done, but the true saints of God will rejoice to hear the trumpet give no uncertain sound, and will respond to the unmistakable ring of authority that marks John Metcalfe's ministry.

However, undoubtedly the great emphasis of the book is positive. It proclaims the Lord Jesus as the Messiah, the King of Israel, the Saviour of the world, in a way that cannot but bless and edify the reader who is serious after God. May many such readers be found for this book, and may the thoughtful reading of it and the sober consideration of the issues that it raises contribute to the bringing in of obedience to the faith among all nations, for his name.

Christian Wilhelm Puritz, Esq. B.A. (Oxon) Ph.D.

CONTENTS

* Ch. and v. references apply to The Gospel According to Matthew.

THE MESSIAH

INTRODUCTION

THE FIRST gospel declares the life of Jesus Christ so as to show his royal line of descent from the seed of Abraham. By right of inheritance Jesus Christ is heir to the throne of David the king. He is the long-awaited Messiah, the Anointed of God.

Hitherto in Israel the Old Testament kings had been marked out with anointing oil in the name of the Lord by the priestly house of Aaron. But no longer. For with the advent of Messias that time was fulfilled; it was over forever. Now at length the fulness of time was come. The Day had dawned: light had broken forth from the east, and lo, the Sun of Righteousness arose with healing in his beams.

Immediately the people which sat in darkness saw great light; to them which sat in the region and shadow of death the light sprang up: it was the visitation of the Dayspring from on high, and with the dawning the shadows fled away. The Son of God had come, the true seed of Abraham and real Son of David, the Elect, the Chosen of God whom the Father himself had anointed — not by man with oil, but

1

with the Holy Ghost sent down from heaven — King and
Priest of the most high God.

The gospel according to Matthew proclaims Jesus to be
the Messiah; the evangelist heralds him as the Anointed of
God. This revelation of Jesus Christ is set against the
background of the kingdom of God. Not only does the
writer relate the life of Jesus to the kingdom, but moreover
Matthew unfolds the nature of that kingdom itself: a thing
without which no man would grasp its character. Typified
materially and physically by Israel in the Old Testament,
with the coming of the Son of David came the heavenly
antitype and spiritual fulfilment of the kingdom of God.

The old earthly kingdom had waxed old and was ready
to fade away: the new heavenly kingdom was at hand and
should endure forever. Of this kingdom Jesus Christ the
son of David the son of Abraham was the heir. Hence
Matthew demonstrates that to understand the life of Jesus
Christ one must see it as a life inextricably bound up with
the kingdom of God. That is what his life is about.

Although the kingdom of God was at hand, it was not
an evident reality to men: it was a heavenly vision. It was
not a tangible fact: it was a spiritual conception. But Jesus'
eye discerned that vision, his doctrine formulated that
conception, his heart yearned to bring it in for God, and
his life and death were dedicated to its realisation. But both
he, his vision, his doctrine, and the very kingdom itself
were despised, rejected and totally repudiated by the Jews
in particular and Israel in general. For these things' sake
was the kingdom of God perpetually taken from them as a
people — to whom naturally it had pertained — and given
to a spiritual nation bringing forth the fruits thereof. These
are the things about which Matthew writes and which are

unfolded so methodically in his narrative of the life of Jesus Christ.

What Jesus saw, and what the Jews saw, were always two entirely different things, and this is reflected throughout the book. What God would bring in by Jesus Christ, and what the Jews wanted God to retain were also diametrically opposed; this colours the book vividly. Notwithstanding, the purposes of God are sure, and stand forever. These purposes commence unfolding very early in the gospel, and do so with a sovereignty precisely commensurate with and parallel to the ever-increasing malice and enmity of the Jews and their Judaistic system against both the Messiah and his kingdom.

To this heavenly kingdom the Jews were utterly blind; it eluded them completely. Yet they were adamant in their conviction that they could see clearly what God willed: where his delight was. Was it not obvious from the scriptures? Settled forever was the kingdom of Israel, the holy land of earthly inheritance. Jerusalem below with its temple, altar, sacrifices, hierarchy, priests, ceremonies. Yonder were the synagogues, beyond the Diaspora: had they not compassed heaven and earth to gain one proselyte? Had they not blessed the world, taken truth to the Gentiles? And truth, objective truth, not subjective feelings and opinions: it was the law and the prophets; the psalms and the oracles. As to interpretation, this was traditionally settled: there were the proper scribes to expound it. Ah, venerable Talmud; Oh, reverend tradition. Blest sabbath rest to contemplate such divinity!

Behold, the great feasts, the high days, the holy-days, the fast days, the solemn assemblies! Lo, the stately processions, the dignified ritual, the resonant accompaniment. See, the ringlets of the Nazarites, the excellent phylacteries, such learned Rabbis, such long robes, such enlarged fringes. Ah, what learning, what ancient doctrine, what a body of interpreted laws; such external order and glory: all this! What else could be the ultimate expression and embodiment of God's final thought? Were they not the circumcised? Had their bodies not been washed with pure water? Were they not all the children of Abraham? Well then. All that remained was for Messias to come and assert the glory and renown of Israel. Then at last the ignorant and obstinate Gentiles would appreciate the facts. Meantime they of Israel were the custodians of all that God could ever really value, to which he was irrevocably committed. As to this Jesus fellow, he seemed utterly blind to these things, they seemed to elude him completely.

These absolutely contrary views of the kingdom of God appear throughout the gospel. What Jesus envisaged as opposed to the entire system of the Jews' religion — morally as well as materially — were two completely different things. That heavenly vision to which the Messiah was not disobedient, but which drew his willing feet, was nonexistent to the Jews. It simply wasn't there, and moreover couldn't be! How could they then understand his speech or comprehend his pathway, when his object was an invisible kingdom and God in a way clean foreign to all their understanding of him? However they were sure that they were the kingdom — who were in fact but the shadow of it — and that their knowledge of God was the correct knowledge — notwithstanding the obscuring veil.

From the very beginning, what the Jews expected God to justify individually and nationally, and that for which Jesus came and which he yearned to bring in for the Father's good pleasure, were two things totally opposed in very principle the one to the other. The realisation, the surfacing, the clear emergence and the final conflict of these two great principles strongly appears in Matthew. Indeed, without appreciating this, or realising these facts, it is doubtful if the book can be understood aright. It is no good looking for 'peace' in Matthew. As to the religious system of Judaism, in very essence it is that to which Jesus came to bring a sword. Look for the sword. But it is the sword of the Spirit. On the other side of its clean verbal cut lies a free justification, a heavenly kingdom, a spiritual house, an interior circumcision, and an inheritance in the world to come.

Therefore I repeat, the first gospel presents the life of Jesus Christ in his progress on earth as Messiah, uniformly and constantly, and always against just this conflicting 'kingdom' background. Everything else, including chronology, as well as the mere recitation of his wonderful life and work, everything else is made subservient to the grand end of demonstrating from Jesus' life the kind of Messiah that he is, and the sort of kingdom which he establishes.

● ● ●

I THE ADVENT OF MESSIAH

AND THE KINGDOM

CHAPTER 1:1 TO CHAPTER 4:25

MATTHEW CHAPTER ONE

¶ The genealogy of Jesus Christ. Ch. 1:1-17

The Gospel according to Matthew opens immediately with

'The book of the generation of Jesus Christ,
'the son of David,
'the son of Abraham.'

Mt. 1:1

This commencement is unique amongst the four gospels. Of the other three only Luke gives a genealogy at all and this does not occur until the second half of the third chapter, in connection with the Lord's ministry. Moreover it differs from that in Matthew. Only Matthew opens with a genealogy, and only Matthew gives a genealogy in order to *prove* by it Jesus' descent and therefore rightful inheritance. That is the object in view as Matthew begins his book.

The copying of the book of the generation, plus the account of the virgin birth, takes up the whole of the first chapter. Matthew is writing after the departure of Messias out of this world, so as to demonstrate to the Jews in retrospect that this same Jesus whom they took and by wicked hands crucified and slew, whom God raised up, was and is indeed the Anointed of God, the very Christ.

In view of the power and glory which the Jews associated with the coming of Messiah, and his kingly reign, to them such a claim was incredible. It was preposterous. It could not be entertained, if on no other ground than that of the obscurity and miserable poverty of those whom they supposed were Jesus' natural parents. So insignificant! They could not possibly have any royal descent; and if not, neither could their offspring.

Therefore of necessity Matthew's first consideration must be to repudiate this slur, and to establish that claim. In verse one he deals with the slur by the emphasis upon 'David'. Of what poorer appearance, supposed they, was Jesus than that unheeded shepherd boy who was despised by his brethren, discounted by his parents, and overlooked by Samuel the prophet? And who was less than poor Abram at the beginning of his sojourn, when he forsook all that he had and went forth not knowing whither he went, but confessing himself 'a pilgrim and stranger on the earth'?

Besides this, let the Jews consider — since they got their proud name from Judah — under what circumstance and from whom

'Judas begat Phares and Zara' ! *Mt. 1:3*

Matthew pursues his advantage: Ye that boast in Abraham, Judah, and David the great king: of what profession originally was Boaz' mother? You who glory in appearance, what was Boaz' wife more than a poor and obscure Moabitess? Yet the one was an ancestor, and the other the great grandmother of David your king! Come to that, how and of whom did the great king beget Solomon? Then why so many slurs on grounds of poverty, obscurity or meanness, upon the true Son of David? Such 'slurs' rightly interpreted, are not disqualifications at all: they enhance Jesus' claim. Conversely, they demean his traducers.

As to the claim: it was perfectly just. This was his genealogy in fact, as any Jew might trace; though none bothered. They had the records: they kept the books: doubtless Matthew referred to their own copies. Why did they not go and examine the matter? What more interesting? It is a king's descent and more: a royal line of divine origin. He is Messiah. His is the kingdom. Is it not written in the book of the generation?

Regarding the kingdom of God, all the enlightened in Israel must admit what was well known: it originated in the promises made to Abraham, confirmed through Isaac, and established in Jacob. However, the Jews mistook the shadow for the substance, the form for the reality, the figure for the true. 'For they are not all Israel, which are of Israel: neither, because they are the seed of Abraham, are they all children: but, In Isaac shall thy seed be called.' This long-awaited seed was Christ. Jesus, sprung of Juda, called in Isaac, was the one intended by this passage. Therefore in the profoundest sense he qualifies as 'the son of Abraham'.

Far more so than Isaac, if the Jews could but perceive it!

8

Let them consider: Isaac was begotten by Abraham in a figure: first by promise, second by the Spirit, and thirdly from the dead.

Now, firstly, Isaac was promised to Abraham in his old age; but Jesus was promised to humanity from the dawn of time. If the literal son of Abraham had been the true child of promise — and not but one of a vast number of types or shadows of that child, beginning ages before Isaac was conceived — of what further need was there long after Isaac was dead, for the prophets to continue speaking of a promised seed yet to come? And if so, then of whom did they prophesy? Of Jesus, the seed of Abraham, the child of promise.

Secondly, Isaac was figuratively born of the Spirit. That is, Abraham had been circumcised. This was a figure — for the time then present — of the removal of the flesh in connection with the conception of Abraham's seed. Symbolically, Isaac was not born after the flesh. As regards his birth, it had been taken away. Then how and of what was he born? Circumcision was the sign that he had been born of God and therefore born through the powerful operation of God's Spirit. But it was not really so: it was figuratively so. But figurative of whom? Why, of the Son of Abraham yet to come, even Jesus Christ.

He was born wholly without the processes of nature: there was nothing, but nothing, of the flesh in his conception. A Virgin conceived. This was by the powerful operation of God's Spirit in fact: 'The Holy Ghost shall come upon thee, and the power of the Highest shall overshadow thee: therefore also that holy thing which shall be born of thee shall be called the Son of God.' That which was conceived in her was of the Holy

Ghost. And who other than the true Isaac, the seed of Abraham?

In the third place, Isaac was begotten from the dead in a figure. What figure? That figure when 'Abraham considered not his own body now dead, when he was about an hundred years old, neither yet the deadness of Sara's womb.' Out of those conditions Isaac was born, conditions sufficiently staggering to warrant the statement that he was 'begotten from the dead in a figure'. If so, then a figure of whom? Why, of him that was to come, the true Son of Abraham, who was begotten from the dead in fact. That is, Jesus; there is none other.

Consider this Son of David. Perhaps the most important qualification to the Jews in looking for their Messiah was that he should be of David's royal line. But that is precisely what Matthew asserts of Jesus from the very first instant:

> The book of the generation of
> Jesus Christ, the son of David.

As he himself said to them, 'What think ye of Christ? whose son is he? They say unto him, The Son of David. He saith unto them, How then doth David in spirit call him Lord, saying, The LORD said unto my Lord, Sit thou on my right hand, till I make thine enemies thy footstool? If David then call him Lord, how is he his son? And no man was able to answer him a word.' Of course not; because the most important qualification for which in fact they ought to have looked in their Messiah they not only seemed to have regarded as a disqualification, but its evidence mounted their fury against him to a raging frenzy! Because he was the Son of God. But above all, Messias should be the Son of God. Of necessity, he must be David's Lord, the mighty God, Emmanuel, God with us. *Therefore* a virgin shall conceive and bear a Son.

No doubt as to his manhood Messiah should be of Judah, of the royal line. It must needs be that of the fruit of David's loins, according to the flesh, God would raise up Christ. Verily Jesus Christ was the king's son, and that from the virgin's womb: 'Of the seed of David according to the flesh.' But of far greater moment was the truth that he must be also the Son of God, come from everlasting Deity. David knew this, and prophesied of the same, in spirit calling Jesus Christ 'Lord'. Why did not the Jews?

David said, 'The LORD said unto my Lord, Sit thou at my right hand.' But who has been by the right hand of God exalted? David himself? No. David prophesied of another, the Messiah. It is evident that David never ascended into the heavens because he said himself, The LORD said unto *my* Lord, Sit *thou*. Not David. Besides the patriarch David is both dead and buried, and his sepulchre is with us unto this day. Then of whom did he prophesy? Evidently of one exalted to the heavens! But who has ascended to those heights? Solomon? Certainly not; he died and was gathered unto his fathers. Therefore David prophesied of one whose humiliated life at the hands of the Jews on earth would be so honoured of God after his death that he should be exalted to God's right hand. But this is precisely what happened to Jesus Christ.

Jesus Christ was David's Lord and was also his son. As to his deity, he was ever One with the Father. He thought it not robbery to be equal with God. He was God. So David called him Lord. As to his humanity, Mary was his virgin mother, a daughter of Zion, sprung of Juda, offspring of David, and married to Joseph. Therefore he was David's son. This same Jesus hath God raised up to the right hand of the Majesty on high. He is a king and a priest. King of righteousness, for he brought in everlasting righteousness by his own blood. King of peace, for the effect of righteousness shall be peace: we have peace with God through our Lord Jesus Christ. A priest forever after the order of Melchizedek.

None but Jesus could ever have the remotest shadow of qualification for the unique demands made by this title

'the son of David'.

Yet Jesus fulfils every qualification, meets all the demands, surmounts them, exceeds them, transcends them, and answers uniquely and superabundantly to the title over and over and over again. Then why did the Jews crucify him?

The 'book of the generation of Jesus Christ' occupies the first sixteen verses of chapter one; it runs from Abraham through David to the captivity and on until the birth of the Messiah. Doubtless this genealogy was copied from the Jewish records apart perhaps from Matthew's dry comments about Judah and David's proclivities, and the mention of Salmon and Boaz' wives. Also it is very obvious that Matthew has contributed verse sixteen, the birth of Jesus Christ.

The Jewish records copied by Matthew were not quite the same as those recorded in the Chronicles. For example, the line from David to the captivity in I Chronicles 3 included three kings which the copy deliberately expurgates. However a precedent had been set by the biblical original, for in I Chronicles 3:11 the entire six-year reign of Queen Athaliah was completely ignored, as if it had never occurred. And not only the reign; the very name of this woman — the offspring of Ahab and Jezebel's house — was omitted from its place. She is blotted out of God's book.

Therefore it is not without precedent that the Jewish copy goes one further. Nor without justice either, for, Exodus 20:5

'I the LORD thy God am a jealous God
'visiting the iniquity of the fathers
'upon the children
'unto the third and fourth generation
'of them that hate me.'

So the Jews set to work with a will, and, not being satisfied with the removal of Queen Athaliah's name alone, they blotted out her children unto the third generation, expunging Ahaziah, Joash and Amaziah. And why not? The Holy Ghost by Matthew accepts the testimony of their copy in the book of the generation of Jesus Christ.

As to the origin of the 'book of the generation', there are those who have imagined that Matthew himself composed it, transcribing the genealogy from the book of Chronicles. But if so, then with an absent mind! Quite apart from Athaliah's three kings, yet a further instance of discrepancy — between I Chronicles 3 and the 'book of the generation' — might be pointed out from Matthew 1:11-12, where the expression 'Jechonias and his brethren' substitutes for the actual names of those 'brethren' in I Chronicles chapter three.

It would have carried little weight with the Jewish hierarchy had Matthew — a private individual — taken it upon himself to alter I Chronicles 3 by the arbitrary omission first of three kings and then of Jeconiah's absent brethren. Especially were such cavalier treatment to form the basis of an appeal to Israel that the genealogy *now* gave three lots of fourteen generations from Abraham to Christ! They would have laughed Matthew to scorn. Well, why not leave out a few more, ironically the Jews might have recommended, making it cycles of twelve to equal the number of the tribes? Or why not — but then, the permutations of arbitrariness are endless. Stupid conjecture! Whatever has happened since, the church in Matthew's day was not led by asinine fools, forever proposing monumental inanities.

Imagine the apostle Matthew testifying for Jesus Christ to the Jews upon a basis of figures conjured up by his own deliberate and sly manipulation of their sacred scriptures! But it was both inspired and brilliant to commence such an advocacy by invoking their own official priestly records rather than appealing directly to the longer Chronicles, from which those records had been condensed. It was their own testimony, and, their own children being witness, it had led directly to Jesus Christ.

What more apt than for Matthew to use the Jews' own witness to the son of David, the son of Abraham? Especially when, unwittingly, the very records of Judaism had created a veritable *coup de grâce* against themselves. As a result of their own sense of fitness and abbreviation, the span of time from Abraham to Jesus — punctuated by the salient events of Israel's history — now fell perfectly into symmetric intervals of fourteen generations each. They had said it!

They scoff? Will they then treat lightly their father Abraham? God forbid. He was the very beginning of Israel, it was his seed. Very well then; what was the next event in Israel of commensurate importance? The establishment of the kingdom under David the king. Granted. It was fourteen generations. So let them count in their book until a further fourteen generations. At what point do they arrive? At 'Jechonias and his brethren'. But that was the third major crisis in Israel's history: the carrying away into Babylon.

It is by two or three witnesses that — saith the law of Moses — every matter is established. Now therefore let the Jews search their record beyond the two lots of fourteen generations created by no arbitrary count, but by the commencement of Israel, the establishment of the kingdom, and the dissolution of the kingdom. Already they have the witness from Abraham through fourteen generations on to David and again a further fourteen up to the captivity. Seek a third to establish the testimony of time beyond a peradventure: count fourteen again in the Jews' book. *Verily, it was their own lifetime!* Well, what of paramount, superlative — it is not *more* than three witnesses — importance had occurred around and about that moment in their own lifetime? *Nothing*, they say?

Well, maybe a vision in the temple. Something; like, a repetition of Sarah's conception, a priest struck dumb, and of course Elijah the prophet born. Nothing much, you see. Oh, and there was that star seen in the east. Nothing?

Nothing but a virgin great with child. Nothing but heavenly messages, divine dreams, angelic visitations. Nothing save a thousand scriptures fulfilled and fourteen generations threefold determined. Nothing but Anna's prophecy and Simeon's departure. Nothing but a dumb tongue loosed to declare the fulfilment of ancient promises, the answer to the sure mercies of David, and the redemption of the oath made to our father Abraham. Nothing but the power of the Highest, nothing but the Holy Ghost, nothing but the Son of God.

Nothing but the angel of the Lord, nothing but the archangel Gabriel, nothing but the glory of God flaring and lighting heaven and earth. Nothing but a multitude of the heavenly host praising God and saying 'Glory to God in the highest, and on earth peace, good will toward men.' Nothing but God manifest in the flesh; nothing but God, the Word, made flesh; nothing but Emmanuel, God with us. Nothing but a baby. Nothing. Nothing to you, ye Jews that passed by. Nothing. Less than nothing. Fourteen generations of nothing.

*

Evidently the very records kept in Judea to preserve the knowledge of David's royal line were those used by Matthew to form the basis and substance of the 'book of the generation of Jesus Christ'. They bore overwhelming testimony from the Jews against themselves concerning the one whom they had both despised and rejected. The records themselves decreed the claim of Jesus Christ to the throne of David. A title, incidentally, which the ancient prophecy of Jeremiah had made impossible to realise for any other of David's successors since King Jechonias. A claim, therefore, reserved for the unique exception of Jesus Christ.

Consider the impasse created by the prophecy of Jeremiah 22:30 to King Jeconiah, also called Jehoiachin, Jechonias or Coniah

> 'Thus saith the LORD,
>
> 'Write ye this man childless,
>
> 'a man that shall not prosper in his days:
>
> 'for no man of his seed shall prosper,
>
> 'sitting upon the throne of David,
>
> 'and ruling any more in Judah.'

So ended David's dynasty. True, for a few years the King of Babylon — having deported everything and everyone except the poorest in the land — made Jeconiah's uncle, Zedekiah, a kind of vassal governor over the squalid remains of Judah. But the last king of David's line had fallen, and ever since the throne had remained vacant and the claim void.

Jeremiah's curse of reprobation upon the dynasty since Jeconiah prevented any of the blood-royal descendants from inheriting the vacant throne.

On the other hand, constitutionally they were the proper heirs. Thus the throne could not legally pass from them to others of David's house not directly in the line of succession. A complete impasse. First; the promise required the seed of David to occupy the throne forever. Second; the curse prevented the exclusive royal line ever from occupying that throne. And finally — effectively blocking any attempt to break the deadlock by a series of abdications — tradition forbad the voluntary passing of the throne rights from the close royal family and seed to other more remote relations who were notwithstanding still of David's house.

17

Humanly impossible, legally insoluble, this predicament
of divine ordination shut up the Jews to the salvation of
God. Its perfect resolution was declared in the book of the
generation of Jesus Christ. This unique son and heir of
David annulled the curse yet retained the inheritance!

As the son of Mary, Jesus was really and truly of David's
flesh — *made* of the seed of David according to the flesh —
although by her he was not of that branch of the family in
line of succession to the throne. Therefore as the seed of
the woman alone considered, Jesus could not inherit the
throne: but on the other hand, he could not inherit the
attendant curse either! He was not of that direct royal line
in the flesh, albeit as to the flesh he was by his mother
truly of the house of David. Thus he fulfilled the vital
qualification that 'Of the fruit of David's loins, according
to the flesh, God would raise up Christ.' But then, what of
the crown-rights exclusive to the royal succession?

Now, Joseph was of David's house no less than Mary his
wife and her son Jesus. More. In Joseph's case the branch
of the family *was* of that exclusive royal line: and in direct
descent, too. Therefore by birthright to Joseph pertained
the long-neglected crown: he was the true heir to the
throne of David. But of course, as such, by prophecy he
must also inherit the curse of Jehoiachin — he could never
occupy the throne nor would he wear that crown.
Moreover, as this had come to him, so it would pass by
birth to his son. That is, to his *natural* firstborn son; for the
curse was to the actual *seed* of Jehoiachin in perpetuity.

However the unique connection between Jesus and
Joseph the husband of Mary, brought Jesus into the
position of firstborn and heir to Joseph without being of
his flesh. As such Jesus inherits all the legal and titular

18

rights of the direct heir to the throne and crown of David the king. He was *born* King of the Jews. Yet absolutely, he is in no way whatever connected with the *seed* of Joseph, and therefore it follows neither was he of Jehoiachin: consequently, he could not possibly be subject to the prophetic curse of disqualification from the throne.

So it came to pass that what baffled all the ingenuity of man to resolve, God easily achieved. Though it had seemed impossible, sublimely the Lord God soared over all the perplexities giving to Jesus the throne of his father David, so that he should reign over the house of Jacob forever, and of his kingdom there should be no end. Only God could — but according to promise God did — raise up an horn of salvation for us in the house of his servant David, as he spake by the mouth of his holy prophets, which have been since the world began.

The symmetric cycle of three fourteen generations clearly demonstrates that upon neither Jesus' predecessors nor upon his successors does the finger of time fall so unerringly. Time itself cried from the skies 'Thou art the Man!' Forty-two generations since Abraham. The covenant was fulfilled. The promise to the twelve tribes had come to pass. Indeed, divided by twelve, the very generations themselves witnessed the mystical 'time and times and half a time' to the coming of their Prince.

It is the royal line to the King of the Jews. Matthew 2:2 'Where is he that is born King of the Jews?' This genealogy is that of Jesus' royal title of inheritance in Joseph. His right to the throne of David which had passed — over the generations — in direct succession to Mary's husband. Of this the angel of the Lord testifies, Matthew 1:20, saying 'Joseph, thou son of David, fear not!'

The 'book of the generation' is the record of the proper royal succession. As such it does not necessarily show an unbroken line of descent from father to son. It is the legal line of title, a line of inheritance. It is a question of the one to whom prior right pertains.

For example, suppose a king — an only son — having no issue, or only female issue; should he die in battle, having neither sons nor brethren the crown might well pass to his surviving uncle. And thereafter to that uncle's son. Yet in the genealogy the names of the King, the Uncle, and the Uncle's Son would be connected in succession by the word 'begat'. A royal genealogy therefore shows the passage of the crown, which must always pass to the nearest qualifying male of the blood-royal: but by no means is that necessarily a son.

So it came to pass that the long-neglected title to the throne of David came to Joseph not by direct descent but by proper legal succession. That is what the genealogy in Matthew is about, and why the formula of connection from one heir to the next is ἐγέννησεν: *beget, give origin, produce*. A much more broadly based word for succession than that indicating 'the son of', which allows no latitude at all. 'Beget' may refer to a son; but just as easily it might be used of a nephew. Or even an uncle. It is wholly a question of an heir to the throne 'produced' by the incumbent who ἐγέννησεν, 'gives rise to', a successor. He has 'begotten' him *to that throne*.

The legal form of royal genealogy traces the crown from generation to generation irrespective of the *exact* personal relationship between one king and the next in line. To do so the record uses the broad formula 'begat': not 'to give birth to a son', but *to give genesis, constitute* a new king.

Of course, usually this will be a son. But at least in one case the nephew was succeeded by his uncle; this would be indicated by 'begat' just the same as if the nephew were followed by his own offspring. The thing to grasp is that such a royal genealogy is *the ancestry of the crown*. And that is precisely what we have in Matthew, onwards from 'David the king'.

Not so in Luke. The genealogy in the gospel according to Luke is actually a register of births from father to son. Save that the order of names descends in Matthew — David to Joseph — whereas it ascends in Luke — Joseph to David — the generations are recorded between David and Joseph in both gospels. Yet between the two, the names vary considerably: they are quite different. The reason being that whereas the one follows the legal title to the throne the other propounds a personal family tree. In other words, both Matthew and Luke span the generations between Joseph and David, but whereas Matthew records the crown, Luke traces the seed.

Because of this fact the word used in Luke to connect the generations differs from Matthew. In Matthew it was ἐγέννησεν 'beget', or, 'produce'. In Luke however the English translation reads 'the son of', indicating a difference in the original between Matthew and Luke.

Observe Luke 3:23.

'And Jesus himself began to be about thirty
years of age, being (as was supposed) the
son of Joseph, which was *the son* of Heli.'

After the initial υἱός, *son*, the connection between generations is given consistently by the word τοῦ, *of*, so as to

21

read 'the son of' right to the end of the genealogy. Since Luke commences that genealogy by asserting categorically that it belonged to Joseph, and Joseph alone, we must not be surprised that many theologians, clerics, doctors and learned brethren have laboured hard and long in the vain attempt to prove that the ancestry actually belonged to Mary. This was because they could not explain why the two genealogies differed since both are said emphatically to be 'of Joseph'. Unwilling to admit defeat, they made one 'of Mary'.

¶ The birth of Jesus Christ. Ch. 1:18-25

Now the birth of Jesus Christ was on this wise: When as his mother Mary was espoused to Joseph, before they came together, she was found with child of the Holy Ghost. It is amazing that so simple and restrained a statement should be used to usher in such tremendous truth. 'She was found with child of the Holy Ghost.' The narrative is almost matter-of-fact. Yet beneath this calm announcement lies revelation sublime beyond measure, surpassing the very creation itself for the manifestation of the glory of God.

But the restraint is designed. Furthermore it is not unique to Matthew. Indeed, of the four gospels, two do not record these events at all. Not a word. Luke however does expound them, developing in order and at far greater depth the circumstances of the birth of Jesus Christ from the work of God in and toward Mary. The reverse is true of the other account — the first gospel — in which Joseph is prominent, Mary hardly figures, and brevity is the rule.

22

What is the reason for these differences? Are we to con-clude that Luke discovered sources unavailable to Matthew, and that conversely Matthew remembered details hidden from Luke? Is that likely? On the contrary, we may be sure that Luke knew virtually every detail with which Matthew was acquainted, and certainly Matthew — being a ready scribe in the kingdom of God — would have had perfect understanding of all things from the very first. If so, then the inclusion or exclusion of detail depended upon nothing more nor less than the leading of the Spirit of God.

Besides, from what we know of the four evangelists, Matthew and Luke were the two least likely to have had the best 'sources' concerning Jesus' birth and childhood. However, the Spirit elected them and them alone to write the record. By critical standards, Mark — associated with Peter — and John would have been far more eligible for the distinction. Because Peter and John were the ones most intimate and personal with Jesus, frequently being favoured with especial insights and confidences. Early reminiscences from both Jesus and his mother were far more likely to have been their privilege than that of the others.

Yet Mark and John wrote never a word about the actual birth, in spite of such knowledge. Indeed, they would hardly have needed sources: they were the sources! But the Spirit was Lord, and he chose not to use them but to use their brethren. To this Peter and John gladly submitted without envy or rancour, knowing full well that what they were restrained from writing — to which intellectually they were so suited — their fellow-servants were commanded of the Lord to express.

Well then, what about Matthew and Luke? Luke wrote the full account: Matthew touched on the matter.

But — since we must be rational — of the two, logically, which one would most readily have had access to 'sources' acquainted with the circumstances of Jesus' birth?

Matthew? Called almost from the beginning, he saw the Lord with his own eyes, looked upon him, handled him, heard him. He ate, drank, slept, travelled in company with Jesus and the disciples for years. So almost certainly he would have become acquainted with such as Zacharias, Elisabeth, John the Baptist, Mary and Anna.

Or Luke? He was not in Galilee or Judea with the Lord for the whole period covered by the Lord's earthly ministry. Luke never knew Jesus. He was not one of the disciples as we know them in the gospels. Luke never appears in the New Testament until after the ascension, and only then in association with Paul and in connection with the evangelisation of the Gentiles.

So tell me: To write the full account of the early days at Bethlehem, which of the two would have been the rational choice? The opposite to the one chosen! Therefore in the things of God one should remember that it is written — and repeated — 'I will destroy the wisdom of the wise, and will bring to nothing the understanding of the prudent.'

Now someone — anxious to put man and not God at the source of things — will say to me, 'But Luke had this special access and exclusive relationship to Mary, whom he alone questioned so profoundly: she was the source for the early Lucan chapters.' Oh? And are we to conclude that Mary was not so free with the apostles of the Lord Jesus that she only unlocked this information for some new believer from abroad? Or must we presume that Matthew, Mark, and

John were so desultory in 'searching diligently' that such data lay beyond their endeavours?

Or perhaps we are required to swallow that Luke was the one to find Mary, lost to the other evangelists? If so, where did he find her: he who sought so long after the ascension of the Son of God? Where? But we know her address.

Perhaps not before the Cross; certainly afterwards. 'Now there stood by the cross of Jesus his mother ... when Jesus therefore saw his mother, and the disciple standing by, whom he loved, he saith unto his mother, Woman, behold thy son! Then saith he to the disciple, Behold thy mother! And from that hour that disciple took her unto his own home.' And there, many years later, Luke would have found her. And John. Maybe Matthew, Peter, and Mark too.

Are we seriously required to accept the sheer irrationalism of academic infidelity, and believe that Mary told this new stranger things hidden from her 'son', and others the eye-witnesses and apostles of the Lord Jesus, her companions those decades past? Then why should Luke know most of Jesus' birth and infancy? He did not *know* most. No more, perhaps less, than any. He *wrote* most, because the Holy Ghost commanded him to declare what he restrained the others from saying. And that was the sole reason.

So then, whether it be Matthew, Mark, Luke or John, all responded with one accord in answer to the mind of the Spirit distinctively to enhance the glory of Christ each according to his own gospel. Fully aware of the stupendous truths richly clustered around the varied incidents making up the life of Jesus Christ, the holy men nevertheless yielded to the restraint of the Spirit as much as to his leading. So it came to pass that Matthew, refusing what was not to purpose, responded in writing to words which the Holy Ghost impressed upon his heart. This set forth in order that alone which was distinctive of the doctrine of Messias and the kingdom.

However, the theological tutors of the clergy and the state religious educationalists — destitute of the Spirit but clamouring for academic recognition — think otherwise. Thinly veiling their sneering unbelief behind the veneer of 'modern scholarship', these worldly men attribute the differences between the gospels to 'sources', to feeble memory, to fallible personality, or to any other thing provided only that it is contrary to sound doctrine and the *Textus Receptus.* Such latter-day Philistines are not at all embarrassed by the total absence of these nebulous sources. None of them exists or was ever said to have had existence by the authors: but whatever does that matter?

These people are too unspiritual to conceive that the Holy Ghost should have led the evangelists into all truth. They are so unholy themselves that they cannot imagine that holy men of God spake as they were moved by the Holy Ghost. It is beyond their conception that the Holy Spirit of promise, having come, could bring *all things* to the remembrance of Matthew, Mark, John and the holy witnesses, acting through their memory and Luke's perception as the sole and exclusive source of the four gospels.

These cynical and worldly-wise opponents of the guileless simplicity of faith have done despite to the Spirit of grace, slandered the Spirit of truth, and insulted the

Spirit of prophecy. For the testimony of Jesus *is* the spirit of prophecy. But of this they know nothing, being destitute of him whom they have blasphemed so utterly. Now let all take notice, and beware of the leaven of these Sadducees.

Conversely we ought to give the more earnest heed to the things which once we heard, lest at any time we should let them slip. We are to remember that the weapons of our warfare are not carnal, but mighty through God to the pulling down of strongholds. Wherefore we should war to the end for the divinity and purity of the doctrine of Christ, casting down imaginations, and every high thing that exalteth itself against the knowledge of God.

As bringing every thought into captivity to the obedience of Christ the Christian looks solely to the divine origin and source of each and all the accounts of the life of Jesus Christ. It is only in the mind of the Spirit that the faithful see the reason for the distinction between Matthew, who records the birth of Jesus Christ in relation to Joseph: and Mark, who records nothing about it at all. The same applies to the difference between Luke, who writes of the circumstances of the coming of the Son of God into the world with regard to Mary: and John, who is silent about what happened at Bethlehem. Divine reason — ὁ λόγος — lies behind it all, waiting for the trembling discovery of awakened faith.

But to return to the first gospel in particular. Asserting the advent of Messiah and coming of the kingdom to an unbelieving Israel, Matthew commences by presenting the overwhelming testimony provided by both the genealogy and birth of Jesus Christ. The first seventeen verses show the Coming One to be the son of David, the son of Abraham. From verse eighteen to the end of chapter one the writer briefly concludes with the circumstances of Messiah's birth. *

It is all the work of God. But whereas Luke reveals the response of Mary to what the Holy Ghost had wrought within her (and the effect of the angelic visitation explaining that work), here in Matthew it is the reaction of Joseph that is recorded.

First Matthew writes of Joseph's answer to the report that Mary was with child of the Holy Ghost. Next, of his reaction to the divine dream sent to guide him through the consequent dilemma. Verse nineteen 'Then Joseph'. Again, verse twenty-four 'Then Joseph'.

The reason for this emphasis upon Joseph lies in the fact that his response to the advent was typical of the godly remnant who were supposed to be looking for Messiah. So wary, so fearful, so mistrusting, Jewish godliness of itself at its best simply could not rise to believing faith. Deeper work was needed. It took the especial enlightenment of the heavenly vision before Joseph wholeheartedly answered to the wonderful gift of grace.

Their minds were blinded. Until Israel turns inwardly to the Lord with all the heart for the interior spirit of wisdom and revelation in the knowledge of Jesus Christ, the veil must remain untaken away.

Matthew does not so much detail the birth of Jesus Christ in and of itself: rather the truth is unfolded just as it

* See 'The Birth of Jesus Christ', Chapter One 'The Apostolic Foundation of the Christian Church', a separate volume in this series. It is imperative that this series be taken as a whole.

appeared to the awakening consciousness of one who was representative of the poor godly Israelite. Joseph was so typical of the simple pious remnant in his reaction to the divine and heavenly things now taking place all about him. O Jew — Matthew seems to yearn by the record of Joseph — a deeper work is needed than either the law or the letter can give thee!

When it was reported to Joseph that Mary was found with child of the Holy Ghost, not many months had passed since that day when the multitude had prayed outside the holy place during the time of incense. The priest, too long having remained within, at last reappeared beckoning and speechless. It was well known that he had seen a vision in the temple. Like ancient Sarah, now his aged wife was with child; but the priest continued dumb and stricken. Anna had been prophesying. In the temple old father Simeon, bowed with years, declared that he should not die till he had seen the Lord's Christ. Expectancy was in the air. 'Art thou he that should come?' was a question pregnant and ready to be born upon the lips of a newly-aware people.

But when it was reported to Joseph of his own espoused wife that *his* was the virgin with child: that was another thing. 'She was found with child of the Holy Ghost.' It was not so much that he doubted the report, he received the report; but what should he do about it? 'Then Joseph her husband, being a just man, and not willing to make her a public example, was minded to put her away privily.' It was not that he believed ill of her: *justice* demanded that she be found blameless, and Joseph *being* a just man, answered to it. Still, it was all too much for him, he simply did not know *what* to do.

Should he take her to him, or not take her? If not, what

would become of her? If so, what might become of him?
Greatly troubled, he feared these things.

Had he thought her guilty, and put her away privily,
that would not have been justice, it would have been
mercy. Then it would read, being a merciful man, or a
compassionate man. But justice is not mercy, it is not a
word for overlooking faults, but a word of judgment. And
judgment told him, in all justice, *that what was said was
true.*

But it was far too much for poor Joseph and what was
uppermost in his mind was, put her away privily. He feared
what was happening, he wanted to wash his hands of it, he
was too frightened to answer to its staggering repercussions.
Like all that are under the law, however virtuous, he just
dare not come nigh by faith. The very proximity of the
work of God set him trembling in acute anxiety.

Besides what he himself might accept was one thing:
public belief and reaction quite another. And public opinion made him fear. But, 'fear not to take unto thee Mary
thy wife: for that which is conceived in her is of the Holy
Ghost.' And if so, was not the Almighty able to safeguard
the consequences of his own wonderful work without the
assistance of Joseph's 'put her away privily'? Joseph feared
the opinion of man and he feared the imminent proximity
of the work of God, too. But 'fear not, thou son of David.'
Or, as was said in another place, Fear not, thou worm
Jacob.

Forthwith comforted and strengthened by the heavenly
messenger appearing to him in a dream, Joseph, being
raised from sleep, did as the angel of the Lord had bidden
him. For now the word of the Lord had been brought

home to him by an inward revelation. The truth had been divinely impressed upon his interior consciousness. This was what was needed to toll the death-knell of unbelief; henceforward Joseph is changed into another man. He loses the spirit of fear, and gains that of power and of love and of a sound mind. He rises triumphant as a true child of Abraham, who went forth not knowing whither he went. He appears conspicuous as a true son of David, who tenderly followed the ewes great with young.

The actual message of the angel of the Lord together with Matthew's expository comment — 'Now all this was done that it might be fulfilled' — form the central part of the unveiling of the incarnation in the gospel according to Matthew. This follows the genealogy and should be summarised as

The birth of Jesus Christ. Matthew 1:18-25.

The passage has been dealt with in detail under that title in the previous part of 'The Apostolic Foundation of the Christian Church'.

That which now follows is connected closely with the genealogy and birth of Jesus Christ and may be summed up under the heading

The testimony to his birth. Matthew 2:1-23.

31

MATTHEW CHAPTER TWO

¶ The testimony to his birth. Ch. 2:1-23

Matthew commences the public testimony to the birth of Jesus Christ with the arrival at Jerusalem of certain strangers from the east, renowned for their wisdom. They were not kings, there were not three of them, they visited neither crib nor manger, and it was not the 25th December. Incidentally, neither was Jesus' birthday: nowhere near it. The arrival of the wise men took place something like two years after the birth of Jesus Christ and on a different occasion entirely from any recorded in Luke. In Matthew we find Mary and the young child — some two years old — in what was presumably Joseph's own hired house.

Upon the subject of rebutting the stupid errors perpetuated by a softly-decaying and apathetic church — which, as it happens, does very well out of it, in league with the commercial system — I would add that the church was neither required, commanded, nor intended to remember Jesus' 'birthday' once a year. Much less on completely the wrong date. But then the heathen 'converts' had to be placated for losing their lascivious and idolatrous drunk festivals, and so the 'Christian' calendar — itself a worldly expedient and invention not an apostolic command — must be moved to fit the dates of ancient pagan revelry. Like 'Christmas' day.

Then were no dates or feasts commanded by the Lord Jesus and his apostles to be kept by a faithful church? Yes, one only. Not once a year at Easter mixed with 'fertility-rite' eggs and filthy heathen reminders, but a holy memorial of the Lord's death in breaking the bread and taking the cup 'as oft as ye do this': certainly at least weekly; by inference, more often.

It is nothing but an inaccurate fable that depicts 'three kings' worshipping an infant in a manger: and by a certain subtle juxtaposition places Mary in the oblique line of obeisance. Sheer fable.

The fact is, an unspecified number of wise men bringing each certain three symbolic gifts came nearly two years later to some house acquired during the interval and worshipped the young child alone. To state or imply otherwise is to perpetuate an untruth. But to proceed upon the basis of that untruth and reproduce each year — clean contrary, I say, to the gospel — numerous pictures and models of 'cribs' with 'kings' and an 'infant-Jesus' with a nun-like 'Mary': this is not merely an inaccuracy; it is a damnable idolatry, in breach of the second commandment.

The arrival of the wise men at Jerusalem caused consternation in Israel. And not surprising, seeing that it was the Gentiles from afar off who alerted the house of God, priest and scribe, Levite and Pharisee to the celestial portents lately moving over their heads. Then why had they slumbered on, hands folded, somnolent eyelids drooping, heavy with false security?

Out of the distant isles in darkness came the enquiring uncircumcised who had long waited for Christ's law, vigilantly seeking the Star of Jacob. But in the 'enlightened' land of promise, within the commonwealth of Israel, the children of Abraham were steeped in languorous stupor, hypnotised by the metronomic ritual of Jewish tradition. No wonder, then, that 'When Herod the king had heard these things, he was troubled, and all Jerusalem with him.'

Herod, of course, was troubled by the ominous 'Where is he that is born King of the Jews?' It wasn't his throne, he wasn't born to it, he had usurped it, and so his murderous heart engaged to remove heaven's challenge to his false position. Not so the Jews as a whole. As yet unaware of any threat to self-interest, they expose none of their latent malice against divine interference with their religion. But the signs are there. Messiah? King of the Jews? Joyless, *sans* gratitude, in unison with Herod they narrow their eyes, tense their lips, and 'are troubled'.

Yet the Jews had good cause to remember the cruelty and malice of the Edomite king whom the Romans had appointed over Judea, and must have observed Herod's ruthless dispatch of any who even remotely threatened his position.

Then how could they fail to discern Herod's motive when with mock solicitude he asks them, on behalf of the wise men, 'where Christ should be born'? How miss perceiving the murderous intent which lay behind his beseeching the wise men themselves to return 'that I may come and worship him also'?

Imagine such shrewd and machiavellian operators as the chief priests and elders of the Jews naïvely trusting such a murdering old politician as Herod, when the latter suddenly catches religion in his old age and proclaims his desire to worship the 'King of the Jews'. Worship the one born to the throne he himself had usurped? Very likely.

But then, why did the Jews do nothing whatever to protect their young Messiah? Why did they not even accompany the wise men to warn them of Herod's likely intentions?

It was not beyond the Jews' subtlety to penetrate what lay behind the king's otherwise uncharacteristic and inexplicable behaviour. His anxiety itself ought to have alerted them. Why did Herod 'privily call the wise men and enquire of them diligently what time the star had appeared,' verse 7? Did it matter to him? In the issue it was two years before; but what was that to Herod? Verse 16 gives the tragic answer. Herod slew 'All the children that were in Bethlehem, and in all the coasts thereof, from two years old and under, *according to the time which he had diligently enquired of the wise men.*' The time that the star first appeared in the east fixed the death-age of the children that were slain to the west.

As far as King Herod was concerned, the moment the wise men entered Jerusalem uttering the words 'King of the Jews', the fate of the young child was doomed. The rival title sealed his death. Feigning an anxiety to worship Messiah equal to that of the eastern travellers, the guileful manipulator begins to engineer their simple piety. Having enquired of the prophetic scriptures from the Jews, Herod directs the strangers to the birthplace of Christ. Too subtle to accompany them himself, the wily king requires — 'that I may come and worship him also' — their immediate return upon success.

But suppose the wise men were not so simple after all? What if they really divined King Herod's evil intention? Even before sending the wise men on their way, Herod prepared against such an eventuality. From the very beginning he laid contingency plans for an alternative murder scheme.

Supposing that the wise men failed to return, Herod would be prevented from discovering the exact location of the young child. Therefore before their departure he determined the general age-group to which the 'King of the Jews' belonged. Equating the age of the child with the first appearance of the star, with diabolical purpose — and innocent airs — Herod questioned the wise men to this end. Two years? Suppose that the star marked his conception and not his birth? Just over a year. Hmm. Safest 'two years old and under.'

Thus was the slaughter determined, and 'when Herod saw that he was mocked of the wise men' he did not shrink from the execution of his horrific second plan in consequence.

Yet notwithstanding all the devious schemes of Herod to murder the young Messiah, and in the face of all the massive indifference of the haughty Jews to lift so much as a finger to save him, the child Jesus was delivered out of the hand of the wicked. By what means? Was the acuteness of the wise men alerted? Were these devout Gentiles disillusioned of any hope in Jewish virtue?

Not at all. It was neither through the wisdom of the wise nor by the understanding of the prudent that the young child was saved alive. It was by the command of the Lord God sending revelation in dreams of the night. 'And being warned of God' — warned by an oracle χρηματίζω just as was Noah of things not seen as yet — 'in a dream that they should not return to Herod, they departed into their own country another way.'

It was nothing to do with man. 'God speaketh once, yea twice, yet man perceiveth it not. In a dream, in a vision of the night, when deep sleep falleth upon men, in slumberings upon the bed; then he openeth the ears of men, and sealeth their instruction, that he may withdraw man from his purpose, and hide pride from man. He keepeth back his soul from the pit, and his life from perishing by the sword.' And that was it: God speaketh. The deliverance owed nothing to men.

Moreover, in the event the wise men owed nothing to their visit to Jerusalem. They came enquiring the whereabouts of the one born King of the Jews. Alarmed, the chief priests and scribes woke up and blundered to their books muttering, What king? And Herod schemed his perfidious plot. Triumphing out of Micah, the Jews recovered their gravity, adjusted their learned robes, and placed the machinery of destruction into the hands of Herod with a sigh of relief.

But they need not have bothered. For 'The star, which the wise men saw in the east, went before them, till it came and stood over where the young child was.' Then were the wise men wrong to have enquired at Jerusalem? By no means. But whilst they thought to ask the way, God intended that their testimony should rebuke blind and obstinate Israel. And, it may be, provoke them to jealousy.

From his own the King of the Jews received neither welcome nor recognition. Nevertheless, the rich from among the Gentiles came to honour him from the land that was very far off. They travelled some two full years on no more than the glimpse of a star in the dark. The wise men entreated the favour of the Son of David, opening their treasures of gold and precious spices brought from out of the ivory palaces, whereby they made him glad. But his own saw no beauty in him that they might desire him.

About this time Joseph received his second vision from

the angel of the Lord in a dream, commanding him to take the young child and his mother and flee from Herod into Egypt, there to remain till heaven's intimation of safety. After the death of Herod the angel appears again to Joseph in Egypt, in a dream instructing him to go to the land of Israel. Taking the young child and his mother, Joseph returns. Yet not before the Prince and Saviour had been shown in a symbolic figure to be identified with Israel in all his troubles and deliverances.

Hearing that Herod's son Archelaus reigned in his father's stead, Joseph is afraid. He appears to contemplate returning to Egypt. He is warned not to do so, but to obey the word of the Lord. This brings him to Galilee. A city called Nazareth to be precise. Perfect.

'He shall be called a Nazarene.' So spake the ancient prophets. But which prophets, and where? The answer depends on what is meant by Nazarene! If it be intended merely an inhabitant of Nazareth, no prophet spake of it. If Nazareth be named after something of which the prophets spake, then again, which prophets and where? And why 'prophets', in the plural? The latter suggests — since all of the major and minor prophetic books are singular — a compilation like Chronicles, Kings, or Judges, in which several prophets spake and were perhaps involved in the writing. That narrows down the search, but still the question remains, What is meant by a Nazarene?

Some have suggested that *Netser*, Shoot, Branch, is intended. But it is unlikely as a derivative for Nazareth. Why not *Nazar* or *Nazir?* It means 'separated' which in the derogatory sense of separate from Judea was certainly applicable in general to 'Galilee of the Gentiles', and Nazareth — 'Can there any good thing come out of Nazareth?' —

in particular. If *Nazir*, twelve times this word — meaning separated — has been translated Nazarite, surely this is applicable to him who was 'separate from sinners'?

Only once in the Old Testament is an individual person referred to as a Nazarite — 'He shall be called a Nazarene' — every other reference is plural or general. The singular reference is from the book of Judges concerning Samson. 'Thou shalt conceive, and bear a son,' — how appropriate to this context in Matthew — 'and no rasor shall come on his head: for the child shall be a Nazarite unto God from the womb: and he shall begin to deliver Israel out of the hand of the Philistines.' This was the one who accomplished deliverance more by his death than in the whole of his life. Now let Israel get a hold of that!

MATTHEW CHAPTER THREE

¶ The testimony to his ministry. Ch. 3:1-17

The ministry of John the Baptist was no separate entity: its selfless motive was found in extolling the ministry of Another. The great significance of John's testimony lay in his heralding the person and work of the coming Messiah: just as its climax was reached in the graphic threefold description of the ministry of Jesus Christ.

The work of John achieved its stupendous conclusion that day when Jesus rose all drenched from the waters of Jordan and discovered the very heavens opened, all deity conspiring with the baptist to proclaim the peerless worth and utter significance of the only-begotten Son of the Father.

Actually John preached to multitudes of the people and vast numbers flocked to his ministry. In particular they of the land of Judea and all the region round about Jordan with the whole of Jerusalem attended his word. He addressed this multitude; all the people; the Jews, priests and Levites; the Pharisees and Sadducees; publicans and soldiers; and finally spoke most closely to his own disciples.

Matthew however, according to purpose, limits his narrative to the Jews in general and the Pharisees and Sadducees in particular: a combination unique to this gospel.

John preached in the wilderness. So doing, he was on the outskirts of the land and separated from the corruption into which the Jews and their priesthood had plunged the house of God with its service. The baptist was outside the camp. And so was the testimony of God. For the glory had departed, God's temple had become a den of thieves, and the Lord stood upon the altar. Of all this, John's position was witness.

More. From the boundaries of the land of promise the prophet's call brought the people to depart their inheritance and flock in alarm to the banks of Jordan. Mute proclamation! What Israel had become in the promised land of sabbath rest was not what Jehovah had intended when he led their fathers from Egypt through the wilderness into Canaan for an inheritance.

The land never was their ultimate rest, nor was it the true sabbatism; but they had settled for it — bad enough —

and worse, had corrupted their way within it. Return to Jordan! Repent of the old positional presumption, and go back! Back to the banks of the river their fathers' feet had passed over dryshod from the far wilderness, and back in heart besides. Enter again, enter afresh in heartbroken and penitent confession of the failure of Israel and the corruption of all flesh before Jehovah.

An urgency lay in the call to Israel for repentance. Not of the imminence of the sabbath of the land itself; rather of the immediacy of the ultimate rest which that land signified. That was what was at hand. A new, a unique prophetic element had been introduced. In a word, not a new kingdom of Israel, but the real kingdom of heaven was at hand.

Far from being eagerly expectant for the coming promise of the gospel, the Jews — uncircumcised in heart and ears — even then resisted the Holy Ghost over the present truth of Israel. Hence John thunders, Repent. Go back to the borders of Israel and beginnings of the people. So come again into the land with fruits meet for repentance as prepared for the breaking forth of the Dayspring from on high.

Of such a ministry Isaiah had foretold, and so had many of the prophets. This was not simply another in the great line of prophetic men of God. Here was the forerunner of the coming of Jehovah, the last prophet of Israel, 'The voice of one crying in the wilderness.' This was Elijah the prophet sent before the coming of the great and dreadful day of the Lord.

John the Baptist's very appearance declared it: his meat shows it forth. Some eight hundred and seventy-five years previously King Ahaziah son of Ahab sent to enquire of his idols for a word of prophecy. But his messengers were intercepted by a man, and returned with this word 'Is it not because there is not a God in Israel, that thou enquirest of Baal-zebub the god of Ekron?' Twice over the wrathful king sent to destroy the man with a captain of fifty and his fifty. Twice over not one survived and nothing remained but charred bones. What manner of man was this? 'He was an hairy man, and girt with a girdle of leather about his loins. And Ahaziah said, It is Elijah!'

And the same John had his raiment of camel's hair, and a leathern girdle about his loins; and his meat was locusts and wild honey.

Locusts and wild honey. John's meat in itself indicated the iron hardness of the man who has learned to live off the most barren and inhospitable of deserts, and therefore of one in whom fleshly softness and worldly indulgence has been rigorously mortified: burned out by a fierce contempt for earthly comfort.

But there is more to it than that, particularly in the first instance. The baptist's meat is symbolical. The food by which the prophet's life is sustained is indicative of the ministry which he exercises. Just as Ezekiel saw in vision a hand with the roll of a book totally covered in writing, full of lamentation, mourning and woe, and was made to eat that book: so also John the Baptist's meat is significant of his work. He eats the symbol of judgment continually.

Locusts are significant of the devastating judgment of God. To a rural people wholly dependent upon agriculture such a plague can spell the end of everything. Indeed the first mention of locusts in the Bible occurs in the eighth plague sent by God upon Pharoah and his people. The locusts of judgment stripped the land of Egypt of every green thing, ensuring long starvation and poverty in consequence. Jehovah judged backsliding Israel by sending mildew and blasting, with the plague of locusts accompanying the word of the prophet Joel. The last book of the New Testament uses the figure of dreadful locusts to depict the enormity of God's terrible warning plagues upon the world in view of the last judgment. The very conception of this had entered into John's belly.

As to the locusts and wild honey. It has been imagined that this duality suggests the baptist's legal ministry of condemnation to Israel, a ministry of judgment, being tempered by the sweetness of his pointing to Christ. This notion then fortifies itself by the analogy of Samson slaying the lion and afterwards finding honey in the carcass: 'Out of the strong came forth sweetness.' That is, the sweet savour of honey came by way of the death of the young lion which had roared at Samson.

But to me this kind of fanciful speculation just shows the result of uncalled persons publishing abroad their wishful thinking and dreamy meandering. They jump to immediate conclusions, and know nothing of the disciplined study, mortifying exercise, and spiritual prayer of those truly called to the ministry. Hence the inconsistency of their silly and erroneous guesswork.

Not to press the matter, the unsuitability of a 'roaring lion' — the figure of the devil — being applied to Jesus in this context is rather obvious. The same applies to honey, which they say indicates the sweetness coming from the offering up of Christ on the cross. If so, what of this: 'There shall be no honey in any offering of the Lord made by fire.'

Has 'honey' no significance then? Yes; if considered in the context of the baptist summoning the people to the wilderness on the far side of the river. Symbolically they are being called again to enter into the land through the waters of Jordan in a new and spiritual way. Israel is to approach and re-enact in heart and interior understanding the ancient types and figures of their fathers brought up from Egypt to possess the promised land.

The locusts are consistent with this, calling upon the penitents to judge themselves and rend their hearts and not their garments. Thus might they be led by the antitype of the pillar of cloud and fire. Then they must be sustained by the hidden manna for such a baptism as brings them into 'the rest that remains for the people of God'.

In the ancient pilgrim context, manna was seen as 'like coriander seed, white; and the taste of it was like wafers made with honey.' This was Israel's wilderness meat of which the reality was at hand. But ceased these millenia past, what could suggest it? Wilderness honey. Certainly, it sustained John the Baptist in his pilgrimage below.

John the Baptist's ministry consisted of three main branches. First, of awakening Israel to the righteousness of the law. Secondly, of prophesying of the advent of Messiah and his kingdom. And finally, baptising the coming Lord in the waters of Jordan.

In Matthew John the Baptist addresses himself particularly to the Pharisees and Sadducees. These two groups indicate the natural propensities of religious man. Especially they portray the party notions to which the self-righteous and those born in religious circumstances invariably incline in any generation. John roundly condemns them both.

44

They were Pharisee and Sadducee, but as easily might have been Calvinist and Arminian, Church and Chapel, Fundamental and Liberal, Brethren and Baptist, Evangelical and Modernist. The polarisation is the same. The work of God and the kingdom of God are other things. A plague on both their houses.

Both Pharisee and Sadducee presumed on position. On favour by exterior confession, religious tradition and party connection. They felt eternally secure. No doubt — respectively — they were the people and wisdom should die with them. Then why did they come to John's baptism? Did they know that wrath was kindled against them? Or did their presumptuous hearts still trust in false assurance? Well, let them not think to say within themselves, We have Abraham to our father. They were not as privileged as they thought: in the sight of God inert stones were as useful.

They were a generation of vipers. Not only were they vipers but their fathers were vipers. They had such trust in those from whom they had inherited their religious security: but, cries John, *they* were vipers too. The children were a generation, an offspring, of viperine parents. It was a serpentine stock, and instinctively the baptist distrusted their repentance. And so it is to this day.

John's prophecy of the advent of Messiah and the kingdom is really second-coming preaching. It is a prophecy of the day of judgment. The day of the Lord was at hand. In a very real sense John never truly understood the purpose of the first coming of Christ. His expectation was that Messiah's advent would be synonymous with the final coming and day of judgment. This view eventually led John to enquire on the basis of absent vengeance 'Art thou he that should come? or look we for another?'

This was also true of the disciples. To them the first coming of Christ was the time of retribution. It was to be the day of judgment. Vengeance should be exacted. Certainly at this time the kingdom must be restored to Israel. They could not have erred more completely. They were utterly wrong. They understood neither the Gentile church nor the present purpose. Much less the eternal purpose.

Millenia apart, the first and second coming of Christ stand like great signposts over the chaos of time. Yes, millenia apart; but only if seen at remove and in perspective. Stand aside and the milestones appear for what they are. But approach too close, decrease the angle, stand in line, and the near signpost obliterates from view the far distant one in direct sequence; but one — large and near — appears. Everything else in line is obscured. So to John there was but one advent and with it was associated all that we connect with the great and terrible day of the Lord at the second coming of Christ.

Nevertheless the graphic threefold witness that John bears to the ministry of Jesus Christ must always remain the perfect summary by which the work of the Lord is to be discerned. The work that Messiah does answers to the separation that his character demands and the purity which his nature requires. That is the message.

Separation is of the essence of Messiah's work. It is the hallmark by which his ministry is distinguished. He hates with a perfect hatred the spurious profession of the hypocrite and he has the will, the power, and the means to purge and banish all false mixture from out of Zion.

Abruptly it is no longer a matter of what the Jews are to do about Messiah. That time is past. Now, now the axe is laid to the root of the trees. Suddenly it is a question of what Messiah will do about the professing people of God. Three things; and he has the means by which to accomplish them. To one end: that he might turn to the people a pure language, for in that day all the earth shall be devoured with the fire of his jealousy.

The forerunner cries an alarm of the coming of the righteousness-rewarding, sin-avenging Jehovah. With cutting directness he hurls his soul-exposing message into the teeth of the hypocrites in Zion. Profession and confession are swept aside as worthless and irrelevant to judgment. Fair appearance is meaningless. The root shall be hacked up and lie all exposed. The righteous shall see it and rejoice. The poor and needy shall weep aloud for joy.

Observe Messiah's instruments, equal to his task. The woodman's axe; the baptist's effusion; the winnower's fan. Separating instruments all, they tell his work and declare divine necessity in its very nature. It is not a question of what God would like: it is the imperative of what he must have, and will have. It is, I say, the demand of his being. He will of necessity separate mixture, put things in their place, name them appropriately and forever treat them accordingly. Messiah sees this, and he is determined to achieve it, that the pleasure of the Lord should prosper in his hand.

Consider. The avenging woodman from heaven is come down to the garden of the Lord with the axe of judgment. It is sharpened, it is also furbished, it is whetted to make a sore slaughter, it is furbished that it may glitter in the hand of the slayer.

Passing through from one end of the garden to the other

47

every tree is narrowly searched out. Nothing passes the
scrutiny of the one whose eyes are as a flame of fire. Many
trunks are marked. Chips fly at the casual flick of the axe
as the white blaze is scored again and again. *That* one? But
it was thought the very best? Nothing but leaves. This? But
the time of fruit is not yet come. Continued immaturity is
a blight like cankerworm: down it must come. The truth is
that every tree which bringeth not forth good fruit is hewn
down.

From the far end of the garden the ringing of the axe
sounds in a great fury as tree after tree is rent and crashes
to the earth in a great cloud of dust. Sparks fly as iron
strikes stone cutting out the root from its place in the
earth forever. Soon the garden is transformed. Solely the
planting of the Lord remains, distinguished by fruit
hanging rich and heavy for his pleasure alone. Everywhere
else upended trees lie along the ground, a mass of stricken
trunks, tangled branches, filling the glades.

But this is not the end. Every tree that Messiah's
heavenly Father hath not planted shall be rooted up and
more so: it shall be cleared away to its place. Dragged off
to the sinister valley the stricken trees are hurled into the
dark ravine till at last they choke the void with a tangled
mass of leaves and branches. Cast into the darkness the
roots glare starkly white against the blackness of the
deep. The orange flame leaps from tree to tree, sheets of
fire roaring up in the draught, great banking columns of
oily smoke roiling upwards lit from within by the lurid
conflagration. This is the end. 'Is hewn down *and* cast into
the fire.'

The baptist's effusion. This is not upon trees. It is upon
persons. It is not one axe to distinguish between both kinds,

but two different baptisms outpoured respectively upon those kinds already distinguished. It is judgment begun at the house of God. Messiah has two kinds of baptism to answer to the righteous and the unrighteous among the professing people of God. Just as his woodman's axe gave judgment between the fruitful and the barren.

The great baptist from heaven pours out the Holy Ghost from on high upon those that obey him: the penitent, guileless, Israelites indeed. This is the reward of the righteous from the right hand of the Most High. In the last days it shall come to pass. The groaning of the oppressed, the sighing of the needy shall be turned to joy, and their mouth filled with laughter as the blessed outpouring rises to ankles, knees, loins: yea, waters to swim in from out the mystical house of God on high. What a Prince and a Saviour.

But another baptism is reserved for Pharisee and Sadducee, scribe and legalist, lawyer and priest, the multitude of the hypocrites at ease in Zion, and this baptism is certainly not that of the Holy Ghost. It is that of fire, of the wrath and indignation of Almighty God. It is reserved in heaven for the stiffnecked and rebellious among God's people, the uncircumcised in heart and ears, the alway-resisters of the Holy Ghost. These insinuate themselves amongst the people of God, and steal all the high places withal. These are the very curse of his house. They shall be separated to await *their* baptism from the heavens.

Spots are they in the feasts of charity, feeding themselves without fear. Clouds they are without water, carried about of winds; trees whose fruit withereth, without fruit, twice dead, plucked up by the roots; raging waves of the sea, foaming out their own shame; wandering stars, to whom is reserved the blackness of darkness forever. Upon these cursed in Israel, these leprous in the house of God, these pedlars in false evangelism, these unctuous mendicants that fill the church, Christ shall pour out from the vials and bowls of his sevenfold fury something quite other than the Holy Ghost to which they so often pretend.

They shall be baptised with fire, just as the hewn trees were cast into the fire. Make no mistake; upon these wretched hypocrites, these ebullient deceivers, the molten contents of the bowls of wrath shall be jettisoned. Fire shall stream from on high, livid sheets serrating the heavens from the mouths of the sevenfold vials above the sky shall engulf and immerse them and their seed forever. Christ shall tip his baptiser's vessel and from it shall erupt the blood-red fire of eternal fury. Molten heat jetting down the skies, searing, enveloping, overwhelming, submerging: so the second baptism — *'and* with fire' — of Christ shall sink the wicked in Israel forever beneath its rising tide.

The final figure used by John to describe the ministry of the coming Messiah whose advent had been so clearly testified to the Jews now follows.

The birth of Messiah was attested with abundant testimony. What had the Jews done about it? By now Christ was a young man. What did the Jews care of it? Yet in the mouth of two or three witnesses every matter is established. The forerunner of the ministry of Messiah testifies to the wicked leaders, blind followers, and indifferent members not only of the woodman's axe and the baptist's effusion but finally of the winnower's fan.

The harvest had come. The sheaves had been brought

in. How the synagogue members, the assembly, the great congregation would congratulate themselves on being brought into the Lord's floor according to assured expectation. But only now does the threshing begin. The servants of the Lord of the Harvest respond to his signal. The flails rise and fall faster than the eye can follow. The vast heap of corn jumps and leaps as a living thing, the dust rises in choking golden clouds, the shout of the reapers, hiss and thud of the flails, stamp of feet fills the atmosphere of the barn.

At last the servants thrust into the heaps upon heaps of flailed corn gathered from the reaping of the fields. Hurling the laden scoops high into the air golden showers cascade everywhere. A new figure appears. The mighty winnower stands in the midst of the threshingfloor and his fan is in his hand. The corded sinews and bunched muscles of his right arm vibrate the great fan: the draught roars through the tossed grain. The light chaff is blasted away into the corners. The solid wheat falls to the ground. Hour by hour, hour after hour: he shall not slack: he will throughly purge his floor.

The light chaff cannot withstand the blast of his fan. But the weighty grain falls at his feet. All is purged. Yonder the airy chaff. Nigh the solid seed. He will gather his wheat into his garner. Not a single trace of that chaff which once had seemed inseparable. Do you hear that, you light frivolous neo-calvinists? Hear it, you airy arminian evangelicals? Do you hear that, you non-extremist, middle of the road, o-so-careful outward chaffy brethren?

Yet this is not the end. For the trees had been burned. The baptiser's fire was poured out. And now mark this: He will throughly purge his floor, yes. And gather his wheat into the garner, certainly. But then, then he will burn up the chaff with unquenchable fire. It is not the godless world John is talking about: it is Christ's ministry to those who profess to be his own. They profess; but they are light as chaff, childish and empty as the children they delight to instruct, but in fact deceive. Now hear this:

> Blessed is the man that walketh not in the counsel of the ungodly, nor standeth in the way of sinners, nor sitteth in the seat of the scornful.
> But his delight is in the law of the LORD; and in his law doth he meditate day and night.
> And he shall be like a tree planted by the rivers of water, that bringeth forth his fruit in his season; his leaf also shall not wither; and whatsoever he doeth shall prosper.
> The ungodly are not so: but are like the chaff which the wind driveth away.
> Therefore the ungodly shall not stand in the judgment, nor sinners in the congregation of the righteous.
> For the LORD knoweth the way of the righteous: but the way of the ungodly shall perish.

★

Now appears the final branch of John the Baptist's ministry. He baptises the coming Lord in the waters of Jordan.

Three of the four gospels record the event and each is distinct from the other. Matthew, Mark and Luke must be considered separately: that is the mind of the Spirit. To amalgamate these accounts into one 'Life of Christ' — as numerous ignorant, unspiritual and unconverted priests, doctors and theologians have done — is to grind into unnatural discord the perfect harmony of heaven's melody of Jesus.

Not only are the three accounts of the Lord's baptism very different but each is set in a context distinct from the other; even going so far as to hint — for entirely doctrinal purposes — that the time at which the occurrence took place varied!

But the Spirit is under no obligation to satisfy the petulant irritation of 'intellectuals' over chronological exactitude. In presenting the true God and eternal Life who bears the titles of Lord of the Sabbath and Ancient of Days the object is salvation and the service of sonship. To meet the inward cry of poor seeking sinners: not provide a living for parasitical religious academics. To sanctify the believing and loving saints: not produce a text book for illegitimate clericalism. To edify the separate and hoping body of Christ: not maintain those denominations which have split from its one true unity.

To this end time and sequence in the gospels are made to serve THE LORD that he may be clearly apprehended by the longing heart. The LORD does not serve time: he made it. He was before its existence. He is above its duration. And he will be after its cessation.

The gospel according to John gives no account of the baptism of Jesus. However it expounds at greater length the significance of the descent of the Spirit. Twice over John the Baptist asserts that he did not know Jesus. 'And I knew him not.' Yet Matthew tells us the baptist met Jesus with the following words: 'I have need to be baptised of thee, and comest thou to me?' Implying that he did know him. The difficulty is resolved by detecting the distinction of the Spirit's presentation of Christ in each separate gospel without confusion.

As over against the unique birth, the perfection of manhood, the impeccable character and peerless spiritual insight of Jesus, John saw one the latchet of whose shoes he was not worthy to unloose. Much less to baptise the Man of God's right hand who should take the axe, the vessel and the fan. 'I have need to be baptised of thee.' That much he knew of Jesus and this is the context of Matthew.

In John on the other hand we see Jesus — before ever he meets the baptist — as the Word, God, the Creator, the Life, the Light, the Authority, the only begotten Son in the bosom of the Father, the divine Christ, the Lamb of God, the Son of God: all that! Deity incarnate. It is in that context that we hear a cry wrung from the very depths of John's heart as he perceives *how much more was in Christ than at first he had dreamed:* 'And I knew him not.' And I knew him not.

But variety is the rule. At the baptism even the names of the Spirit differ in each account. In Matthew he is the Spirit of God; in Mark simply the Spirit; whereas Luke refers to him as the Holy Ghost. Wonderfully rich, the Spirit selects from the immense variety and depth of the divine manifestation that which accords with the doctrinal purpose of each gospel respectively. Again, for example, in

Matthew the voice from heaven speaks of the Son to Israel. But in Mark and Luke the Father speaks to the Son of himself. Who can tell the depths of divine communication? On this thrice-holy ground the Spirit is Lord. Let all mortal flesh keep silence.

Matthew directly and doctrinally connects the ministry of the spiritual woodman from God, that mighty baptiser of heaven, the great winnower for the day of judgment — *'Then* cometh Jesus' Mt. 3:13 — with the coming of Messiah to John's baptism. The last thing John expected: but up till then he had not conceived of the sacrificial Lamb or of the day of grace or of the times of the Gentiles. So that seeing Messiah only in terms of the judgment, he could not comprehend him in terms of meek submission to inferior hands. But so it was. ' ... He will burn up the chaff with unquenchable fire. *Then* cometh Jesus ... to be baptised of John.'

Hitherto John the Baptist's view of royal Messiah was one common to Israel. So that his protest at what he considered the inconsistency of David's son taking so degrading a position, expressed much of the Jewish objection to Jesus.

Here was a Messiah vastly different from the one which the Jews had designed for themselves by the selective use of scripture. However, unlike the majority of the Jews, John was led by the Spirit and knew the meaning of soul affliction and hence his heart was swift to obey the word of the Lord. It is to humility therefore that the words are addressed 'Suffer it to be so now.'

Maybe. But for all John's broken and contrite spirit stern rectitude abides. Not at the expense of what is right,

55

Messiah though thou art! But wait; 'For thus it becometh us to fulfil all righteousness.'

Immediately the Spirit beams his penetrating rays and floods John's soul with wondrous revelation. Eye had not seen it, nor had the ear heard; neither yet had it entered into the heart of man to conceive the immeasurable, the unspeakable, the unutterable, the overwhelming love of God, the staggering stoop of love divine. But now streams of light break forth from the heart of the deity, suffusing the soul of the great forerunner. 'Then he suffered him.' Then.

John's shocked objection to baptising Messiah was upon two grounds. First, that of Jesus' spotless purity exempting him from any requirement for baptism. Secondly, John baptised with water — of which Jesus had no need — but the mightier than John would baptise with the Holy Ghost — of which John had every need: 'I have need to be baptised of thee.'

No power on earth would have moved the just baptist from this objection, so heart-felt from the poignant sense of his own unworthiness. But heaven had somewhat to say to him, on grounds altogether superior to what was merely personal.

Jesus' reply — like John's complaint, unique to Matthew — falls into two parts. On the personal level John is quite right. Jesus accepts the justice of John's objection. But higher things are in view and the two have a figure to enact which soars into sublime spiritualities: on that account John must suffer any personal feelings or sense of unfitness. He is to embody the legal office: suffer it to be so that the figure may be fulfilled.

The second part of Jesus' answer is the first clear revelation in the New Testament of the justifying righteousness of God. Its importance cannot be overestimated, and it is more than enough to tear the veil from the heart of the whole of Israel, so blindly set upon the pursuit of legal righteousness.

Let Israel but once consider the import of Jesus' explanation to John. 'For': on account of the picture created by John's baptising Jesus; its tremendous clarity and importance. 'Thus it becometh us': John and Jesus; so enacting the ministries of law and gospel which they embody respectively. 'To fulfil': in a tableau, a picture. 'All righteousness': not only of the law, a righteous rule prescribed of God to Israel. Nor only of nature, a moral law, inscribed upon the heart of mankind, an inner consciousness. Not only the obligation stimulated by the things that are made, laying a moral necessity upon the creature to worship the Creator. Nor even only the righteousness of God manifested in the justice of his judgments in dealing with mankind hitherto. But above all the unique, the deity-declaring, heaven-opening, divinely-satisfying, gospel-displaying righteousness of God in itself: the revelation of its own intrinsic character through Christ Jesus.

All righteousness. More than simply the righteous assessment of the relative worth and virtue of Jesus as compared with John. *That* righteousness forbad his baptism. But *all* righteousness required it notwithstanding.

The righteousness of the law required it. That is if Jewish sinners under the righteous curse of the law were to be pardoned and yet the law remain honourable and inviolate. Then the law's righteous requirement demanded the spotless Jesus' baptism in the guilty sinner's place beneath its curse. The figure declared this reality. John, standing for the law, laid Jesus beneath the waters of death.

But infinitely superior the righteousness of God required it. That is, if the sinful children of wrath are to be ransomed, pardoned, redeemed and justified. If they are to be delivered from the power of darkness and translated into the kingdom of God's dear Son, receiving the place of sonship as the heavenly children of God. Then the righteousness of God required that on their behalf Jesus should undergo a dread baptism in which all Jehovah's waves and billows of almighty wrath should pass over his head, sinking him into deep mire where there is no standing.

This is that by which God's own nature is glorified. It is the revelation by the gospel of the righteousness of God without the law. It is *another thing altogether than legal righteousness already made known*. Now, this is a distinction clean missed by traditional orthodox protestant theology.

Luther — the most illuminated, apostolic, and experimental of them all — saw it, and saw it clearly: but rather in the sense of wonderful fleeting glimpses of heaven's blue through the racing clouds of ragged obscurity. But that great-heart was failed by others and curiously mislaid in much of the reformed tradition.

On this head, Calvin certainly lost ground to Luther. The coldly logical Frenchman was more methodical but by no means so visionary.

Imperious puritanism missed it completely, although many simple 'uneducated' brethren raised a cry for disencumbered truth. A cry which caused restless irritation in the high places of human education. Thither the letter-learned doctors of the law had carried the poor bruised faith — battered by endless pedantry and bound with legal chains — there to indulge their knowing pride and exclusive academic hauteur.

Poor humble men had dared to point out to the high priests of puritanism that justifying righteousness was never called in scripture 'The righteousness of Christ', as the learned doctors taught. That it was never said to be wrought by way of the law. Much less through the illegal, unevangelical, unreformed and uncalvinistic notion of 'The active and passive obedience of Christ to the law'. A novel invention. The plain brethren observed from their Bibles that justifying righteousness was always called 'The righteousness of God' and it came 'by faith of Jesus Christ' alone.

They were commanded to silence as dangerously uneducated in divinity. They had not been to college. But the fact was, they observed, neither had the Lord Jesus nor his apostles. To them divinity school was no better than a contemptible Jewish substitute for the Holy Ghost. But the clergy disregarded this. Immaterial. The system had been established and that was that. These unlearned troublers should go to school, not Christ; and they should learn, not think.

But uneducated or not, were they not *right?* What had that got to do with it? Tradition had been settled.

Now appears authoritarian Reverend John Owen, clerical son of a Welsh clergyman, product of Oxford University, 'Doctor of Divinity', as ecclesiastics quaintly called it.

Armed with worldly honours and a piece of paper, he attempts to overawe the 'ignorant' believers in Christ with a vast show of Latin, Greek, and Hebrew letter-learning. Through academic degrees of intellectual prowess awarded by the universities, such clergymen ever attempt to triumph over the simplicity which used to be in Christ. Blind as a learned bat on the subject, Owen attempts to shut up the poor seekers after righteousness with a long face and a lifted lip.

Baring his academic teeth hideously at the sheer temerity of rustics daring to think for themselves, he darkly hints at their danger. Slyly he mutters the names of ancient heretics. As though there were the remotest connection! Heresies had nothing whatever to do with the light breaking upon the poor simple enquirers. Typical. No wonder J. N. Darby so rightly entitled his tract 'The notion of a clergyman dispensationally the sin against the Holy Ghost'. Everything Owen said against these brethren applied equally to 'the carpenter's son' and the 'unlearned and ignorant men' called apostles. So who is the heretic?

The early 'Plymouth' brethren made the distinction between the righteousness of the law and that of the gospel. They owe this to John Darby and his loyal fellow-labourers. Modern Brethren — in various divisions, alas — ought not to have forgotten either the spirit, teaching or teachers of their forbears in the faith.

Let them be sure: God is no more obliged to their mere traditions than he was to those of the denominations from which their fathers rightly separated to come together into the unity of one body.

J. N. Darby's great contribution on the subject was the

separation of the righteousness of the law from the righteousness of God revealed in the gospel. On the other hand, he placed justifying righteousness in union with a risen Christ, which scripture certainly does not. The doctrine is, that righteousness of God in the gospel is placed for faith's apprehension entirely, absolutely, exclusively and completely in the blood of Jesus. This is what the resurrection declares.

And that is what the baptism prefigures. It is a vivid picture at the commencement of Jesus' ministry of the real goal and tremendous climax at the conclusion of it. The baptism shows — demonstrably in Matthew — what his ministry is all about, come straight to the centre of it. The declaration is this: his ministry is about righteousness.

And that is the heart of the gospel. 'For I am not ashamed of the gospel of Christ: for it is the power of God unto salvation to every one that believeth; to the Jew first, and also to the Greek.' But *why* is it the power of God unto salvation? Because of righteousness. '*For* therein is the righteousness of God revealed from faith to faith: as it is written, The just shall live by faith.' It is all about righteousness. Otherwise it is no gospel at all.

Jesus had no need to be baptised of John. On the contrary, being a baptism of repentance for the remission of sins, the One without sin — who knew no sin — and who was separate from sinners could never rightly be baptised on his own account. But he wasn't baptised on his own account. He was baptised, in a figure and in the event, on behalf of others. And if so, then to fulfil all righteousness.

This was not demanded of Jesus. He laid down his life of himself. The law found no fault in him, put upon him no obligation to lay down his life for others. John, the figurative embodiment of that moral rule, cried aghast in protest to forbid what was altogether beyond its scope. Jesus' rectitude had *earned* life: why then throw it away on the worthless? That was not right. Not legal compulsion, no; but it was the revealing of the heart of God, the ultimate expression of love divine in freely given grace.

Here it is what John represents that baptises Jesus into death, puts him under the wrath of God. It is the law in its offended sanctions and outraged curse against guilty transgressors. For them Jesus submits to its reluctant hands to be submerged beneath the waters of judgment on their behalf in death.

'And for this cause he is the mediator of the new testament, that by means of death, for the redemption of the transgressions that were under the first testament, they which are called might receive the promise of eternal inheritance.' And again, 'Christ hath redeemed us from the curse of the law, being made a curse for us.' In a figure, John the legal ministry of condemnation, seeing Jesus helpless and submissive as upon the cross of Calvary — a willing spotless sacrifice — laid hands upon him and thrust him under the curse of the law to death.

However, so far, this is not a revelation of the righteousness of God in and of itself. First, it is not a revelation: what Israelite — be his generation never so ancient — ever doubted that God was righteous in his dealings according to law? Or doubted the validity of legal sacrifice? But the gospel claims more, far more, than this: 'But *now* the righteousness of God *without the law* is manifested.' Secondly, such legal appeasement as is figured in John's baptism is not in respect of the righteousness of God absolutely in itself considered: it is in respect of what the law calls forth from that righteousness. It regards the fact that God is righteous when he deals with men on a legal basis, and that he forgives them with due respect to law.

Really, the law measured the exact righteous sentence for God to pronounce upon men and their actions, as their just and lawful Judge. But the intrinsic divine righteousness itself, that which was without measure and according to the divine nature: the absolute essence of righteousness within the deity — quite apart from the relatively paltry legal measure — this, I say, this is another thing altogether. But it is precisely what is revealed by the gospel: 'the righteousness of God without the law'.

God is a Spirit and therefore his righteousness could not be depicted at the baptism in the same way that John embodied the appeasement of the offended and outraged law. However — baptism being a figure of Jesus' death — every possible hint was given that not only was the law satisfied, but moreover righteousness of God itself was met at Calvary.

The law was a rule whereby in the doing of all things written therein continually, a man would earn life. 'Cursed is every one that continueth not in all things which are written in the book of the law to do them.' And, 'The man that doeth them shall live in them.' But on earth. The law promised bliss and long life on earth, in this world for which man in Adam was made. This rule of righteousness for men therefore, even if met vicariously, could never open heaven: it could only leave the pardoned transgressor, newly forgiven and cleansed, on earth. But 'lo, the heavens were opened.'

The satisfied law accepted a legally justified son of Adam by the vicarious death of Jesus. But the righteousness of God acknowledged his own beloved Son, another head for men than Adam: 'In whom' — not with whom — 'I am well pleased.' An entirely new standing for a completely distinct relationship with God. This brought to the Father in Sonship. Only righteousness met justly according to God's own nature could do that, a basis — an objective basis — upon which men in Christ might be partakers of the divine nature.

'All righteousness' is by definition far more than legal righteousness. It is all the righteousness that there is or can be as such. Legal righteousness might bring a man as far as the Levitical priesthood acting on his behalf at the brazen altar: but there remained the unrent veil beyond the reach of legal priesthood. And at best a long and happy life in Israel during this present world. And then? But by the gospel of Christ God brought in everlasting righteousness beyond the power of death with no veil at all and an inheritance of everlasting glory in the world to come for the ages of eternity by way of a better resurrection. Satisfied law could never, never, never do that. But divine righteousness did it, and did it in such a way as forever to take the faithful out of reach from the law and its curse world without end.

The descent of the Spirit was not because of satisfied law, although of course it could not be without it. Law must first be satisfied. But that in itself could not have brought the baptism of the Holy Ghost. 'Received ye the Spirit by the works of the law, or by the hearing of faith?' Not when Moses was being read, but whilst Peter was yet speaking the Holy Ghost fell upon them all.

Jesus Christ baptises with the Holy Ghost precisely

because — when in death he honoured the law by vicariously meeting its curse for sinfulness — he went also in the measure of his sufferings infinitely beyond the afflictions required by the penal sanctions of legal justice.

Above all that the law could require, conceive, or even imagine, there soared the ever-increasing anguish of the passion of the great Sufferer. Beyond mortal endurance. At Calvary Jesus' affliction on behalf of others scaled the heights of infinity so to meet and quench the absolute ire of the outraged justice of God. But meet it, quench it, he did. He drank to the dregs the cup of the wrath and indignation of Almighty God not only for this world but also for that which is to come. He brought in everlasting righteousness.

At Calvary the very righteousness of God searched out eternity to the last for a single vestige of what was unsuited to the divine nature in any one of those vast numbers whom the crucified had bound to himself as one, and whose salvation he had undertaken to secure. He was their sacrifice. They were as him; he was as them; they were one. Nothing. There was nothing. Righteousness divine could find nothing. It was finished.

For his own true Israel Messiah has been to the divine heights of the offended justice of Jehovah, and satisfied God in his own nature that he might be agreeable to the reception of sons by Christ Jesus. That is what he did. It brought in everlasting righteousness. It opened heaven. It pleased the Father. And it brought down the baptism of the Holy Ghost. This Jesus. This Messiah. This son of David the son of Abraham. 'In whom I am well pleased.'

MATTHEW CHAPTER FOUR

¶ The beginning of his ministry. Ch. 4:1-25

Temptation is the beginning of his ministry. Temptations so subtle and refined that to any but one led of the Spirit — far from appearing temptations at all — they would seem to extend unique opportunities for the greatest good of the world. Yes, including the third temptation in Matthew. It is not a matter of a clear issue between right and wrong. It is a question of discerning between what appears to be right to man and what is actually revealed from God.

The Temptation is unique to the Person tempted. There can be no drawing of petty 'lessons' reduced to ordinary human circumstances. There is no comparison between these and our temptations. They are altogether above us, they are too high for us, they are exclusive to the Lord of Glory. The Temptation proper is solely to do with the Redeemer, Jesus Christ the righteous.

To perceive the significance of the Temptation, mentally we must soar above in time and space and view history stretching back to the creation, imagine it reaching forward till the end of time. Amongst all the countless teeming myriads of mankind emerging and submerging by birth and death in multitudes of rising and falling civilisations throughout the rolling ages of destiny, only one compares with the man led up of the Spirit to be tempted of the devil. There can be but one comparison. It is between the first man Adam in the garden, and the second man Christ in the wilderness.

Such a view shows that the long dark night had reigned

supreme over the world: thick darkness had covered the people. Fallen in Adam, shapen in iniquity, conceived in sin, born under sentence of death, the time of mankind's temptation in the light was long, long past. Since then it was all groping upon the dark mountains.

But now at last comes the Lord from heaven, the unique man, conceived of the Holy Ghost and born of the virgin Mary. The second Man and true Messiah, this spotless Saviour appears as the Light of the world, the only One since the creation of Adam to be without sin. Therefore it follows that his person, his position and his temptation are all unique. So is his challenge to the god of this world, the prince of darkness, the devil, to redeem his people from under that ancient and universal sway.

The three temptations constitute The Temptation because singly and together they are ultimate. There is nothing that could be added to any one, and there cannot be more than three.

Nothing could be added to any one temptation because each represents the diabolical ultimate within its sphere. Beneath it, myriad forms of that temptation may appear: but above it nothing exists because it is the absolute quintessence of devilish subtlety within that realm.

There cannot be more than three such temptations, because there are no realms of existence common to Man beyond body, soul and spirit. Correspondingly, there are no further spheres of obligation beyond the personal, the social, and the religious. Try these to the limit and nothing is left.

That is why there are three temptations to The

Temptation. Because Man in his interior nature is threefold and in his exterior environment has three ascending spheres of obligation. The reason why the second and third temptation are reversed in Luke from Matthew, respectively, is because Matthew emphasises the King and Kingdom and therefore the exterior realm of royal obligation ending with no less than the whole world. Whereas Luke stresses the Man and hence human nature, ending with the highest sphere of obligation: the spiritual and the religious.

Although of course the Lord Jesus was physically in the wilderness and actually fasted, it is both childish and superstitious to think of an embodied devil, to insist on a literal transportation to the temple, or to envisage a real mountain capable of flattening out the round globe and compressing all time to a moment. These are simply expressions used to convey the invisible, moral and spiritual realities far more vividly than difficult abstracts. And they are eminently satisfactory to enable the humble to get at the heart of the matter without being troubled over what lies beyond human comprehension.

John, emphasising the incarnate Deity, naturally ignores The Temptation. Mark, on the other hand, tells us that Jesus was 'thrown out' or 'cast out' by the Spirit into the wilderness, but gives very few details. In Luke, Jesus was 'led' and in Matthew 'led up again' into the wilderness, and in both cases we read of The Temptation in detail.

Matthew commences with the word 'Then', Mt. 4:1. That is, immediately after Jesus' baptism. Since John baptised 'beyond Jordan'—and therefore on the far bank—immediately to be led up again from thence, placed Jesus on the far side of the river in the selfsame position as Israel wandering through the wilderness before crossing Jordan to enter the promised land. So that if Jesus' baptism typified his vicarious substitution in death for Israel, 'then' his ascent up to the wilderness position showed Jesus' sympathetic identification with Israel in all that suffering pathway.

The unexpected wording 'led up again' of the Spirit is clearly suggestive. Jesus himself was never said to have gone up before! But Israel long ago came from the howling wilderness, and once more we see the hint of identification with his people in all their pilgrim tribulations. He *wants* them to know that in all their history he felt for them and in spirit shared with them throughout their pathway here below. 'Up again' suggests that this was not the first time that the sympathetic High Priest and King of Israel had felt what it cost the people to be Jehovah's in an alien wilderness.

This emphasises that the Messiah who had come to save his people from their sins, 'So he was their Saviour' Isaiah 63:8, identified himself with that people in the place of their humiliation, perhaps not for forty years, but sufficiently to show his true priestly pity for them. They had been — as Israel God's servant — humbled in the wilderness and the place of temptation. He is going — as Messiah their deliverer — 'again' into the wilderness led up of the Spirit to be tempted of the devil.

But there is this grand distinction: they failed, he never fails. They fell, he remained upright. They were corrupted by the heathen, he is ever separate from sinners. They discovered the plague of their hearts, he was a Man without sin after God's own heart. Indeed the very words used by Jesus to defeat the devil in the wilderness were those words used by God to admonish Israel when the devil defeated them in the same environment.

Of course it goes without saying that there is nothing whatsoever that is vicarious about Jesus' identifying himself 'again' with Israel in the wilderness. It is all sympathy, pure sympathy, total sympathy. He is deeply touched with the feeling of their infirmities in the very place which brought those infirmities to light. How kind! It is like the prophet; though never so stern in his rectitude, his bowels are moved with compassion and 'I sat where they sat, and remained there astonished among them seven days.'

This demonstrates far more eloquently than words the willing submissiveness of a Messiah so compassionate — one who is not ashamed to call them brethren — that he is certain to act on Israel's behalf as their dying substitute. For the time must come that Christ their passover should be sacrificed for them. 'O Israel, thou hast destroyed thyself; but in me is thine help.' Throughout his pilgrimage on earth Jesus showed the perfect qualifications for so noble a laying down of his life at the last.

How else could Messiah undertake at Calvary to save his people from their sins and their abysmal failures, unless first in contrast he had demonstrated the sheer worth of his own spotless life and the peerless success of his every undertaking? How else, unless voluntarily he entered into the circumstances and fully succeeded in the very place and situation where their weakness and corruption had been brought to light? So it came to pass that 'Jesus was led up of the Spirit into the wilderness to be tempted of the devil.'

Therefore having written 'So he was their Saviour' immediately afterwards Isaiah the prophet continues 'In all their affliction he was afflicted,' and that is exactly what we see here. He went up 'again' into the wilderness. But, I say, where they fell, he stood; and where they succumbed, he triumphed. And like the sabbath year for the land being neglected for four hundred and ninety years but reclaimed year by year in the seventy years of the captivity, so for every one of the forty years of Israel's wandering affliction in the wilderness Jesus voluntarily, pitifully, but in sinless perfection fasted a day for a year, and showed total success where they had manifested utter failure.

The first temptation came as a result of Jesus' forty days and forty nights fasting. 'He was afterward an hungred. And when the Tempter came to him, he said, If thou be the Son of God, command that these stones be made bread.'

The first is the only one of the three temptations in which Matthew uses the name of 'Tempter' for the devil. It is not used at all in Luke's account, and the name never occurs anywhere else in the gospels. In fact, it is only found in one other place in the New Testament, when the apostle feared the approach of 'The Tempter' to the early church.

Used in the precise sense — the ultimate — there were only three occasions for the Tempter. This is to apply the name absolutely: considering whom he comes to tempt as pure and unfallen from the hand of God. First; the whole world and age in Adam at the garden: the Tempter's success was complete. Second; the Lord Jesus in the wilderness: the Tempter's defeat was total. Finally; the early church in the unity of the body of Christ: before scripture closed, the Tempter's success was shattering. That is why the name occurs only two times in the New Testament. The truth is that after the fall the devil need and could appear only twice in this guise.

As to the name 'devil', this is simply the most appalling

71

case of what denotes superstitious ignorance being put in the place of proper translation. Derived from the very old English 'deofol', it is a meaningless word used by witches, wizards and clergymen to frighten the ignorant and childish into subjection. It is a word conjuring up all the nameless nightmares, all the frightful bogeymen in the dark corner of the stairs, all the dread childhood horrors of darkness. But the New Testament ὁ διάβολος — literally he who *throws-through* — actually pinpoints the meaning with cold logic and exact precision.

In New Testament Greek the word is used in the forensic context of Counsel-at-law for the prosecution. Ὁ διάβολος therefore means 'The Prosecutor', the one who 'throws through' the courtroom his convicting accusations, who 'casts across' the great Assize legal arguments so overwhelming that the poor Accused is left without defence. It is not a personal name. 'The devil' is never given a personal name. It is a functional description, the sole office of which consists in proving transgression at law so as to bring in a verdict of 'Guilty' from the Judge against the Defendant.

However it is by another, more rare, functional name that 'the devil' — it seems impossible to change that word! but at least let the *meaning* be understood — approaches Jesus, weak with fasting, in the first of the temptations. He appears in the function of 'The Tempter'.

That Jesus was 'an hungred' is easily understood. But the temptation was not to end the fast. The temptation was to command the stones to be made bread: a power surely exclusive to the Son of God. Then what was wrong with using it? Might it not *enhance* the virtue of Jesus' forty-days identification with Israel's affliction, for them to know afterwards that at any second Jesus could have ended his fast miraculously? But he did not do so. Now that the fast period had concluded, would not his previous voluntary self-denial be exemplified by the demonstration of power that had been ever present but always restrained? Then what made this a temptation?

'Command that these stones be made bread.' In Luke it is the substance itself, hard and inedible to the hungering Jesus: 'this stone'. Here it is 'these stones', the appearance of the substance, scattered as hoar-frost, white pebbles like Israel's manna upon the desert floor. A visible reminder in itself of the propriety of heavenly intervention to provide bread where none was to be found. I repeat, Where was the temptation?

Consider: 'If thou be the Son of God, command that these stones be made bread.' That was the temptation. Taking occasion of actual bodily hunger, the heart of the matter lay in the Tempter's subtle misconstruction of the message uttered from heaven at Jesus' baptism.

The Saviour's triumph over the temptation stood in his perfect understanding of the baptismal message, and therefore of the *means* by which his ministry should bring in the kingdom of God. Not by the Tempter's means! And equal to Jesus' perception, was his unswerving, unflinching zeal to fulfil the Father's will and to finish the work which he had been sent to accomplish. He could not be hoodwinked and he would not be deviated.

The voice from heaven had spoken out of the Hebrew scriptures. The first part of Jesus' baptismal message was declared from the psalmist; the second spoken out of the prophet Isaiah. Primarily the speech extolled the divine relationship and kingly destiny of the Son of God. But secondarily it heralded the path of lowly humiliation and intense suffering by which that predestined crown should be gained. Death was inherent in the heavenly prospect of glory. But not the way the Tempter twisted it!

'This is my beloved Son.' Quoted from Psalm two, these words come from a Messianic passage declaring the kingdom of Christ against which the heathen, the people, the kings of the earth, and the rulers set themselves. They appear to cast away the Anointed of God. But he that sitteth in the heavens laughs: resurrection is in view. He shall smash the heathen like a potter's vessel; he shall utterly tread down all his enemies; he will break all their bones with an iron rod: they shall be utterly and perpetually overthrown. Then shall the King reign for ever: of his kingdom and dominion there shall be no end. This is his sure destiny. The mouth of the Lord hath spoken it. The promise of Almighty God is behind it: 'Thou art my Son.' Power is in the word.

'In whom I am well pleased.' This passage, taken from the forty-second chapter of Isaiah, is part of a series of prophecies concerning the suffering servant of Jehovah. It is found in a context which culminates in the most terrible anguish and piteous affliction for the poor servant. He is bruised and struck down to death by none other than the very Jehovah whom he had served so faithfully. Yet this was the only way to save his people from their sins. Therefore what is in view here is Jesus' meek humility and obedient suffering even unto death.

The baptismal message sets before us One who, being in the form of God, thought it not robbery to be equal with God. But for all that, it was in his mind to become a suffering servant for the Father's good pleasure. He made himself of no reputation. He took upon him the form of a servant. He was made in the likeness of men, and, being found in fashion as a man, he humbled himself, and became obedient unto death, even the death of the cross. Though this servant were a Son, yet learned he obedience by the things which he suffered. And suffer he did, even unto death. Therefore it is said 'In whom I am well pleased.'

What is entailed in these temptations is the suggestion that Christ should use the divine power described in the first part of the baptismal message not merely to alleviate but actually to avoid completely the ignominious path marked out for him by the second. Indeed it is proposed that *that* is why the power and authority of the Son are given. '*If* thou be the Son of God.' Surely the consequence must be to demonstrate this Sonship in such a way that humiliation and indignity are avoided altogether?

The Tempter stresses that the glorious and omnipotent authority by which the kingdom will be established after the resurrection — 'Thou art my Son' — should in fact be used *now* to circumvent the bitter humiliation and suffering unto death suggested by the words 'In whom I am well pleased.' He submits promises pertaining to the glory beyond the resurrection, in order to obviate the prophecies pertaining to suffering and death before it.

In fact the Tempter *never even mentions* the second part of the baptismal message. On both occasions he quotes only the first part, relating to the risen glory of the Son of God and the establishment of the kingdom. Consistently he ignores the latter half of the message, altogether as if it had never been spoken. He proposes action — 'If thou be ... then' — on the basis of the promise in the primary part of the message alone. He clean takes away the second that he may altogether establish the first: a temptation affirming the divine necessity of avoiding suffering altogether.

'Man shall not live by bread alone, but by every word that proceedeth out of the mouth of God,' v.4. It was not that bread was an exception to the proceeding. Bread did proceed from the mouth of God. The Creator had spoken it into being along with everything else. And as with most living things, its seed was in itself: thereafter it propagated itself; but originally it came by his word of mouth at the beginning. So did man, and he should not live by that word alone.

Jesus' reply comes from Deuteronomy 8:3. A most suited context for Israel's Messiah identifying with his people in affliction. 'The LORD thy God led thee these forty years in the wilderness, to humble thee, and to prove thee, to know what was in thine heart, whether thou wouldest keep his commandments, or no. And he humbled thee, and suffered thee to hunger, and fed thee with manna, which thou knewest not, neither did thy fathers know; that he might make thee know that man doth not live by bread only, but by every word that proceedeth out of the mouth of the LORD doth man live.'

And the LORD, Messiah's God, led him up by the Spirit into the wilderness for forty days, and the LORD humbled him, and proved him, and suffered him to hunger. Not for forty years, only forty days, but it was enough to know what was in his heart. Neither was Jesus sustained with manna, for the LORD his God did not send it, and it was to come from heaven from the mouth of the LORD or not at all; it was not for the Servant to abuse the power entrusted to him to *make* manna. The Servant was in the place of God's dependent Man, not God himself! *Man* shall not live by bread alone. Besides, it was legitimate that Israel might be sustained with manna from heaven those forty years. But the sent Messiah who hungered these forty days could have none of it: he came to give, and give again, and give to the uttermost. He *was* the Manna.

Jesus' reply is absolute. A word more about 'bread'. Even superficially it is obvious that the word encompasses the whole conception of food. But in such a context and at such a spiritual level, much more is involved. Bread implies *the principle* of earthly necessities. Bread, and the body sustained by it; bread, and the shelter that body needs; bread, and the life it supports; bread, and the propagation of life. Needs for the body: in this life and the present world.

One can see immediately, the whole of the temptation of Adam and Eve in the garden was fully encompassed in no more than the *first* temptation of Christ in the wilderness. The primeval Temptation was entirely a question of 'food' and of 'eating'. Of what might and might not be eaten: 'And the serpent said unto the woman, Yea, hath God said, Ye shall not eat of every tree of the garden?' It was the allurement of 'bread' in the excitement of the appetites: 'And when the woman saw that the tree was good for food, and that it was pleasant to the eyes, and a tree to be desired to make one wise, she took of the fruit thereof, and did eat, and gave also unto her husband with her; and he did eat.'

'And when Jesus had fasted forty days and forty nights, he was afterward an hungred. And when the Tempter came to him, he said, If thou be the Son of God, command that these stones be made bread. But he answered and said, It is written, Man shall not live by bread alone, but by every word that proceedeth out of the mouth of God.'

Furthermore, as Messiah, it is a question of the Kingdom. The Tempter knew that. Not just bread for *himself:* bread for *the people.* The Tempter is suggesting that although man is of God, that this Man is the Son of God, what God *means* by being the Son of God must first be considered in connection with providing for the basic human needs. It is for the great need of the world. Bread. Everything must be subservient to the visionary conception of procuring food for the peoples. The hungry cry for bread. If the ability of the King to provide it cannot be proved alone in the wilderness, how can it be proved before multitudes in the world? 'Command that these stones be made bread.'

In the name of humanity the devil cries to the Son of God, and humanity cries with him. In a continent of millions who are on the edge of starvation, said a great world leader, 'The only form in which God dare appear to the people is bread.' But 'he humbled thee, and suffered thee to hunger.' Why? 'To know what was in thine heart, whether thou wouldest keep his commandments, or no.'

No. The cry reveals man's agreement with the devil in his conception of Messiah: 'Ye seek me, not because ye saw the miracles, but because ye did eat of the loaves, and were filled. Labour not for the meat which perisheth, but for that meat which endureth unto everlasting life.'

But what of the body? Its appetites and sensations demand to be fed, clothed, cared for, cherished, sheltered. To this end — utterly mistrusting the God of providence — the Tempter's philosophy of bread was bequeathed to the world in the fall and death of Adam. It states that the crying injustice of mankind is that men are still hungry, that they call out in need, lie in pain, suffer neglect. That man has a *right* to live, a *right* to happiness; a *right* to education, career, marriage, security, medicine, diversion. Then, 'If thou be the Son of God,' surely sonship means the use of all this power and authority to create bread for the deprived and under-privileged peoples of the world? *This* is to be King. To give the people bread. Where is this King? Where is his kingdom?

'When Jesus therefore perceived that they would come and take him by force, to make him a king, he departed again into a mountain himself alone.'

This philosophy asserts that all man's spirit, soul, religion, worship, every heavenly connection, all should be brought down and focused upon this present earthly life, as though the material level were the supreme, and man's short period in this world were all that pertained to him. Bread is the one thing needful. And quickly; life is short. Man practically proclaims in all honesty, in the name of God, religion, morality and human rights: *Thou shalt love the world with all thy mind and heart and strength.* And God and thy neighbour as a means of promoting its temporal welfare.

But Messiah totally rejects this whole conception. The present life is death: the life to come is immortality. He that loseth his life shall find it. The present world is fallen: the world to come is everlasting. 'Labour not for the meat which perisheth, but for that meat which endureth unto everlasting life.'

To that end, gnawing hunger, bitter affliction, degrading humiliation: all are seen as blessed help obtained from God that one may sit loose to this passing evil world. The contrary philosophy, so ably expressed by the Tempter, so much demanded by the people, so consistently presented by the rulers: it is all so utterly *alien* to the kingdom of heaven. As it is to the Son of God.

Therefore hear the last word. It is written, 'Man shall not live by bread alone, but by every word that proceedeth out of the mouth of God.'

The Second temptation in Matthew concerns Christ King of Israel as the priestly leader of God's people. It has in view Messiah's sense of religious responsibility and spiritual government towards men, in things pertaining to God. He is the chosen of God, the one mediator, the unique apostle and high priest ordained to give counsel to the people and to approach God on their behalf. He is the heir, to him is the kingdom and of his rule and dominion there shall be no end. Son over the house of God, his peerless worth, unique humanity, and divine sonship all demand his exaltation as absolute authority over the people of God in all things religious.

But how are men to know this? Given these prospects, by what means is Jesus to attain them? How is he to gain recognition in the eyes of the people as their royal priest ordained of God? *Diabolos* has a suggestion. It is the second temptation in Matthew.

Not so in Luke. In Luke this temptation is placed third and last. It is precisely the same incident but it is viewed from another aspect and at a different level. Therefore it requires placing in an alternative sequence.

Luke consistently stresses the manhood of Christ. He

.always keeps Jesus' humanity in view. Hence in each temptation the third gospel emphasises the successive areas of human responsibility addressed by *diabolos*, and, appropriately, arranges the three in ascending order of importance: body, soul and spirit.

The last temptation in Luke concerns the final and ultimate sphere of obligation proper to human nature. Not moral rectitude regarding the appetites. Nor social responsibility towards the world. But subject worship of Almighty God. Man was made neither for himself nor for others. To the contrary, man was created for the glory of God alone. Therefore the true realisation of manhood must be found in revealed religion; just as the ultimate fruition of human nature — its final justification for existence — must be expressed in spiritual worship.

However in Matthew the whole emphasis is different. The outlook is towards another perspective: the King is in view and his government envisaged. This is so whether it be considered in respect of providing bread for the masses, priesthood for the worshippers, or world-dominion for the nations. It is a royal question: it has to do with divine administration.

Matthew is environmental and exterior, whereas Luke is personal and interior. Matthew views Christ the King tried in relation to each governmental realm of the kingdom. Luke sees Jesus as Man, exposed to temptation throughout every sphere of human obligation.

The first gospel makes clear that the Man born King of the Jews is also the chosen and anointed high priest of God for the people. However the presence in Israel of the centuries-old Aaronic priesthood and hierarchy —

ordained of God under the hand of Moses — posed certain questions.

The Jews revered the house of Aaron. The tribes cherished the priests and Levites raised up and preserved by the God of Abraham, Isaac and Jacob even to the latest day. Ministering before the children of Israel, they were the visible custodians of that renowned glory made known to the fathers from of old.

Three times a year and more the tribes ascended to Jerusalem, their feet standing within her gates. Thither the tribes went up, even the tribes of the Lord, unto Israel's testimony there, to give thanks to the name of the Lord. Within the house of God Israel was led by the priestly seed of Aaron. The priests mediated between the tribes and Jehovah, appearing before God in their behalf and turning to bless the people in the name of the Lord.

'O Israel, trust thou in the Lord: he is their help and shield. O house of Aaron, trust in the Lord: he is their help and shield. The Lord hath been mindful of us: he will bless us; he will bless the house of Israel; he will bless the house of Aaron. So shall peace dwell within thy walls, O Jerusalem, and prosperity within thy palaces. Let the house of Aaron now say, His mercy endureth for ever.'

Now then, seeing these things were so, what further need was there that another priest should rise from the house of Judah, of which tribe Moses spake nothing concerning priesthood? By what scripture, with what sign, and on what principle will this Jesus dispense with Aaron's house and present himself to Israel as the Governor over the house of God and its service? Certain questions indeed.

How were the people to know that this same Jesus was taken from among men and ordained for men in things pertaining to God? For the taking, ordaining and sending were all invisible. But the ancient priesthood, the sacred garments, the holy service: they *were* visible.

And Aaron's house had been established by the immutable decree of Jehovah himself since time immemorial. Here were things Israel could look upon, behold, handle, and see with their very eyes: visible things, age-old things, things certain and tried, things proved and proved eminently satisfactory again and again by the fathers from old time. Then why change in the last days for something which was neither apparent nor visible? Hence the questions. In effect the Jews said, Moses I know, and the Levitical priesthood I see; but who are you?

The great problem then was this: what visible sign ought Jesus to give that the Jews might recognise the divine origin and human necessity of his new testament priesthood? What exterior manifestation of that inward spiritual grace?

It was suggested from the sacred scriptures, opened in the holy city, spoken within the divine precincts, situate upon the pinnacle of the temple: 'If thou be the Son of God, cast thyself down: for it is written, He shall give his angels charge concerning thee: and in their hands they shall bear thee up, lest at any time thou dash thy foot against a stone.' A sign indeed.

Suddenly caught by flaming spirits as wondrously manifested, the hurtling figure arrested in mid-air by ministering angels, the amazing vision would appear to Levite and scribe, priest and people alike! What doubt could ever remain in the Jewish heart? See him gently lowered to the earth by the radiant hosts of heaven! Who else but the true Messiah, Melchizedek indeed, King and Priest of the Most High God?

But is *that* the way to establish the kingdom? A way of exterior glory, miraculous exhibition, of visible signs?

And mark, the question is not, Did miraculous signs attend the Lord Jesus in bringing in the kingdom of heaven? For undoubtedly they did. However, not one of *them* was arbitrary. None was superfluous. All had coherent purpose. Each possessed spiritual reason. And all were perfectly balanced with Jesus' preaching and teaching.

Divinely sent signs were given so as temporarily to depict in the exterior body, the permanent wonders done before God for the interior soul. In this light *diabolos'* proposal was impertinent and irrelevant. The spectacular would produce the very opposite to the desired effect. It would draw attention to the Lord Jesus, certainly. But not in a way which exemplified his doctrine. Rather in a way of exhibitionism totally alien to the kingdom of heaven. This was clean contrary to the means by which the kingdom must be established.

For divine signs to *attend* whilst Jesus actually *brought* in the kingdom by the doctrine of the gospel: this was one thing. Even so, men must not mistake the ephemeral sign for the permanent signification. However, for *diabolos* to substitute false and misleading signs in place of the true and altogether instead of the kingdom itself: that was another thing. Yet it was precisely the deception upon which this proposal was based. All sign — and false sign at that! — and no kingdom.

What shall we then say to these things? Was — and is — it not the diabolical purpose that men should be deflected and stupefied by signs and wonders? Once upon such a course, what will satisfy the novel appetites but more and more startling diversions? Where will it all end but in religious conjurers feeding self-deluded pretence?

Once men are ensnared, how many charlatans will run to meet the demands of the incredulous with an ever-changing and ever-increasing series of tricks and pretences? Will this not perpetually charm and captivate the bewitched *away* from salvation? *Does* it not? Then, instead of enlightening rather would it not permanently blind men's eyes to the one thing needful?

What of the Fall? What of inbred depravity? What of the mountainous unforgiven sins against law and gospel? What of the resurrection and the impending judgment to come? What of the immortal state world without end? What of eternity beyond the grave when time is no more? What of meeting Almighty God?

The answer to these questions will establish the kingdom of heaven. Not exterior signs and wonders titillating the senses of men whose rock-hard and unchanged hearts remain those of unregenerate and unforgiven sinners.

Salvation brings in the kingdom, not miracles. The kingdom of God is not signs and wonders but righteousness, peace and joy in the Holy Ghost.

A crucified Saviour is what the eye of faith must behold, not a wondrous signal. A solid gospel not a superficial entertainment. The kingdom of an inward heaven is required not the deceit of an outward distraction. To be built on the rock not splashed by the froth. Revelation on the truth: this is the need of men.

Exterior signs and wonders had their temporary purpose. *Diabolos'* sign had no purpose at all. It would have produced the diametrically opposite effect to the end required in true religion.

It is useless to bedazzle spectators with what would be in fact a worldly display — albeit miraculous — to captivate the attention. It will but draw the heart *away* from those essential truths needed to save the soul from death. Truths which must be received by preaching and teaching. Faith comes by *hearing* not gazing. And hearing by the word of God.

As with the first temptation — though not the last — the second is based upon the presumptuous corruption of the baptismal message. The first part of that message, speaking from Psalm 2, tells of the glorious Son of God, raised from the dead and ascended on high, destined to have dominion over all the earth.

However this glory to come is *on the basis* of the humiliation first to be endured and suffered in this present world. So the apostle assures us: 'He became obedient unto death even the death of the cross *wherefore* God hath highly exalted him.' It is this prior humiliation to which the second part of the baptismal message refers.

Yet the temptation totally ignores this qualifying prophecy! It stresses solely the Messianic glory of Psalm 2. Yet the whole basis of that glory, I say, the whole basis of it, is the work done in meek submission and lowly servitude on earth.

Diabolos proposes the crown without the cross. The saving of the life without the losing of it. The glorifying without the suffering. But the cross, the losing of life, the suffering, are in fact the sole path to the crown, the salvation, and the glory yet to be revealed.

Dispensing altogether with the tribulations of this life — without which the kingdom of God cannot be inherited in the next — *diabolos* transfers all the glory reserved for the world to come, and proposes it here and now in the world at present. A neat disposal of the strait gate and narrow way that leadeth unto life.

The divine oracle at Jesus' baptism shows that earthly tribulation is just as much the lot of our great high Priest as it is of those on whose behalf he ministers.

His priesthood does not obviate his being touched with the feeling of our infirmities, it requires it. His high dignity is not airily to dismiss the temptation, on the contrary it is humbly to submit to it. His ability to work miracles is not a licence to do so; rather, he is charged to learn obedience by the things which he suffers. His priestly glory is not given that angels should smooth away his suffering path; it is that alone he should offer up himself without spot unto God a sacrificial victim. And so it was. But it is this very principle that the second temptation contradicts.

For here is the heart of the enemy's attack: the responsible exercise of the priestly ministry of the Son of God. On what principle should he exercise his royal priesthood? The temptation is, a lordly one. The truth is, a sacrificial one. Sacrifice is of the very essence of his priestly rule; it is the basis on which that rule is exercised over the people of God. This is what *diabolos* attempts to confound through the misrepresentation of the purpose of the Father and the unbalanced interpretation of the word of God.

The second temptation must be seen as a trial exclusive to Messiah's priestly government. The altered environment shows this. Consider the difference of the setting from that of the first temptation. The former was beyond Jordan in the solitary wilderness; the latter is at the holy city in the fruitful land. The first was far off in the cursed and forsaken wastes; the second nigh within the blest and thronging precincts.

Previously Jesus had wandered the stony-ground of the barren desert floor. Now aloft the temple-courts he beholds the ancient priesthood attendant upon both altar and worshippers far below.

Formerly it was to do with stones and bread. Here the lofty view portrays the desperate need of better sacrifices than those of Aaron, and of a nobler priesthood than that which for itself must first offer both gifts and sacrifices for sins. Yet high above stood that singular priest for ever after the order of Melchizedek — spotless son over the house of God — able by one offering to perfect forever them that are sanctified.

But how shall they look up to him? That was the question.

Clearly the very setting proposes the question. *Diabolos* taketh Jesus to the holy city. Then into the temple. Then up to the wing of the holy place, on the edge, high aloft. So looking down on the priestly courts, on altar, laver, priesthood; on the tableau that depicted all the unresolved religious questions of the centuries. These very questions which the Son of God had come to resolve. Thus the second temptation.

Whether in the body or out of the body I cannot prove; God knoweth. But if a physical and literal interpretation be demanded, it is well to remember that no such demand is feasible of the final temptation. Jesus was physically transported? Think of the difficulties. The context of all three temptations is explicit: 'Then was Jesus led up of the Spirit into the wilderness to be tempted of the devil.' So where was he at the second temptation? Is it seriously proposed that this invisible spirit, *diabolos* — for miles horizontally and feet vertically — physically transported the incarnate Son? And how arrive on the wing of the temple?

How could Jesus *not* have been seen? And seen talking to himself? Now for my part I read, 'Then the devil taketh him' *in conscious sensation.* That is, so as to convey to the mind and imagination the panoramic sight with all its concomitant spiritual questions just as vividly as though Jesus were really there.

In the heightened and detached mental state following upon so long a fast, given such strong mental impressions from so powerful a being, the sensations would be fully equal to the simple description. Therefore in this unique passage the description is one of the manner in which *diabolos* conveyed Jesus' *mind.* Thus it is quite proper to take the passage in this light. But if any wish to think otherwise that is their affair.

Proceeding to the actual wording of the second temptation, a great deal of irrelevant comment has been devoted by some to the fact that *diabolos'* speech is couched in the language of the psalms. 'The devil quotes scripture' we are told at length with many a flourish and much embellishment. It seems to me that such commentators pounced upon the obvious with relief, because here, at last, was something about which they could enlarge.

But surely the reason for *diabolos'* quotation from the prophetic passage is that it is the form appropriate to the particular context and peculiar scope of this temptation. Neither the first nor the last temptation quotes from the scriptures. Yet if but half of what these commentators have written about 'the devil quoting scripture' were true, he would have done it not only before and after the central trial but virtually upon every occasion on which he opened his mouth. However, it is because the second temptation distinctively surveys and addresses the priestly realm that of necessity the language is taken from Holy Writ.

The issue was one of interpreting the mind and ways of God as concerning the means by which Messiah's priesthood and government should be made known. This having been written and long foretold in the prophetic scriptures, it is to this source that Jesus would look for guidance. Then from where else should *diabolos* quote when seeking to deflect Jesus by subtlety from the straight and narrow path of spiritual and divine principles?

Again, much is made of the fact that the quotation from Psalm 91 differs from the original in that a clause is omitted and a phrase added. However, for what it is worth, the Septuagint supplies the additional phrase. And since it is not altogether illegitimate to quote only one half of a verse providing the absence of the remainder makes no difference to the sense, really one might dispute as to whether this is a misquotation or not.

In any event, to me the end of the question is this: Has the old serpent lost his subtlety that he blunders over a simple matter of record? A straight-forward quotation from the psalms? And what kind of an insult is it to Jesus' intelligence to suppose that he would not notice? An observant child would notice: but this is a temptation so refined and diabolically subtle that it is impossible without the revelation of the Holy Ghost even to know what it is! As if *diabolos* would risk *that* by blundering over a simple quotation. Since Jesus says nothing against it in his reply, we may conclude that he was not so punctilious as to fault the discrepancy of a word or two making absolutely no difference to the sense.

'It is written again, Thou shalt not tempt the Lord thy God.' Jesus' reply to *diabolos* refers to the unbelief and failure of the children of Israel not many days after leaving the land of Egypt, Exodus 17:1-7. Having passed through the Red Sea as by dry land — which the Egyptians assaying to do were drowned — soon the tribes entered into the wilderness proper. But not without continued and manifest tokens of the care and providence of Almighty God, for they were led by a pillar of cloud every day and the fire failed not by night. And as if this were not enough, also for six days each and every week abundant manna fell from heaven thick about the camp, especially with sufficient to provide against the sabbath on the sixth day.

Then how could they ever doubt him? But they did, for pitching in the place Rephidim — afterwards called Massah and Meribah, Temptation and Strife — they found, apparently, that there was no water. They strove against the Lord and Moses that day. Bitterly complaining against Jehovah and railing at the adverse providence discovered in

91

this dry place, they took up stones ready to stone Moses the man of God.

Why did they not trust Jehovah? He had led them there: and would he then suffer them to perish in the wilderness? Why not leave the provision of water to the God of providence? Why create such an issue that if God did not provide water at that very moment they would slay Moses the same instant and doubtless thereafter return to Egypt? Why threaten Jehovah with such dire and immediate consequences? 'Why tempt ye me?' With their strife they forced the issue in the day of temptation in the wilderness: Let him answer or no: 'Is the Lord among us, or not?'

Ought they not to have submitted with meekness to all that befell them, and *then* in that submission to have trusted and proved him by faith? But no; striving against the providence of God, denying the God of providence, they tempted God to answer. They forced a situation of their own making. They themselves created circumstances which obliged Jehovah's intervention to preserve his own honour, not to mention save the threatened life of Moses. But, 'Ye shall *not* tempt the Lord your God, as ye tempted him in Massah,' Deuteronomy 6:16.

Exactly. The aptness is perfect. This prohibition forbids precisely what *diabolos* proposed to the Lord Jesus. The creation of circumstances forcing God to answer in order to redeem his word given in past promises; not to mention save the endangered life of Jesus. But with this motive: the people would then immediately recognise their Priest and King. And in addition the sly innuendo was somehow conveyed that this whole precipitation was actually required by the words given at Jesus' baptism.

But the ears of the man led by the Spirit into the wilderness were open to the Father: he knew the message. He knew that if he was to be crowned with glory and honour, first he must be humiliated with shame and ignominy. If he was to bring a people into the Father's house, he himself must first have not where to lay his head. If he was to be the beloved of God he must receive no honour from men. If he was to dispense the bread of life his own body must first be broken in death. If he was to be head over all things to the church then he must first wash the disciples' feet. Oh yes, he had the message.

In a word, if he was to be glorified amidst myriad praising angels, then he must first be traduced amongst the mocking, reviling multitude. Moreover, like Israel of old, he must not use his power and privilege to alleviate the path of thorns. He must not exercise the authority of his Sonship to alter the disposition of his Father's providence. He must not use the frailty of his manhood to appeal for God's special intervention: he must never create a situation obliging God to intervene dramatically in order to preserve his life. No, he must submit and trust and learn obedience by the things which he suffers in meek resignation to the providence that befalls him. In fine, he must not tempt the Lord his God, as they tempted theirs at Massah.

The Third temptation is the last, for the sequence in Matthew undoubtedly records the actual order of events. Consider the word which introduces each temptation; also that used to conclude the whole. The first commences with

'Then', Matthew 4:1. The second temptation, 4:5-7, begins with the same word as the first clearly showing that this follows immediately afterwards. Of necessity the remaining temptation must be the last.

Although the third and last temptation commences with the word 'Again' — perhaps not quite so definitive — nevertheless it is followed straight away by yet another 'Then' in the wonderful little verse which declares that all is now over. 'Then the devil leaveth him.' The verse goes on to speak of the comfort and succour given by ministering angels to the gaunt victor. Since this took place immediately after Matthew's last temptation and also concludes the whole, it follows, the first gospel gives the correct sequence.

But for all that we must not think of these three temptations merely as incidents. In another sense they are summaries: the crystallisation of events at the climax of their duration. Thus it is written, 'Being *forty days* tempted of the devil,' Luke 4:2. There had been increasing pressure in just these three areas for well over a month culminating only when the senses could no longer be heightened by continued fasting, and when prolonging the issue could prove nothing further than had already come to light. Sufficient time had elapsed to demonstrate for good and all the inviolate integrity of Jesus' virtue. '*Then* the devil leaveth him.'

There is no subtlety about the last temptation. No 'If thou be the Son' or sly craftiness with the baptismal oracle. It is a blatant all-or-nothing offer which in the very making shoots *diabolos'* last bolt. Seeing that deception avails him nothing at all he piles upon the counter of temptation — heap upon heap! — all that he has ever acquired to trade for the tender shoot of Jesus' spiritual virtue.

Without finesse he boldly displays one glittering panorama upon another of vast and overwhelming richness and glory. Breathtaking! Time gathers her mantle and sweeps the ends of heaven and earth at his bidding, flashing the hidden but swiftly unfolding pleats of her richly embroidered cloak, opening past and present with a flicking twirl of fabulous revelation. But in so doing *diabolos* sacrifices subtlety whole upon the altar of massive prospects and glittering gain. So much it means to him; and thus his malice lies all open and exposed.

The 'Exceeding high mountain' must be regarded as the figure of a supernatural elevation commanding such advantage that all the world that ever there was appears spread as a textured carpet at one's feet. The peak of this spiritual aerie soars above all space to pierce a dimension of time in which the rolling ages are focused through the glass of *Now!* All duration contracts to a moment of time: 'All the kingdoms of the world and the glory of them.' 'All the kingdoms of the world in a moment of time.'

'The World'. Although the same in the English, in fact the original uses two entirely different words. So that once again and for entirely doctrinal purposes Luke differs from Matthew. Luke has οἰκουμένη whereas Matthew gives κόσμος. Both were involved; each is selected. One respects man; the other regards the dominion. Very wrongly this distinction is hidden from the English reader by the single word 'world' used in translation.

The Greek word selected in Luke is that from which we derive *economy*, and in the broader sense this makes an excellent rendering. Οἰκουμένη, *oikoumene*, is derived from οἰκέω, *oikeo*, a verb meaning 'to inhabit'. It is generally associated with a well-ordered household. An economic household. The expanded word used in Luke therefore implies the well-ordered economic structure of mankind: the economy of households and nations, therefore, the inhabited or civilised world. Personally, I understand the correct translation to be 'civilisation'. 'All the realms of civilisation in a moment of time.' All that is or has ever been civilised, cultured, educated, artistic and refined; what is governed by reason, wisdom, sagacity, with a due regard to the proper respect owed to dignities; a propriety exists, a politeness, and with it a nicely balanced religion. Civilisation.

Matthew uses the much more common κόσμος, *kosmos*. Whereas the word translated 'World' in Luke 4:5 occurs but fifteen times in the New Testament, *kosmos* is found one hundred and eighty-eight times. From it is derived the English cosmos, cosmic, cosmopolitan and cosmetic. Basically the word means 'adornment, harmonious arrangement, constitution or order,' and usually the reference is to outward appearances although this is by no means always the case. The basic meaning may have several applications, for example a woman's adornment — 'Whose adorning, *kosmos*, let it not be that outward adorning' — but almost invariably in the New Testament the word refers to the harmonious arrangement, constitution or order of the creation.

Kosmos, then, denotes the appearance of the world, either of the whole creation as an entity or else of created man exclusively. If the latter, it is not individual; it is the very state of mankind, the whole system of world man, corporate humanity. When *kosmos* is used in this sense, as it is in Matthew 4:8, there is always an alien connotation: not Adam viewed as innocent in the garden, but his guilty posterity expelled from it, man as seen in the flesh.

The word so used refers to the vast system or arrangement of mankind in the fall and alienated from God. It is a corrupt seed spread over the face of the earth in the continuity of successive generations. Thus mankind is considered as an entity. Humanity is seen using this complex of cosmos to disguise from itself the truth of the whole shocking arrangement. That is the world. And it is precisely what *diabolos* offered to Jesus. 'All the kingdoms of the world and the glory of them.' All that he had gained and man had lost in the fall.

It is easy to see how the presentation of the cultured *oikoumene* in Luke appeals to the highest in man, whereas the cosmic dominion reviewed in Matthew challenges ability in the monarch. Incredible, fantastic offer! Who but the one that spurned it wholly and with contempt could utter so profoundly 'What shall it profit a man, if he shall gain the whole world, and lose his own soul?'

The truth is that Christ did not come to 'christianise' the world or to make this nation or any nation his, but to bring into being a chosen generation, a royal priesthood, a holy nation, a peculiar people not at all of this world but altogether of that which is to come. He came to call out such a people as separate from the world, to create the spiritually conceived church of God, the ἐκκλησία — *the assembly called out* — which at the last shall be enabled to cry in response: 'Thou wast slain, and hast redeemed us to God by thy blood *out* of every kindred and tongue and people and nation.'

Though he purchased the field, it was to gain the treasure: this was his vision and all else is loss. This prompted him to say 'I pray not for the world but for them which thou hast given me.' And again 'They are not of the world even as I am not of the world.' The truth is, he does not *want* the world as it is, nor the nations as they are, neither man as he stands. He calls the poor and needy, the lost and sinful, the worthless and self-condemned, and new creates the whole into one new man. Hence it is said, 'If any man be in Christ, there is a new creation: old things are passed away; behold, all things are become new.' Such a people together with their Lord look beyond this world for a city in the world to come, whose builder and maker is God.

But *diabolos* showed him 'All the kingdoms of *this* world and the glory of them; and saith unto him, All these things will I give thee, if thou wilt fall down and worship me.' And again he saith 'For that is delivered unto me, and to whomsoever I will I give it.'

But is it his? And can he give it? Certainly Jesus called *diabolos* The prince of this world. And the apostle waxeth very bold and says of him, 'The god of this world', speaking in another place of 'the rulers of the darkness of this world'. Again Paul refers to 'The prince of the power of the air' governing the 'course of this world' by acting through 'the spirit that now worketh in the children of disobedience'.

Moreover the enticement in the temptation itself is based upon the reality of *diabolos'* possession and gift of the world and civilisation: 'To whomsoever I will I give it!' If it be said, That is a false claim; I reply, Then it is no temptation. But it is called a temptation.

Notice the wording. 'If thou *therefore* wilt worship me, all shall be thine.' But *wherefore?* Because the possession and dominion claimed by *diabolos* were in fact his, and his to give, and he would on one condition give them: *'therefore'.* Significantly the offer is not *contested* by Jesus:

98

it is simply and outright *rejected*. Hence by implication in
itself it was perfectly valid: it was just that it was so
contemptibly objectionable. The world and all those things
and all that glory, *were* his to give, as he said, 'For that is
delivered unto me, and to whomsoever I will I give it.'

How did he get it? Whose was it? Moses the servant of
God writing by the Holy Ghost in the book of Exodus
records that tremendous day when 'the mount burned with
fire' and there was 'blackness, and darkness, and tempest,
and the sound of a trumpet, and the voice of words; which
voice they that heard intreated that the word should not
be spoken to them any more: For they could not endure
that which was commanded, And if so much as a beast
touch the mountain, it shall be stoned, or thrust through
with a dart: And so terrible was the sight, that Moses said, I
exceedingly fear and quake.' That day God came down and
spake all the words of this law. And the LORD thy God
said 'In six days the LORD made heaven and earth, the sea,
and all that in them is, and rested the seventh day.'

On the sixth day, it is written: God said, Let us make
man in our image, after our likeness: and let them have
dominion over the fish of the sea, and over the fowl of the
air, and over the cattle, and over all the earth, and over
every creeping thing that creepeth upon the earth. So God
created man in his own image, in the image of God created
he him; male and female created he them. And God blessed
them, and God said unto them, Be fruitful, and multiply,
and replenish the earth, and subdue it: and have dominion
over the fish of the sea, and over the fowl of the air, and
over every living thing that moveth upon the earth. And
God saw every thing that he had made, and, behold, it was
very good. And the evening and the morning were the sixth
day.

The earth was given to man. It was his dominion. All these things God gave to him, and the glory of them, for that was delivered unto him, and he should fall down and worship the LORD his God, the Creator, and bring in the blessing. And it was very good. It was, but man lost everything. Not only did he lose everything, but since losing it he has rearranged his cosmos to assure himself that he has lost nothing. Indeed, that it never happened. And that the creation never happened. And God never happened.

From that day to this, mankind has with one consent made excuse for himself. The whole world has been blinded in the error and persuaded in the delusion. But the Genesis truth stands sure: turning from his Creator to the tempter, man has sold himself into slavery for a falsehood and delivered up his dominion for a lie. Hence 'that is delivered unto me.' Yes, for no more than an illusion. In return the god of this world has blinded that world to the shocking truth of the awful thing that it has done to its Maker.

Yes, and continues to do. For the modern method of 'scientific' profanity is no less blasphemous than the ancient system of superstitious idolatry. The object is the same. Prove the fallacy of the Creation; the error of the Fall; the nonsense of the Devil. And if you dare, the falsehood of God. The end justifies the means. Collect as many scientific facts as possible; scatter them as widely as may be: only, embed them in a structure of 'evolutionary' clay whatever. Invincible proof now appears to all who see it.

No God, no creation; no fall, no revelation. No redemption. Only evolution. Assert it with anthropology: argue it with archaeology: boast it with biology: clarify it with chemistry: guarantee it with genetics. Confirm it through geology: prove it by zoology: say it with science.

Put posters in the primary, cry statistics in the secondary, sound dogma in the highest. Measured by its mythical time-scale, towering with heady iron logic, the atheistic idol of socialist science nevertheless rests on the trembling clay feet of theory and conjecture. No doubt covered with discretion.

However, this poor latter-day idol has fared worse than old philistine Dagon who fell upon his face. This stands on its head. The heady facts of cast-iron logic must needs support the speculative feet of plastered earth. Professing a scientific detached outlook at once curiously subjective and myopic, these devotees tirelessly polish each metallic gleam: so to prove the idol all of metal. Then why the clay?

Away with unbelieving questions. Only believe! Merge fact and fiction, blend photograph and illustration, confuse experiment with speculation, confound truth with theory. Bewildering? But every fact screams Evolution! Gravity itself seen aright now demonstrates the ascent of man. Every iron-hard truth embedded into an evolutionary — revolutionary! — system of moulded clay, it becomes utterly obvious to the intoxicated worshippers that all is of one.

'Get thee behind me, Satan.' Not only because the Tempter is himself in very essence The Wicked. Neither because the condition he requires is so blasphemously evil. Quite apart from that, aside altogether from the character of the one who offers — the world in and of itself is so corrupt and deceitful. Its very nature is to wonder after the beast. 'The *diabolos*, and Satan, hath deceived the whole world.' So it is written. And again, 'All the world becomes guilty before God.' Thus it is concluded: 'The whole world lieth in wickedness.'

101

'Get thee hence, *Satan.*' Occurring for the first time in the Temptation, the first time in Matthew, and the first time in the New Testament, the ancient Hebrew title used by Jesus finally to dismiss *diabolos* opens up a wealth of accumulated revelation from the Old Testament.

Hitherto the narrative had employed the descriptive names 'Tempter' and 'Prosecutor' from the common Greek tongue. At last, however, the Old Testament Hebrew is quoted giving the name revealed from of old time — Satan — as if to emphasise the final identification of this Wicked Being now pin-pointed in the wilderness.

Here is one who is not subject to the ravages of time, but is as fresh, alive and alert today as he was in the day of creation; he has neither slumbered nor slept. Here is one who is so mighty a being that he maketh war in heaven, inhabits the heavenlies, and with his hosts rules the globe and its celestial environs, instantly present throughout the world. Here is the god of this world, the prince of the power of the air, the ruler of the darkness of this world, the principality of the spiritual wickedness in heavenly places. It is he. Saith Jesus, 'Satan'. The ancient adversary of the people of God.

'Satan' is a descriptive Hebrew title, just as is 'diabolos' in the Greek. Neither is a proper name; both are functional words indicative of activities. The Wicked One is never given a proper name: his titles, respectively, describe his several works. Therefore as *diabolos* is Greek for 'The Prosecutor', so in the same manner *Satan* is Hebrew for 'The Adversary'. Because these words are simple and straightforward descriptive titles neither is exclusive to the Wicked One. They may be, and are, used generally: provided only that the description fits the person concerned.

Hence 'The Prosecutor' applies to anyone fulfilling that function in a court of law. It is the context in the New Testament which makes the title so inescapably definitive when the great and dread prosecutor of heaven is intended. The same principle applies to the Hebrew 'Adversary'. This is made abundantly clear in the case of Numbers 22:22 where the word *satan* is used of the Angel of the Lord when taking the part of an adversary. However, once again, there is no doubt at all when that ancient foe from the garden of Eden is intended: the context is always definitive.

This Hebrew word occurs over thirty times in the Old Testament, and of these occurrences well over half are exclusive to the dreadful and heavenly adversary of the people of God. As to the rest, the word *satan*, generally translated 'adversary', is applied indiscriminately whenever and wherever suitable.

However the most part of the references without doubt are to *the* Satan, that is, to the malevolent being later to be made known in his function of *diabolos*. But it must be remembered that the word 'satan' is of itself not a name; it more describes an attitude.

The word is a transliteration, a carrying over, of the Hebrew as Hebrew, and this bad habit of the translators renders the meaning unintelligible to the English reader. So that in practice some seventeen times the translators simply ceased to function and lumped us with the foreign Hebrew word. Well, for 'Satan' read 'Adversary', because that is what it means and what we are intended to understand.

The word occurs thirty-seven times in the New Testament Greek. The Holy Ghost deliberately used the Old Testament term to cast back the well-taught saints into their Bible

— the Old Testament scripture was the Bible of the New Testament church — to get the good of the revelation. *'Satan'* is very strictly an Old Testament concept and the Lord Jesus and his apostles use the word so that their hearers and later readers would draw truth from the Hebrew root of revelation.

And revelation indeed it was! Commencing with the Book of Job, in the opening chapters we are given a sudden mysterious insight in the hidden realms far beyond what is visible and apparent, and we glimpse within those heavens that lie altogether outside the sky and past the mind of men to conceive. There, in that spiritual other-world eternal in the heavens, two interviews with the Most High take place when the Adversary comes to present himself with the mighty angels.

In the first, gazing with cynicism through the veil onto the world so far below, 'Satan' requests permission to take away that in which he supposed Job's piety rested. Secondly, foiled at the first by a love in Job quite past the Adversary's comprehension, he requires that he might sift Job as the very wheat is sifted. And that is that. The book drops to the earth and there the rest is enacted. But the first scene was the cause of the whole. And that is the message.

We find *Satan* no more till virtually the end of that New Testament Bible, the Old Testament scriptures. So long a time had passed! Is the Adversary dead? Then whatever has he been doing these millennia past since Job? Zechariah, in the dreams of the night, with revelations from the Highest, by visions into the heavenlies, finds a door open in heaven and ascending up thither beholds the courts of the Most High.

It is the fourth vision of Zechariah. Joshua the high priest stands in filthy rags accused and vehemently persecuted by 'The Adversary'. The malevolent spirit stands at the right hand of Joshua 'to be an adversary'. He is undiminished in years. He is unwearied in function. He is undeterred in purpose. Ever since Job, day and night on high he has unceasingly accused the brethren before God in the courts of heaven. This is the last mention of 'Satan'.

Till Matthew. And not before the third temptation. Tempter, *Diabolos*, yes. But now, 'Get thee hence, *Satan.*' You! Yes, *he* was the Prosecutor, *he* the Tempter. He had come down from the heavens, narrowly tracing the descent of the Son of God. No doubt marking the incarnation, considering the beginnings, pondering the flight into Egypt, brooding over the events at Nazareth. Now, free to do his worst in the wilderness, though still hiding his ultimate identity this invisible spirit — appearing if possible, it might be, as no more than impression or sensation — comes in two other forms of influence. But Jesus' use of the ancient title at last reveals his real personality. *'Satan'* identifies both the Wicked Being and also his vicious and perpetual hatred for the people of God. By the old Hebrew title this heavenly enemy is finally exposed, rebuked, and dismissed by Jesus.

'Get thee hence.' Not for the first time has the Holy Spirit inspired these words of contempt reiterated by Jesus. The former occasion was over seven hundred years before. Speaking of the filth of idols and of idolatrous forms of worship — 'Thou shalt worship the Lord thy God and him only shalt thou serve' — the prophet Isaiah expresses the correct measure of loathing and bitter hatred generated by the Spirit of God against this stinking and abominable evil.

'Ye shall defile also the covering of thy graven images of

silver, and the ornament of thy molten images of gold: thou shalt cast them away as a menstruous cloth; thou shalt say unto it, *Get thee hence.*'

It is an expression of unutterable disgust for an unclean, filthy and revolting article of refuse. It is in these terms that Jesus dismisses that Adversary who thinks to tempt *him* with the gold and silver, pomp and goodwill, gained by idolatry. When loose modern evangelicals, soft latter-day brethren, begin to feel the same intensity of holy loathing inspired by the Spirit of God against *all* forms of idolatry and false worship, then, and not until then, will their pouting mouths be pulled off the breast of the whore Babylon. Only then will Satan cease his successful flattery and begin again his useless persecution. Meanwhile what I object to is this: that such deluded compromisers should take the name and death of Jesus upon lips habitually sated and defiled by such disgusting milk.

However let it be known that there is a growing number of penitent and God-fearing brethren who have returned to fall with weeping and lamentation at the feet of the mighty Conqueror, there to catch and fiercely repeat the tones of his withering contempt for aught that defileth 'Get thee hence, Satan: for it is written, Thou shalt worship the Lord thy God, and him only shalt thou serve.'

★

Immediately following the temptation, the narrative reports the news that John the Baptist has been cast into prison. Jesus hearing of this departs into Galilee, and, leaving Nazareth, comes to dwell in Capernaum. Now is fulfilled the significant ancient prophecy concerning the arising of Messiah's ministry upon the earth. All this occupies chapter 4:12-16.

Virtually a whole year is omitted in the space between verses eleven and twelve. Slipping from one verse to the other there is not a jar, not a mention of some twelve months' ministry of the Lord Jesus. As if immediately after the temptation Jesus departed into Galilee, not the faintest ripple appears upon the surface of the narrative to show that so long a time has sunk into the void without a trace.

But why? For this simple reason: from the life of Messiah on earth Matthew is teaching the truth of Christ as he is in heaven and as he ministers from thence throughout the age. He is not an historical Messiah. He is a living Christ. His is not an anointed ministry *ending* at Matthew chapter twenty-eight. Messiah is on high now and Matthew chapters one to twenty-eight show — using his life as the basis — what Messiah means and what Messianic ministry involves to all who seek him even unto this present.

And one of the first things to grasp is this: Messiah's ministry is neither Mosaic nor Jewish. It is evangelical and universal. Most emphatically it is not a mixture of both the legal and evangelical testaments, nor is it an amalgam of Jewish and Gentile systems, much less is it a merging of law and gospel into a shared doctrinal philosophy. It is a new thing. It is unique. It brings in a new man. Its rule is superior to law and above the legal dispensation and altogether higher than that which is required by the commandments.

Hence Messiah's ministry is never truly received by one

107

single living soul until to that soul the legal time has run its course. Christ must be the *end* of the law for righteousness to every one that believeth, or Christ will be nothing at all. Moses and Elias must fade away completely and there must no man be seen save Jesus only. Moses, Elias and John shut us up in the dark night of the soul's experience, then cease and point to the coming Son, the rising Messiah. Leaving the old legal ministry standing, disciples must follow Jesus as he walks. In a word Messiah does not minister until to the soul he is exclusive. Lifeless men may rustle the dry leaves of the dead letter of Matthew here below but there will be no living streams from heaven by Messiah on high until 'John is cast into prison.' *Then* Christ's ministry begins and the soul set free indeed.

For virtually the whole of the year that is omitted, historically John and Jesus ministered simultaneously although in quite different locations. However this bare fact is enough to cause Matthew — Mark and Luke, too — to omit that part of the history because of the overwhelmingly superior doctrinal reasons. Only when John is cast into prison — and therefore ceases to minister — will the evangelists begin the great sweeping passage of the singular and alone ministry of Jesus Christ.

Here we see yet another example of the way in which spiritual criteria completely govern the writers of the gospels. They were not intellectuals. The basic attitude and philosophy of the schoolmen and of the educationalist was something from which they shied as an abomination to the Holy Spirit of Truth. They wanted nothing to do with knowing pride, reasoning prowess, or intellectual ability. They knew that the world by wisdom knew not God and that the wisdom of this world and the *way* in which the world was wise — its very thought processes, postures, attitudes to and transmission of knowledge — were all foreign to the teaching of the Spirit.

The apostles were taught by the Holy Ghost. Concerning worldly learning, in both profane and religious things they were 'unlearned and ignorant men'. Like their Master, these disciples — as to the great schools of scripture and Hebrew doctrine — had never learned letters, had no 'knowledge'; yet they knew more than all of the Jerusalem doctors put together, speaking with authority and not as the scribes. They were those 'who had heard and learned of the Father', and necessarily they mortified their carnal minds, aware that 'the carnal mind is enmity against God.' They were illuminated inwardly by the spirit of wisdom and revelation in the knowledge of Christ, and to this end utterly eschewed the natural reasoning processes. They denied nature's proud and high-minded conceit in favour of divine enlightenment and spiritual leading upon their mortified, passive and waiting hearts. They wanted the Spirit of prophecy. For the testimony of Jesus is the Spirit of prophecy.

They had turned from the visible, worldly, exterior wisdom to which human ability must address itself by means of the intellectual faculties. All this they regarded as crucified and themselves crucified unto it: they embraced from the heart that invisible, heavenly, 'hidden wisdom, which none of the princes of this world knew, for had they known it, they would not have crucified the Lord of glory.' They renounced the 'earthly wisdom', and espoused the 'wisdom from above'.

Not the storing of memory, neither the gleaning of information, nor yet the searching of scripture guided the apostles into all truth. It was the inward Spirit of Truth,

the interior shining of the radiant light from the face of
Jesus Christ immediately illuminating their hearts and
showing them how and what to write. And into that light
and wisdom within the reader must be directed or else he
shall forever stumble upon the dark mountains.

For it is exactly at this point — and consistently so —
that the various churches have stumbled. Bypassing the
teaching of the Holy Ghost and the inward light of Christ,
they have required their ministers and teachers to address
themselves to the ministry on the basis of intellectual
ability and according to worldly principles of education.
Over the generations the consequence of this is that it is no
longer really the scriptures that are held at all. It has become
a body of tradition more or less shot through with dry
unbelieving speculation and cold infidelity. That is what is
held: as to what is preached, we hear every variety of
sentimental fluidity diluted from this unbelieving mixture.
As a Baptist Superintendent of the Metropolitan area once
said to me 'Our ideal congregation has both 'evangelical'
and modernist members. Our perfect minister is one who
speaks helpfully to both but offends neither.' Precisely.

Thus has come to pass the true saying 'The time will
come when they will not endure sound doctrine; but after
their own lusts shall they heap to themselves teachers,
having itching ears; and they shall turn away their ears from
the truth, and shall be turned unto fables.'

Instead of the secret, inward gift and teaching of the
Holy Ghost preparing and qualifying a man, the churches
have substituted Divinity Colleges, Theological Academies
and Bible Schools, looking to these inventions of theirs to
provide them with Ministers, Teachers, and Evangelists.
By so doing — make no mistake — they have usurped the

prerogative of Christ and dispensed with the person of the Spirit in the call to and preparation for the ministry.

They have treated the ministry and divinity in just the same way and its preparation by exactly the same process as would any worldly educationalist in respect of a purely material subject. To be truly honest they should say 'We have not so much as heard whether there be any Holy Ghost.'

Divinity is not a material subject for men to study; it is a spiritual revelation for the Holy Ghost to communicate. Divine knowledge comes by divine illumination upon the scripture: and this is clean *contrary* to the mind of man over the scripture. Therefore salvation appears solely on the basis of man's crucified mortification: not upon his scriptural education. The intellect must be voluntarily humiliated: not cultivated. As Wesley put it

> When, my Saviour, shall I be
> Perfectly resigned to thee?
> Poor and vile in my own eyes,
> Only in thy wisdom wise?
>
> Let me cast my self aside,
> All that feeds my knowing pride,
> Not to man, but God submit,
> Lay my reasonings at thy feet;
>
> Of my boasted wisdom spoiled,
> Docile, helpless, as a child,
> Only seeing in thy light,
> Only walking in thy might.
>
> Then infuse the teaching grace,
> Spirit of truth and righteousness;
> Knowledge, love divine, impart,
> Life eternal, to my heart.

To this poignant and heartfelt plea, scripture addresses itself. Notwithstanding it lies cold and dead till the Holy Ghost gives inward title to the exterior promise: interior leading into the written truth: an inward illumination on the outward information. Then in a mystery heart and understanding are spiritually opened to see the radiance of Christ glowing in all the scriptures, and, moreover, glowing for oneself.

To fulfil this purpose Matthew writes. Wherefore it is obvious that neither biography, chronology, nor yet 'religious education' are the object of the Holy Ghost in giving the gospel according to Matthew. The full salvation of the reader is the object. If so, then the gospel must be read in a spirit of supplication and prayer to this end; otherwise the whole purpose for which that gospel exists will go over the head and clean escape the reader.

The mere Bible student or so-called divinity scholar — let alone the 'sermon-gleaner' — reads from a viewpoint entirely foreign to the reason for, idea of, and expression within the book. He knows nothing yet as he ought to know, and in that state he never will: he shall but blunder about the dead letter, blindly gathering twigs for the burning. The gospel cannot be understood by intellectual students in the class or lecture room. It is not for the intellect; it is not for mere study; it has no place in the classroom. It is for those desperate for life from the Messiah; it is for the closet. This is clearly understood by the brokenhearted. Not the seekers after knowledge are blest, but 'Blessed are they which do hunger and thirst after righteousness: for *they* shall be filled.'

Not that I would call the passing of examinations, obtaining certificates, gaining degrees, receiving academic acclaim, 'Seeking after knowledge'. I would not. I would call it 'Seeking honour one of another'. Of which Jesus says 'How can ye believe, which receive honour one of another, and seek not the honour that cometh from God *only?*' And I would comment upon it: 'That which is highly esteemed among men is abomination in the sight of God.'

Then if the true seeking after knowledge be so rare, how much more rare is the hungering and thirsting after righteousness? Not least because — within little more than a few decades — multitudes have been dazed, silenced, and then made to fall in awe at the feet of the vast complex of modern learning and education backed by its great scientific and technological achievements. Since all this glory of men is associated with a contemptuous turning away from the old paths, many have been disheartened and discouraged from seeking the Lord by what appears to be the overwhelming 'proof' of man's self-sufficiency and the apparent inevitability of the success of all his works.

Yet verily I say that every last thread of this garment of human praise shall wither and be cast away like an unclean rag — useless and worthless — at the portals of death. Once over the threshold of that dreadful door it will soon appear how feeble — what petty mental probings in the dark! — was the whole complex of human gleaning that passed in the erstwhile world for such overwhelming knowledge. Plummeting into eternity every last fact proves a ghastly liability as the sentence rings out for the soul's immortal and everlasting judgment.

Then what kind of folly is it that the modern churches, assemblies and congregations have themselves trodden underfoot the old hidden spiritual wisdom in favour of adopting the world's system of education for its ministers and teachers? The intellectual instead of the spiritual is chosen. The classroom instead of the closet. The superficial rather than the profound. Brains and memory instead of heart and knees. Information rather than salvation. In a word, education instead of revelation.

The very way of looking at knowledge as well as of teaching it has been copied from worldly principles and methods by the fallen church. Yet the world has not, and never did have, a body of knowledge comparable to the divinely inspired scriptures. Then how shall they know how to teach them to us?

As to their teachers and system of teaching there can be no possible comparison with the church. *The divine Person* of the Holy Ghost has been sent to *indwell* the Lord's people and from *within* to teach them the truth by *revelation*. But the world is completely void of and oblivious to the Holy Ghost. 'Whom the world cannot receive, because it seeth him not, neither knoweth him: but ye know him; for he dwelleth with you, and shall be in you.'

This is that divine interior Spirit of Truth, abiding and shining within, who teaches and leads the saints into all truth. That is, the truth contained in scripture. How then shall we go to the world — which knows neither the scripture nor the Spirit of Truth — in order to adopt their worldly method and system of education so that we may transfer it to the church? A system, remark, based entirely on the total absence and ignorance of the Holy Ghost? And shall we thus go, so as to learn how to teach the inspired Bible, which *they* regard as no more divine than the Canterbury Tales?

Yet this is exactly what has happened. Many have gone

out into the world. And, going out, they have not shunned even to alter the proper text, the true version of our gospel. Moreover they themselves have taken the place of the Holy Ghost. Now, the old true apostles went out to convert the world to the church; but you see how these new false apostles are different: they have gone out to convert the church to the world. And from the world, they have very nearly succeeded. But meantime the glory has departed, and by a mysterious handwriting ICHABOD appears over every lintel.

In direct consequence of this infidelity, the Holy Scriptures — text, version, translation, paraphrase: all varied and optional; as if to say, scripture is not *that* accurate! — are now regarded in a light-hearted and critical way that would have horrified and shocked the apostles, and put our God-fearing and serious fathers in sackcloth and ashes. This is reflected by the unbelieving, unspiritual and downright suspicious way of examining the Evangelists. And no longer is the now-virtually-useless prefix 'evangelical' any guarantee against this attitude. On the contrary.

Men held in honour — who believe little or nothing, and that most flexible — have bent their keen analytical minds to rend the gospel in pieces and quite sift out all spirituality from the scriptures through the sieve of their haughty intellects. By their criticism they have broken the Bible into a thousand shards like a potter's vessel, denied the Potter, questioned the clay, and fouled the fragments; yet if one should dare to criticise *them* they scream 'No charity, no charity' at the top of their falsetto voices.

These things being so, we ought to give the more earnest heed to the preservation of text, version and evangel lest at any time we let them slip. We must resolutely refuse the chaffy fare and seek only the solid wheat of the gospel.

So then, we need not be surprised today if we find false explanations bruited abroad as to the reason for the 'lost year' between Matthew 4:11 and 12. However, as one not without fruit from the Lord, I submit what I have obtained upon my knees from the Spirit. And even — God is witness — upon my face before the God of my salvation. I believe the fair-minded will soon see that this agrees with the method of the writers. And agrees also with the single-minded dependence upon the Spirit that filled Matthew's heart and mind and everywhere pervaded and spread through his gospel.

The setting for the ministry of Jesus Christ and the effect of his presence is now quoted: 'The land of Zabulon, and the land of Nephthalim, by the way of the sea, beyond Jordan, Galilee of the Gentiles; the people which sat in darkness saw great light; and to them which sat in the region and shadow of death light is sprung up.' *The prophecy of Isaiah*, circa B.C. 700. *The gospel according to Matthew*, circa A.D. 60.

This setting is of the utmost importance and must be interpreted spiritually: Where is Jesus to be found? The place sets the tone for that which is to occupy the major part of the book: The ministry of Jesus Christ. The extraordinary thing — it was unbelievably staggering to the Jew — was that Jesus did not work from Jerusalem; certainly, Messiah would work from Jerusalem! But then, Matthew shows otherwise.

Surely Jerusalem was the place for the Christ? All the world expected it; all the Jews knew it. Mount Zion! Where else? Jerusalem was the centre and hub of every religious activity and authority: thither the tribes went up; to this place was the gathering of the people.

The truth was there: exposition, exegesis, hagiology, eschatology, soteriology, christology, theology, apologetics, doctrine. The books were kept there: here were the oracles, the covenants, the ceremonies, the priesthood, the temple; the schools for the scribes, the colleges of both Pharisee and Sadducee; well, *God* was there, and there exclusively.

It was the city of the great king. Abraham had sacrificed there. Solomon had built there. David's seed was buried at Jerusalem. The hierarchy was there: the *system* depended upon the centrality of Jerusalem: the Messiah — the true Messiah — *must* find acceptance and authority from Jerusalem, and thence minister. So also that baptist fellow. 'The Jews sent priests and Levites *from Jerusalem* to John to ask him, Who are *you?*' God may do a thing from heaven and send the Baptist; but Jews must verify it from Jerusalem, and send priests and Levites. Otherwise, how could it be of God? He had obligations, you see.

However, in contradistinction from Jerusalem, Galilee is conspicuous for nothing whatsoever. 'Galilee of the Gentiles', a term of contemptuous dismissal, marks out that land as the epitome of nothingness. But only to the Jew. It was a Jewish expression. It was not that no-one dwelt there, or that nothing grew there, nor was it that there was no water: it was just that there was no *religion.*

The place was outside the pale. Beyond even the accursed Samaritans: Galilee *of the Gentiles.* There; there, saith Matthew, there shall Messiah be found. Then he quotes Isaiah, that most renowned of prophets, to prove it.

The meaning is this: spiritually, Galilee stands for an environment in which there can be nothing *but* the Lord — as to religion — simply because it is a place in which nothing else subsists. For in religion everything existed at Jerusalem. Everything, that is, *except* the Lord. The very reverse is true of Galilee. Therefore 'Galilee' shows those moral and spiritual conditions in which Messiah is always found and found to minister grace to the hearers.

Galilee represents a despised, small, detestable place, unwanted and disliked by the Jews from Jerusalem, by scribes and Pharisees, priests and Levites, Sadducees and doctors of the law. 'Galilee of the Gentiles'. It has nothing. That is why Messias chooses it. To stain the pride of all glory and to bring into contempt all the honourable of the earth. This puts down the mighty from their seats in Jerusalem, who had taken over the temple and the synagogues, the centre and system of religion on earth, and thought to make the Almighty a party to their deeds.

Now contrariwise God has set *his* Man in the middle of nothing and nowhere; to him the disciples flowed, and to him shall the gathering of the people be; and thus it came to pass. And does: you see that there is nothing in today's 'Galilee' but what the rich, full, satisfied and laughing priest and prelate, evangelist and minister, brother and friend, would find despicable, irritating and contemptuous. But in that spiritual place it shall be said: JEHOVAH SHAMMAH, *The Lord is there.*

It is vital to understand this contrast between Jerusalem and Galilee in Matthew. At Jerusalem there was everything but the Lord. In Galilee there was nothing but the Lord. In the one case there was no room for the Messiah. In the other case there was room only for the Messiah.

In Matthew, Jesus does not go up to Jerusalem until he goes to die. This is the first, the last, and the only visit. Matthew omits the many other occasions — about which he knew full well — so as clearly and crisply to bring out the truth.

So great was the enmity of the Jews at Jerusalem that, given divine licence to lay hands on Jesus, they would require no further occasion. Only let the latent malice and envy but once surface, and the city would have no need of a second visit: 'O Jerusalem, Jerusalem, thou that killest the prophets, and stonest them which are sent unto thee.'

If Luke and John reveal other visits, then only the extraordinary and providential restraint of God — exercised for some particular and special purpose requiring Jesus' presence at Jerusalem before his actual death — prevented the inevitable consequence of murder following from the exposure of Messiah to the hatred of the hierarchy. Given that unrestrained exposure, the crucifixion was inevitable. Matthew confines the record to the last visit in order to demonstrate this veritable enormity.

'For they that dwell at Jerusalem, and their rulers, because they knew him not, nor yet the voices of the prophets which are read every sabbath day, they have fulfilled them in condemning him. And though they found no cause of death in him, yet desired they Pilate that he should be slain.' So much is this true, that, saith Jesus, 'It cannot be that a prophet perish out of Jerusalem.'

The gospel according to Mark — contrasting the true and false Service of God — emphasises this same principle. Luke differs a little, because his purpose is to reveal the grace of God for all mankind. And he is at pains to show that this is

'To the Jew first'. Jesus' two childhood visits to Jerusalem therefore are recorded with their special teaching. But after this, in adulthood, as far as Luke is concerned Jesus does not again go up to the holy city save to die.

John however stands alone. The last gospel is unique in openly stressing Jesus' deity: it is God revealed, and God emphasised; not manhood. Since Jehovah chose Jerusalem of old, and ordained the feasts aforetime, and elected the Jews from the beginning, and presided over the millennia of Israel's history; how then can these things be which we have seen come to pass in Matthew, Mark and Luke? Whence this extraordinary Jewish enmity — beginning at Jerusalem, too — if they were the people and that the scene of Jehovah's long and intense cultivation? John tells you; but the special restraint of providence is required to leash the enmity of man that the tale might be told. For it *could* only be told at Jerusalem. There these things were first ordained. And there at the last they must be finally outworked.

Luke lays particular emphasis upon such free and lavish grace shown to all the world: to the Jew first, and also to the Greek. This is asserted when Christ, raised from the dead, commands his disciples 'Tarry ye in the city of Jerusalem, until ye be endued with power from on high.' It is from there that the gospel is to go out. So the disciples return to Jerusalem filled with great joy that such grace is shown even to that wicked city 'where our Lord was crucified'.

Matthew is different. It is a question of the Jewish Messiah and what the Jews have done to him. 'Jerusalem' tells the dreadful tale. When Christ is raised therefore there is no question of the disciples going back to that city of rejection and reprobation. It is: 'Woe to the bloody city.' And as to the inhabitants: 'Reprobate silver shall men call them, because the Lord hath rejected them.'

No longer shall it be called 'The holy city'. It is now 'The great city, which spiritually is called Sodom and Egypt.' It is 'Jerusalem below' the mother of carnal persecutors. It is the centre of that religion and people upon whom the wrath has come to the uttermost. Therefore in Matthew, I say, after the resurrection there is no record — as in Luke — of 'tarrying at Jerusalem'. On the contrary: 'Then the eleven disciples went away into *Galilee*, into a mountain where Jesus had appointed them,' Mt. 28:16. You see again how events and places are selected to suit the doctrine, and how this abundantly confirms the correct interpretation.

Galilee is seen as the region in which Jesus calls and gathers his disciples. One might think it the most unlikely place and source for the Lord's people, but evidently one would be wrong. Matthew makes it quite clear that this is in fact the typical place and that they are in fact the characteristic persons.

Despised by the proper orthodox Jews, the Galileans were considered to be the 'people that sat in darkness'. They were utterly scorned by those with 'the light': the truth, the doctrine. It was not simply that Galilee of the Gentiles was in darkness; Galileans sat in it, v.16. This indicates a miserable, passive resignation in which there was no help, no resource: nothing could be done. And what darkness it was! That of the 'region and shadow of death'. The region of death was one in which sin abounded, for there death had dominion. This was the seat of the king of terrors. As to the 'shadow' of death, this teaches that death loomed over everything; nothing was exempt from its overshadowing. Dwelling in these fearful shades hopeless Galileans were all their lifetime subject to bondage. Death looked over their shoulder. Its long shadow cast a chill fear, a clammy coldness. Well, these people, 'Galilee of the Gentiles', sat there. Inert and helpless.

Till the light dawned. What light was this? v.16 'Great light'. Dayspring, dawning light. On the Bible? From the scriptures? No: these they had long possessed; also, no doubt, artificial light by which to read them: but the people still sat in darkness. Until they saw great light. That was when, v.13, '*He* came and dwelt there', that these very sayings 'might be fulfilled' v.14. This was Messiah, this great light, and his coming was the light springing up. Saith he, I am the light of the world. It is the radiance of his own person; not just passing through, but 'dwelling there'.

Or rather indwelling: for it is not really an exterior shining to which the prophet refers. Multitudes then saw, as multitudes now read of, his exterior and objective person, and even obtain a blessing from his hand. But this is not to receive the true light. His disciples received that light in reality when they could say 'God, who commanded the light to shine out of darkness, hath shined in our hearts, to give the light of the knowledge of the glory of God in the face of Jesus Christ.'

That interior shining is the true interpretation of 'The people which sat in darkness saw great light.' Just as the meaning of 'the region and shadow of death' does not indicate that Galilee of the Gentiles lay in some kind of literal polar twilight half the year round. It refers to the inward thick darkness felt perpetually in the miserable soul crying out for union with the living God. It is this dark night that the shining beams of the coming Saviour dispel completely, when the glory of the Lord arises within the inmost heart.

This light of life broke in upon the poor Galileans after they had been divested of every hope from the law, all help from man, and the last vestige of any trust in their own righteousness. As to the one, 'John was cast into prison' and was beyond helping them now; as to the other, they 'Sat in darkness and in the region and shadow of death' and were quite past helping themselves.

Weary and heavy-laden, self-condemned and seeing no alleviation from their misery, the glimmer of hope which John had kindled — Mt. 3:1,2 'In those days came John the Baptist preaching and saying, Repent ye: for the kingdom of heaven is at hand' — was now at last taken up by Another. And although it was exactly the same message — Mt. 4:17 'From that time Jesus began to preach, and to say, Repent: for the kingdom of heaven is at hand' — the change of preacher made all the difference.

I say, it was precisely the same message. Nevertheless whilst John preached it there was darkness; but when Christ preached, great light arose! So you see, vital as is the correctness and accuracy of the message, it is not just what is preached; it is also, Who is preaching? And as to this, observe that it is the Lord's person and actual presence that makes all the difference. It was one thing — and a good thing — that Messiah and the kingdom were preached. But it is another thing again that he himself should do the preaching.

And this brings a message to the latest day. It is one thing for men to preach Christ — not that that, in truth, is so common! — but it is quite another thing for Christ to preach by those men. For our faith to stand 'not in the wisdom of men, but in the power of God': for our gospel to come 'not in word only, but in power and in the Holy Ghost', then of necessity in the preaching, Christ must come, and come by the Spirit, and come to the heart, and come himself to 'preach peace to them that are afar off'. Then like some poor lost Galilean, the soul that hears the joyful sound shall echo with delight 'Arise, shine; for thy light is come, and the glory of the Lord is risen upon thee.'

Now follows Jesus' call first to Simon and Andrew, then to the two sons of Zebedee, Mt. 4:18-22. From the seventeenth verse to the end of the chapter we find a sweeping general summary of the active ministry of Jesus himself to the poor and needy throughout all Galilee. There are no apostles labouring with him: it is solely his own ministry. This is depicted in broad sweeps upon the canvas of a wide background. But into this sequence, and clean contrary to its generalisation, we find inserted a most minutely detailed passage — nets, boats, occupations, names, relationships — not at all in keeping with the context of Jesus' virtue immediately going out to all the needy people. Rather, it has to do with commanding these four individuals. But there is no hint that they then minister with him; they do not. From verse twenty-three onwards Jesus still ministers alone. The passage is extraordinary and the reader should ask himself, What is it doing here?

In the verse immediately preceding the calling of v.18-22, we read: 'From that time Jesus began to preach, and to say, Repent: for the kingdom of heaven is at hand.' But this theme does not continue until the twenty-third verse: 'And Jesus went about all Galilee, teaching in their synagogues, and preaching the gospel of the kingdom.'

There follows an increasingly graphic and vivid description of Jesus' ministry, continuing until the end of the chapter.

Observe then that the obvious flow of the context from verse seventeen finds its continuity only in verse twenty-three. From thence it progresses uninterrupted until the climactic conclusion of the chapter. Notice therefore that after its beginning this flow is summarily interrupted and driven underground at verse eighteen not to reappear until its stream breaks surface again after verse twenty-two, thence to swell onward through its course. As if there had been no such interruption! Why is this?

Why is it? The answer lies in discerning the mind of the Spirit. It is inexplicable unless interpreted spiritually. Evidently this is not a call to these fishermen to become disciples of Jesus. They were disciples already. *That* call had occurred many months before, John 1:35-42. Furthermore, Matthew carefully abstains from the use of the word 'disciple'. The discerning will perceive that the word used in Mt. 4:18-22 is 'brethren'.

Also it is a question of occupation. They are called to minister; or rather, to learn to minister. No longer fishermen; now fishers of men. No more nets; they left their nets. No 'suffer me first to bury my father'; they immediately left their father. For if they are to preach the kingdom, new life is required, and from another source than nature.

Wherefore note the stress on relationships within so small a compass of verses. First, Jesus saw 'two brethren', Simon called Peter and Andrew 'his brother'. Again he saw 'other two brethren' James 'the son of' Zebedee, and John 'his brother'. They were in a ship with Zebedee 'their father'. Jesus called them and they immediately left the ship 'and their father' and followed him. You see it: two brethren; his brother; other two brethren; the son; his brother; their father; — and again — their father.

This is no coincidence. This is what the Spirit is teaching. Arresting our attention by the unusual context, concentrating it upon the multiplicity of relationships, the Spirit would direct us into the mind of Christ. 'He saw two brethren.' Men could look upon Zebedee and his two sons: and so could Jesus. Yet he who looked not at the things which are seen but at the things which are not seen could discern the purpose and election of the Father in heaven. And perceiving what he did — about two brethren — as seen in the mind of God, he could worship and say to his Father and their Father 'I will declare thy name unto my brethren,' Hebrews 2:12. And again he saith, 'Behold I and the children which God hath given me.'

Taking occasion by the natural, the spiritual is taught, Mt. 4:18-22. They are designated 'brethren', but the emphasis is not upon the natural common father of each pair of brothers, for, 'they left the ship *and* their father.' The *allusion* is to sonship and that from God out of heaven. It is the kingdom of God and not man, of heaven and not earth, that they must first experience, learn and indwell, before ever they can become 'fishers of men' in the sense in which Jesus meant the term.

I say, the *allusion* is to sonship. The kingdom stands in sonship. Mt. 5:9 'children *of God'*. And again, Mt. 5:16 'Your Father which is *in heaven'*. But if the kingdom stands in sonship towards God and the Father, then it must do so likewise as brethren towards one another. But certainly not by natural birth! 'They left their father.' Thus fulfilling the word to the brethren: 'Call no man your father upon

the earth: for one is your Father, which is in heaven,'
Mt. 23:9. That is what is being hinted: sonship must be
granted and experienced to enter the kingdom. And it must
be developed to preach that kingdom.

Therefore the true and spiritual interpretation of
Mt. 4:18-22 is that here is a call to preach the kingdom — or
learn to do so — on the basis of sonship. In the Spirit of
adoption they were brethren. Born of the Father. They left
all — who were long since called disciples — and followed
Jesus *inwardly by the Spirit into sharing his unique life and
place with his Father.* And this they experienced when he
rose from the dead and sent forth the Holy Ghost.

That is what he is teaching them as they follow him.
Look at it in Mt. 28:10, where the risen Messiah says to
the women 'Be not afraid: go tell *my brethren* that they go
into *Galilee,* and there shall they see me.' But already here
in chapter four, Matthew is hinting that the kingdom is
entered by sonship. This is put to us after describing the
commencement of Jesus' preaching and before coming to
its conclusion. It is the heart of the matter.

The first thing about the kingdom must have astonished
the Jews. It was 'of heaven'. However they had calculated
it would be 'of Israel'. The next was like unto it, for
they conceived that the kingdom stood in Jewish paternity
marked by circumcision. It did not. It stood in divine
sonship distinguished by the indwelling Spirit of adoption
instantly crying, Abba, Father.

The other thing was this: so soon as Jesus works, he
associates brethren with him in the ministry. But not yet
to speak; first to learn by obediently observing him in his
life and vocation. They are specially called, but not because

127

of any natural qualifications. To the contrary, the ministry is solely upon the basis of Jesus' choice from among those who were already called brethren. From the midst of the brethren, I say, he calls his ministers and associates them with him in his work.

They were young Galilean fishermen. Not Jerusalem doctors or lawyers. Neither Judaean scribes or Pharisees. Nor yet Jewish priests or elders. Much less were they sage Rabbis or masters of Israel. They were of no account to such people. Fishers. That was what they were. And being called to the ministry, they did not *then* study to become scribes, doctors of the law, Rabbis, or teachers. They did not *then* join the Pharisees, emulate the masters or envy the priests. *Then* they followed Jesus.

The brethren called to Christ's ministry learned, of course. But what they learned was obedience, and that by the things which they suffered. They endured discipline, naturally; but it was not the discipline of a subject in the classroom, it was that of experience under the open sky. And enduring the chastening which they found in the Master's steps, God dealt with them as sons. They went through a schooling, it is true; but then it was the school of life, that of reality, learning the harsh facts of existence. They followed Jesus 'as he walked'. In the actual present exercise of his ministry. And they watched; and waited; and held their tongues.

And eventually it came to pass that when the fulness of time was come they in their turn were sent forth to preach. Then priest, elder, scribe, Pharisee and Sadducee, were all amazed. 'When they saw the boldness of Peter and John, and perceived that they were unlearned and ignorant men, they marvelled; and they took knowledge of them, that they had been with Jesus.' The power and wisdom of God was upon them, who were but poor vessels of Christ's choosing. But those years past, they had been with Jesus, associated as working apprentices with him in his actual ministry. And *that* was what made the difference.

The brethren forsook their nets: the tools of their trade. They abandoned the ship: the means of their livelihood. And they left their father: significant at once of the roots of the past, the security of the present, and the inheritance of the future. Straightway they departed, hearing the call of Christ. They burned their bridges: they did so immediately and they did so permanently. And I may add, they did so for nothing. 'Give us this day our daily bread' was no mere repetitive platitude to them; they meant it: or starved.

There follows a period of intense activity throughout all Galilee marked by Jesus' teaching in their assemblies, preaching out of them, and healing everywhere.

It was the healing which at that time drew the greatest attention to Jesus. Miracles of such infallible immediacy that transformed diseased bodies and minds from the most fearful corruption and appalling affliction to complete wholeness and perfect health before the very eyes of the people. The transition took place in the twinkling of an eye — not even an unfocused blur — even as they watched: you could see it; and every time without fail. Staggering! His fame went far beyond the nine hundred square miles of Galilee. It went throughout all Syria.

They brought to him all the sick. Column upon column of pathetic relatives laden with stretchers, panniers, litters; limping, gasping, groaning. As if all the suffering pain of humanity streamed and converged from the four corners of the earth upon the compassionate Man of Galilee; and he healed them all. How wonderful. O, how heart-rending was his matchless pity. Yet surely there was pain reflected deep within his own eyes, as he watched them come and 'healed them all.'

There followed him great multitudes of people from Galilee, and Decapolis, and Jerusalem, and Judaea, and beyond Jordan. Multitudes, multitudes followed him. But why? Multitudes in the valley of decision.

I say, was it not pain deep within his own eyes, as he watched them come?

MATTHEW CHAPTER FIVE

'And seeing the multitudes, he went up into a mountain.' But why? Not for them to follow. The sick could not, and the multitudes did not. He left them to go up, and his *disciples* — as opposed to the multitude — came unto him. Then we read, 'He opened his mouth, and taught *them.*' Not the multitude; the *disciples*. But why?

Because of the distinction between them. Although it is said, 4:25, 'And there followed him great multitudes,' notwithstanding that 'following' was far different from the following of his disciples. One was so superficial as to be invalid. The other sufficiently profound to be counted valid. You see then that it is not enough to 'follow Jesus'. The 'following' must be examined and analysed to find of what sort it is.

The same is true of 'believing'. It was said of another, and earlier, multitude: 'Many believed in his name, when they saw the miracles which he did. But Jesus did not commit himself unto them, because he knew all men, and needed not that any should testify of man: for he knew what was in man.' Yet previously in the same chapter it had been written 'Jesus manifested forth his glory; and his disciples believed on him.' Evidently in the one case the 'faith' was worthless. Yet in the other case belief was validated. Then 'believing' must also be examined and analysed to find of what sort it is.

So then, following or believing, there is that which goes by the name but cannot be reckoned for the reality. The reason for this is the heart-attitude which lies behind words and actions, and gives them their real character. It is from the heart that the Lord will be followed, and in the heart: that is what the Sermon on the Mount is about. And it is from the heart that saving faith proceeds: 'With the heart man believeth unto righteousness;' and again, 'Ye have obeyed from the heart that form of doctrine which was delivered you.'

But the multitude of superficial believers did not believe from the heart. They believed from the sensations, and their lustful hearts continued unchanged. Just as the many followers did not really follow the Lord: though they appeared to do so. In fact they strayed after their own desires. They followed with the feet; but their selfish hearts remained unaltered. You see then how that the deceitful heart of man towards the Lord Jesus is like the horseleech that hath two daughters, crying Give, Give.

They followed Jesus for their health, who were sick: just like the ten lepers. For their bread, who were hungry: just like the multitude that 'seek me ... because ye did eat of the loaves, and were filled.' Or for diversion and entertainment, who were stupid and empty: just like the mindless creature who blurted out 'Blessed is the womb that bare thee, and the paps which thou hast sucked.' The common self-indulgence of all alike is rebuked with icy disdain: 'Yea rather, blessed are they that hear the word of God, and keep it.' That is, the disciples. The true believers and real followers.

Those who follow in verity do not follow to indulge their selfishness in or from the gospel. Nor to believe whilst the heart remains in an unchanged state of self-gratification. They follow to be made selfless in Christ; to believe for a new heart, and a new spirit, to be made perfect in love. How? The power is in the gospel of Christ and the doctrine is in the Sermon on the Mount. That is what they believe for, and how they follow him with certitude.

The result is the mortification of the old self-indulgence: which after its false and treacherous fashion pretended to believe and follow; and the bringing in of a new heart the character of which Paul describeth on this wise:

> Though I speak with the tongues of men and
> of angels, and have not charity, I am become
> as sounding brass, or a tinkling cymbal.
> And though I have the gift of prophecy, and
> understand all mysteries, and all knowledge;
> and though I have all faith, so that I could
> remove mountains, and have not charity, I
> am nothing.
> And though I bestow all my goods to feed
> the poor, and though I give my body to be
> burned, and have not charity, it profiteth me
> nothing.

> Charity suffereth long, and is kind; charity
> envieth not; charity vaunteth not itself, is
> not puffed up.
> Doth not behave itself unseemly, seeketh not
> her own, is not easily provoked, thinketh no
> evil;
> Rejoiceth not in iniquity, but rejoiceth in the
> truth;
> Beareth all things, believeth all things, hopeth
> all things, endureth all things.

You see, then, how it is the character of the heart which
determines the true value of outward actions. Even though
those actions — such as giving one's goods, or life itself —
appear to be the last word in virtue. But they are not:
without a heart melted by love divine and sweetly endued
by the Spirit of Christ, such 'virtuous' actions are a
downright liability.

Love is of God. Not man. Indwelt by Father, Son,
and Holy Ghost, abiding in Christ and full of the Spirit:
that is to love, and Paul tells of the resultant character in
I Corinthians 13. Otherwise, such exterior acts as giving
one's goods to feed the poor, giving one's body to be
burned, one's life to serve the needy; such generous gifts as
the tongues of men and angels, heavenly knowledge, divine
prophecy: all these are but as an unclean thing. Or filthy
rags, Isaiah 64:6. Outward to men they are admired as
sparkling translucent china: but inward to God they reek
and stink, full of black extortion and excess. It is from
within, out of the heart of man, that the real character of
things — words, professions, actions and intentions — is
determined.

And man's unchanged heart is full, but full, of self-gratification. Not uncommonly through religious means. Or through intellectual satisfaction with the doctrine. Or emotional pleasure out of the sensations Jesus gives. Or blessings, healings, gifts, joys, services, evangelisms. Not these things give the heart its character. It is the heart that gives them their real character.

Therefore despite the appearances, without the indwelling love of God the heart remains morally unchanged, given over to the fixed determination of living to its self-gratification as the end of being and existence. The being lives to indulge the senses and sensations: it loves itself supremely. God and man must serve that end.

Whether it be the gratification of religious appetites as satisfying the virtuous feelings, or whether indulging the base lusts as gratifying the common corrupt desires, neither can alter the end for which the heart lives: not one whit. In both instances it is self-indulgence. In one case the means chosen is, externally, more commendable; though utterly deceptive. In the other everything is transparently obvious. Nevertheless, the end is the same. Self is everything, and selfishness the meaning and ultimate reason for existence. And that, morally, is the whole of sin; the *form* of indulgence, or *type* of gratification — religious or base — being irrelevant.

So then, whether cures, transformations, bliss; yes, and verily I say unto you, whether forgiveness, pardon or justification: if that is *all* the Lord is come to and followed for, it is neither real coming nor true following. It is just a selfish grasping, self-preservation, self-insurance. There is no sure believing nor certain loving.

It is true that we love him because he first loved us; but

that is the *effect* of his love: self is broken, the end of
existence alters, the life-being melts and changes: we *love*
him. If so, then not with an unchanged selfish heart
admiring and gazing upon Jesus outwardly, nor from the
satisfaction of the company or meeting, still less from gifts
and blessings, and assuredly never from the grasping of
salvation in case one might be lost. He is loved for himself:
for his own sake; and loved so as the end of being which
was set upon self-gratification through the indulgence of
the various sensibilities, is now fixed upon *his pleasure
alone.* 'My heart is fixed, O God, my heart is fixed: I will
sing and give praise.'

The language of such a soul speaketh on this wise:

> My God, I love thee, not because
> I hope for heaven thereby,
> Nor yet because, if I love not,
> I must for ever die.

> Not with the hope of gaining aught,
> Nor seeking a reward,
> But freely, fully, as thyself
> Hast loved me, O Lord!

> Then why, O blessed Saviour mine
> Should I not love thee well?
> Not for the sake of winning heaven,
> Nor of escaping hell.

Loved for himself alone! Loved, not in the sense of
emotion, but wholly lived for as the end of all existence and
being. Loved for his own sake from the ultimate intention
of the will and in the deepest pools of consciousness.

Now the Spirit has taken away the old stony heart of unbelieving selfishness. A new heart and a new spirit have been given in answer to the groaning of the oppressed, the sighing of the needy, the heartbroken plea: 'Create in me a clean heart, O God; and renew a right spirit within me.'

Filled with the fulness of God, the love of God shed abroad in the heart, Christ dwells within and the shining of his light, purpose of his love, and breathing of his life fill the soul. His interior language is ever the same: 'I came down from heaven, not to do mine own will, but the will of him that sent me.' 'My meat' — he saith within, sweetly blending with the life of the soul — 'is to do the will of him that sent me, and to finish his work.' To the whole range of affections, desires, passions, lusts; all the sensibility both base and virtuous feelings; he cries in victory from the inward parts of the soul and deepest depths of the will: 'Father, not my will, but thine be done!'

Of that will, for such hearts, Jesus now instructs his disciples in the Sermon on the Mount.

First, however, there is just a little more to be learned about those whom Jesus teaches, besides the place and position from which he teaches them.

As to those whom Jesus taught, they are called 'Disciples', Matthew 5:1.

This descriptive name for Jesus' true followers occurs over two hundred and seventy times. Of these occurrences some seventy are found in Matthew. The first time that the word 'disciple' appears in the New Testament is in this place — Mt. 5:1 — immediately before the Sermon on the

Mount. Implying, right at the outset, that here are the features which characterise the disciple.

The sort of grey, insipid 'devotional' dish that is served up lukewarm today at conventions and the like in the name of 'evangelical' coyly places 'discipleship' as a kind of Christian optional extra. Always providing one happens to feel specially keen. But not to worry if one doesn't. After all, we are still believers aren't we? All Christians together eh? Well, perhaps a few Mohammedans and Jews maybe, these days: you know, those of 'other faiths' isn't it called?

The sheer viciousness of this error — so hard to discern beneath the soft, cosy layers of insipid sentiment which must be peeled away before the light reaches the facts — is absolutely breathtaking in its daring trifling with immortal souls. We *must* be disciples to answer to the description of those who are saved. Our eternity hangs upon it. Be not deceived by this lying misapplication of 'love' which denies, rots and corrupts all judgment and righteousness.

Strictly, the actual word 'believer' — not the verb: the collective noun — so translated occurs only a very few times in the English New Testament. Yet to hear certain evangelicals one would think it the *only* name given to the faithful. Whereas in fact the name Disciple is one of the chief descriptions of the saints. A name given in that great proportion because it is one which is most indicative of the saved. Christ's sheep answer to it: as they do, proportionately and in balance, to all the titles given to the brethren.

Incidentally, the name Christian occurs only three times, two of which are a nickname and all a title originally given by men. But it is what Father, Son, and Holy Ghost call the people of God individually and collectively, in the word of God, that truly describes the elect. Get back to warranting those descriptive titles and none other — as a person and people — and you have got back to the New Testament.

Then what does 'disciple' mean? The Greek word is μαθητής, *mathetes,* and is that from which *mathematical* is derived. The basic word is used to cover the whole range of mathematics, geometry, astronomy, and so on: science. Hence it indicates an attitude of precise exactitude concerning the knowledge taught. The disciple and his discipline are accurate, precise, methodical.

The word therefore utterly repudiates today's — no wonder it isn't used! — quiet dropping of dogmatic doctrine. It pours scorn upon the sly assumption that the faith — but one of many! — is all guesswork, all vague and 'open-ended' loose liberal evangelicalism.

Again, 'Disciple' is a word that totally negates emotional evangelism, the vast mass-meeting, the softening up, the show-biz techniques, the final 'decision' to the gentle cooing of 'Just as I am.' 'Disciple' tells you, it's just as you aren't.

By definition — mark that: *definition* — the disciple has an objective rule of clear precise truth. To it he disciplines himself and also brings everything that presumes to the name of Christ, refusing what is not agreeable to Jesus' doctrine, and actually repudiating what is alien to it. That is a disciple. And, as I say, it indicates what is necessary for salvation.

Mathetes implies that the disciple abhors vagueness.

Everything has a discernible rule or measure and everything is to be gauged by it.

The disciple allows of no intrusion from family or feelings or emotions to sweep him off his feet. Miracles, signs, wonders; blessings, experiences, ecstasies; superficial following, false faith, the stopping short at pardon: the disciple lays judgment to the line and brings righteousness to the plummet, and justly tries them all. His grand object is to learn the truth from the mouth of him that speaketh from heaven. To this end he sits at Jesus' feet, tranquil and calm, that he may absorb the doctrine by his Master's voice in a way that is truly spiritual.

'Disciple' therefore implies teachability. A meek docile receptiveness. A humble eagerness to be taught. But not by anybody. Just by the Man from Galilee. He is the one who teaches life from life and lives the life he teaches. He is the one who speaks as having authority, and not as the scribes. He is the one of whom it is said, Who teacheth like him?

Mathetes implies a body of doctrine; clear precise teaching on everything: not for debate or intellectual speculation. It is the last word. It is dogmatic: the Judge has spoken: the time for argument is long past. The faith has been once delivered. The doctrine of Christ, the way of life, the apostolic doctrine, all give absolute clarity about every subject.

That is what is taught, and since it is divine, what has man got to do with it? Nothing but humbly submit and meekly learn. To receive with meekness the engrafted word, which is able to save the soul. Such is the humble and earnest spirit of the disciple: it characterises him. It is this character that is described in Chapter 5:3-12.

Blessed are the poor in spirit: for theirs is the
kingdom of heaven.
Blessed are they that mourn: for they shall
be comforted.
Blessed are the meek: for they shall inherit
the earth.
Blessed are they which do hunger and
thirst after righteousness: for they shall be
filled.
Blessed are the merciful: for they shall
obtain mercy.
Blessed are the pure in heart: for they shall
see God.
Blessed are the peacemakers: for they shall
be called the children of God.
Blessed are they which are persecuted for
righteousness' sake: for theirs is the kingdom
of heaven.
Blessed are ye, when men shall revile you,
and persecute you, and shall say all manner
of evil against you falsely, for my sake.
Rejoice, and be exceeding glad: for great
is your reward in heaven: for so persecuted
they the prophets which were before you.

In fine, it is clear that *mathetes, disciple,* indicates that
the old life and way of life have been forsaken completely
from the inmost heart, in order that the Master and his
doctrine may be attended with meticulous thoroughness
and mathematical accuracy. To this end disciples actually
follow their Master whithersoever he goeth: it is not a way
of study: it is a way of life. With purpose of heart they
cleave to the Lord.

These in turn are the ones to whom the Master — on hearing that his mother and brethren stand without — will turn, saying 'Who is my mother? And who are my brethren? And he stretched forth his hand toward his disciples, and said, Behold my mother and my brethren!

'For whosoever shall do the will of my Father which is in heaven, the same is my brother, and sister, and mother.'

II THE DOCTRINE OF MESSIAH
AND THE KINGDOM

CHAPTER 5:1 TO CHAPTER 7:29

¶ The setting. Ch. 5:1-2

The place and position from which Jesus taught the disciples provides the setting for the 'Sermon on the Mount', chapters five to seven inclusive. However I think that this address ought to be designated 'The doctrine of Messiah and the Kingdom'. The former title merely indicates the place from which the Sermon was delivered. But the description of this occupies less than one verse. It describes nothing whatsoever about the content of the Sermon itself.

Since the actual Sermon covers the next three chapters and some one hundred and ten verses, and since the whole is vitally significant to the context of the gospel according to Matthew in particular, then a title describing so long and important an address ought to summarise *the address itself*. Not the place from which it was delivered. As to that sermon or address, it is a distinct development in Matthew's declaration of Messiah and the Kingdom: crucial in his exposition of the doctrine. Hence that is what must be described.

Not that the setting is unimportant. In fact it is most important. What I am saying is that the setting is for the Sermon, not the Sermon for the setting. Therefore in a general title for these three chapters it must be the *content* that is described because that is what is pre-eminent.

Probably the Sermon 'on the Mount' was given its traditional name in order to distinguish it from a somewhat similar — if more condensed — form of address found in Luke 6:20-49 but which was delivered 'on the Plain'.

The questions that must be considered are these: Are we to draw lessons from the distinctive setting of Matthew? If so, what are they? And why is the situation reversed in Luke? Would not the conclusions of Matthew 'on the Mount' negate those of Luke 'on the Plain', and vice-versa? How can such contrasting settings both be significant?

First of all, observe just how much Luke differs from Matthew. For example, as to the circumstances preceding the Sermon. In Luke, it is after a whole night of prayer alone with God; in Matthew, the Sermon occurs in the midst of a day crowded with service to man. In the one case Jesus commands and calls his disciples to him; in the other, his disciples come of their own accord. In the third gospel, Jesus chooses and names the apostles; in the first, there is no thought of apostles at all — the name does not occur until the tenth chapter.

Luke has it that Jesus descends to men on earth; but in the other case he ascends towards God in heaven. On the one hand Jesus comes down with the apostles; but on the other he ascends and calls his disciples. One declares that he approaches to the multitude; but Matthew tells that he retired from the multitude. Luke predicates that Jesus stood down in the plain; in Matthew's case, Messiah sits up high on the mountain. In the one instance Jesus speaks to his disciples below; but in the other he is said to teach the disciples from above. In the third gospel Jesus descends to heal and then speak; yet in the first gospel Jesus heals then ascends to teach.

If not a hair on our head shall perish; if not a sparrow shall fall to the ground without our Father's knowledge; if God gave intricate and precise figures of the true centuries before the New Testament began; if Jehovah delivered explicit and graphic types and shadows in Israel from of old time: tell me, in the case of the Son of his love at the end of the world, shall it be that these exact distinctions have no message? They have a message. And verily, it would take more and longer than this book to tell the tale and draw out the riches to the full.

Consider Matthew. Jesus is teaching the doctrine of the kingdom. But it is not educational or exemplary teaching. It is a way of life. And of life altogether superior to anything ever envisaged by men. The world could not rise to this doctrine: human life simply cannot answer to this quality. Israel was unequal to the task: trouble enough with prohibitions and negatives! The sheer positive radiance of the life here described was too high for Israel, it went over his head.

This is the life of the Son of God seen not in himself but as indwelling his disciples. Without such a Spirit of sonship men have no heart, neither life nor power, to dwell in the heavenly kingdom sphere or to live on its spiritual level of being. It was the Day of Pentecost that brought in the unction to fulfil the quality of life described in this address. The effect of the sanctifying work of the Holy Ghost is being declared beforehand to the disciples in the 'Sermon on the Mount'.

If so — whilst spoken then — this was a future reality dependent upon the sufferings of Christ on the cross of Calvary. Full atonement must be made and justification for the ungodly wrought by blood before the Spirit could be given. Risen from the dead, ascended into heaven, Jesus must present the tokens of his earthly travail on behalf of those for whom he suffered in death. Accepted of God the Father, the Spirit in consequence was poured out from heaven upon those waiting disciples below. This is that which actually brought in the life that had been previously described in Matthew chapters five to seven. It was present power from on high to fulfil the word before spoken below.

That is, from high upon spiritual Mount Zion. Having finished on earth the work which he came from heaven to conclude, the ascended Son has returned and is seated on the right hand of the Father in the excellent glory. And so effectively did the Son bind his people to him in redemption that they are said to be sat down with him. From the glory the Lord Jesus inwardly calls them by name — in the unrolling process of time — and calls them into the position which he won for them on Calvary. They are declared to be seated in heavenly places in Christ Jesus.

From the highest glory of heaven the Lord Jesus secretly speaks to his people in a mystery. 'He that speaketh from heaven' — the Son of God — declares from the ascension day until the end of time that heavenly and spiritual doctrine of the 'Sermon on the Mount'. Thus his present disciples even now obtain an inheritance among them that are sanctified by faith in him. There is no power for men in reading the print on earth. The power is in that transforming voice from heaven.

Now all these things are facts. What might be questioned is this: Is the setting of the 'Sermon on the Mount' a figure of these facts? When Jesus ascended into the mountain and sat down, he called his disciples unto him, and taught them heavenly doctrine. Was this a deliberately created *figure* — for the time then present — of later gospel facts? I answer, yes it was. And — though illustrating different truths — so it was with the figure in Luke also. Although of this we cannot now speak particularly.

The indisputable truth is that the doctrine enunciated by the Lord Jesus in the 'Sermon on the Mount' was altogether beyond the disciples until *after* the descent of the Spirit. That is, following the ascension.

Thereupon the disciples are said to have ascended in Christ. Because it was on their behalf that he sat down so far above.

In such a special context 'Mountain' is used mystically to indicate the heights of Messiah's heavenly ascension. This is the meaning of the Old Testament 'Mountain of the Lord'. It is the meaning of the 'Mount of Transfiguration'. It is the meaning of 'A Lamb stood on the Mount Sion, and with him an hundred forty and four thousand, having his Father's name written in their foreheads.' An allegory precisely commensurate with the teaching here.

Precedents could be multiplied. I know we must be

have we not prophesied in thy name, and in thy name cast out devils, and done many wonderful works? But he will abhor them; they are workers of iniquity; profession, gifts, hearing the word, and all. They did not *do* it. That is iniquity. He saith, Depart from me ye workers of iniquity.

But those who hear these sayings — that is, the sayings of Matthew chapters five to seven — *and do them* not only profess justification: they show that they are justified. They not only confess the atonement, they demonstrate that the atonement was made for them. They not only speak of faith, they show their faith by their works.

Being baptised, receiving the communion of bread and wine, professing the doctrine, hearing the word, preaching it, keeping the ordinances, attending the services, being evangelical and evangelistic, tithing and giving, belonging to the 'church', being in the 'ministry': all these are outward forms that are worthless in and of themselves. They are not even miraculous. Those whom Christ is here said to damn in the Last Day, Mt. 7:21-23, went far beyond outward works. They actually did miracles over and above all these human works. But they were unsanctified, and as such, condemned, damned and lost forever.

Therefore it behoves those who profess the name of Christ not only to believe that they died and rose in and with him, but that they are those disciples whom he carried up with him in his ascension. And if so, not solely to look back to the cross. Nor simply to look forward to his coming. But primarily to hear his present voice now speaking to their hearts from heaven as bringing them into the fellowship that is with the Father and the Son. It is the character of this fellowship that Jesus sets forth so ably in the 'Sermon on the Mount'.

One ought to mention in passing that there are
several Jewish expressions found throughout the following
doctrine, in which with kindly condescension to the
disciples' understanding Jesus limits his language to the
dispensation then present. For example 'leaving one's gift
at the altar' is impossible to the Christian. First, there is no
altar: that was a figure of Calvary. Second, we bring no
gift, such as pigeon, lamb, goat, or ox. But they did, and
understood the application. And so must we, for it is a
prophetic principle that the word speaks in some degree
through the conditions that actually obtained at the time
during which the prophet foretold.

This address was delivered to the disciples and only
through them to those who should follow thereafter. Hence
however prophetic, visionary and far-reaching, of necessity
its *medium* was Jewish and accommodated to the present
understanding of Jewish disciples. In that sense the Gentiles
had neither part nor lot in the matter. As to them 'After
all these' — materialistic — 'things do the Gentiles seek.'
Yet after the Sermon became a gospel reality, Israel was
rejected, the Old Covenant forever concluded, and God
took up the Gentiles in the New Testament.

So the fact that in places this doctrine is accommodated
to the then-present light of the Jewish disciples must not
lead us to suppose that it is irrelevant to the Church. It *is*
in fact the Church's sanctification. It *is* the Church. It *is*
Sonship. Seventeen times 'Your Father' or 'Your heavenly
Father' occurs directly. The word translated 'children' here
is υἱός: *Sons*. Relationships, remark, exclusive to the Church
in God the Father and in the Lord Jesus Christ.

¶ Entrance into the kingdom. Ch. 5:3-12

Verses three to twelve of Matthew chapter five — the opening of the 'Sermon on the Mount' — consist of nine 'Beatitudes'. These are so called because they affirm bliss or blessing — a state of beatitude — upon those who are in the condition to which they refer respectively, and because of the priceless promise associated with each.

Is there any significance in the fact that there are *nine* affirmations of beatitude? Yes, there is a spiritual significance.

Numbers are used symbolically in certain passages of both Old and New Testaments, where the scripture adopts a certain form of imagery to portray the truth. It is comparatively easy to discover these places and to detect the intention of the writer to convey ideas by the numerals used.

Where the mode is vivid, with bold colourful strokes sweeping across a large canvas, where poetry and mysticism rise to sublime heights, where numbers are employed for no logical reason yet are applied specifically: there you have it. For example, take the mystical temple in the last chapters of Ezekiel, or the imagery in the latter part of Daniel. Zechariah's visions; the 'little apocalypse' of the synoptic gospels; or the book of the Revelation of Jesus Christ. These are some of the obvious cases: but there are very many shorter instances, where passages of this kind are inserted to illustrate a more conventional and prosaic style of conveying the truth.

Such brief passages are often detected by noticing a specific numerical arrangement. Where the specially significant numbers — three, four, seven, ten, twelve, or their multiples, for example — occur in such a context, then it is safe to apply the rules of interpretation.

These conditions obtain in the case of the Beatitudes. Although found in a larger teaching context, here is discovered a certain poetic style. Clearly there is a deliberate numerical arrangement. Then what is the disciple intended to do but discover what this is, and find out why the Master employed it?

Superficially there is a difficulty in the fact that there are *nine* beatitudes. But, difficulty or not, the Lord Jesus deliberately repeated 'Blessed' — μακάριος, *makarios; blissful, happy* — nine times, and the Holy Ghost specifically records these words by Matthew. Thus we are not only to look for the teaching in each singular pronouncement, but also in the total number and in the whole arrangement.

Symbolically, the number 'nine' is virtually unused! Yet with careful contemplation it becomes clear that no numeral could be more significant to illustrate the Master's teaching in this place.

The first *seven* beatitudes — seven being the number invariably associated with perfection — all refer to *active moral conditions*. They describe the interior state of the blessed. But the last *two* beatitudes are completely different.

They do not refer to the active state of the blessed at all. In the last two cases it is not the blessed who are active, they are passive; it is others who are active towards them. The reference is not to what the blessed are themselves, but to the hostile activity which their sevenfold bliss generates from the world at large.

Immediately the problem of the odd number begins to clarify. There are not nine parallel beatitudes. There are seven parallel beatitudes. Two more are added to these, as if — so to speak — at right-angles to them. The latter two pronouncements indicate an entirely different approach.

But still. Granted that the number of beatitudes is significant. Given that the first seven beatitudes have an integral importance. Why add only two? Since the resultant total of nine has no symbolic meaning, why — for example — not add *three* to the first seven, so as to round off and complete the whole number? Ten, after all, has a significance just as great as seven, and moreover is as often employed in numerical imagery. Why then did the Master deliberately stop short?

But that is exactly the point.

He did stop short.

Consider:

In the first seven beatitudes the Lord Jesus pronounces upon the sevenfold — *perfect* — state of moral and interior bliss to be found by the disciple on earth. Yet this is evidently not what the worldly would consider bliss. Even for the spiritual, one could suppose that it comes short of what might be expected. It is true that the blessed are kind, pure and peaceful. But then they are also poor, mournful, bruised, hungry and thirsty. Is this bliss, then?

Yes, considering the inward consolations. 'Theirs is the kingdom of heaven.' One will reply to me, Well; but whilst this first consolation is indeed in the present tense, the other six are in the future tense! 'They *shall* be'; is this perfect bliss on earth? A proper observation.

But then it must be appreciated that the comforts of this present time *are* largely anticipatory — six out of seven! — and, let us be completely honest about it, these are commensurate with a great deal of spiritual affliction and inward suffering. Nor is that everything. For from without also the last two beatitudes assure us of persecution, reviling, reproach and contempt from the world and the formally religious. Still, for all this, we reckon the sufferings of the present time to be but a light affliction, lasting for no more than a few moments, and not to be compared with the glory which shall be revealed hereafter.

Indeed that is precisely the reason why there are nine 'beatitudes' in all. Ten, a round number, would indicate a fulness or completion. But in terms of blessedness, whatever the heart may now feed upon that is spiritual and heavenly, so long as the soul remains in this present scene, bliss will fall short of completion.

There will be joy. There will be blessedness. Betimes moments of ecstasy. But withal, tribulations without and afflictions within shall be felt as strong and sometimes stronger than any other sensation. This always has been and it always will be the portion and lot of the disciples throughout their earthly pilgrimage below. He that loses his life shall find it. The disciple takes up his cross daily. He dies daily.

In this world we shall have tribulation. But daily we draw nearer to another world, a better resurrection, and a scene in which — though it be said 'These are they which came out of great tribulation' — God shall wipe away all tears from our eyes, and there will be no more crying. Our beatitudes will be complete: crowned *tenfold* in the world to come.

Yet even now we enjoy sweet sensations of this heavenly bliss; such anticipatory thoughts and hopes. There is discovered to the labouring soul an inner blessedness. It is like the grapes of Eshcol borne on the staff with the pomegranates and figs. Like flagons of milk from the land of promise, carried over to refresh the pilgrims on their way until they obtain their desired haven and arrive at the heavenly country. So is our ninefold bliss below. We know where we are going. And already, precious foretastes break in upon the soul and spiritual comforts stay us on our pathway.

To the casual reader the beatitudes could appear as a series of disconnected statements. To the superficial there is no visible sequence. They seem not unlike a number of random proverbs. But upon the barest reflection it is obvious that this cannot be so in fact.

Indeed there is a poignant and exquisite thread of continuity in these sayings, carrying the soul step by step through the spiritual portals of the kingdom. Each 'blessedness' builds upon its predecessor and leads naturally to the successor which follows. At last a perfect — sevenfold — entrance is made and the dual reaction of the world and its religion to the entrants clarified.

The state described in each consequential beatitude gives no hint of dogma. These are not doctrinal steps: they mark the experimental progression of the inner soul into the heavenly kingdom. The beatitudes do not state the objective truth: they describe the spiritual interior. They do not tell us what to believe or what is believed: they record the heart struggle to faith itself and how this profound inner belief was achieved.

The beatitudes are not the dogmatic truths presented for belief to the soul seeking the kingdom of heaven. They are the experiences undergone and the heartfelt sensations made known to the deeply exercised soul as it progresses from unbelief to faith. The beatitudes do not set forth the truths of the gospel. They describe the spiritual journey of the inner man as the Spirit of God acts upon and within the soul, finally to lead into spiritual union with the Father and the Son.

1st. 'Blessed are the poor in spirit:'

Here is the very first step towards the kingdom. The first stirring to God-ward. And yet so certain is the way which is taught by Jesus and declared by him to be blessed, that the kingdom is assured to these elementary tremblings of the poor soul towards the heavenly gates. Theirs *is* the kingdom of heaven.

Consider the poor. Blessed is he that considereth the poor. And blessed be the poor, saith Matthew, but adds 'in spirit'. Wherefore it is not poverty, barely, that is blessed.

One may object: Luke says only 'Blessed be ye poor,' excluding the reference to 'in spirit'. As if poverty as such, of any kind, qualified for the blessing. Not so. Jesus says in Luke, Blessed be *ye* poor. Not any poor as such, but only that kind of poor to whom the Lord Jesus then addressed himself. What poor were these? 'And Jesus lifted up his eyes on *his disciples* and said, Blessed be ye poor.' Or even more strictly 'Blessed poor.' That is, poor *disciples*. Let a man find out wherein disciple-poverty consists and he shall understand the meaning. But Matthew has told us the meaning beforehand: poverty *of spirit*.

So then it is not indiscriminate. Not just any poor that are blessed. To the contrary, being poor can engender a curse. When Job fell into poverty, his wife advised him, Curse God, and die. Hence the wise man asks for deliverance from poverty 'lest I be poor, and steal, and take the name of my God in vain.' The poor man who does that need not think that he shall inherit any blessing from the Lord.

Moreover, 'A poor man that oppresseth the poor is like a sweeping rain which leaveth no food.' And will God bless this poor man? I trow not. Besides, 'If a ruler hearken to lies, all his servants' — even the poorest and most servile, all of them — 'are wicked.' In consequence 'The poor and the deceitful man meet together.' Now these are not the blessed poor. Rather, they are nigh unto cursing. Wherefore observe, it is a *specific* kind of poor that is pronounced blessed of God.

This kind is called the Lord's poor, the poor of the flock, the disciple-poor. Of them he declares: Blessed are *ye* poor. Why? Because their cry is to God-ward: 'This poor man cried, and the Lord heard.' Because the Lord heareth the poor, their expectation shall not perish. God setteth the poor on high, he raiseth up the poor out of the dust. He shall stand at the right hand of the poor.

The Spirit himself maketh intercession for them, crying,

'Forget not the congregation of thy poor.' And he does not, but blesses them. They call upon him one by one, confessing 'I am poor and needy.' But for the oppression of the poor and the sighing of the needy shall I arise, saith the Lord. He shall abundantly satisfy Zion's poor. He hath prepared goodness for the poor. Therefore let the poor and needy praise thy name.

I say, of *this* sort of poor, the Lord's poor, the congregation of his poor, disciple-poor, Zion's poor, he saith 'Blessed be ye poor.'

Theirs is a spiritual poverty. Blessed are the poor *in spirit*. Riches can never alleviate this want. Nothing but Messiah's blessing can bring relief. Moses cannot speak to their condition. 'For they hearkened not unto Moses for anguish of spirit.' But, saith Jesus, They hear my voice.

Only Christ can address this state of soul and lead into abundance from penury. Job felt this when he cried out loud 'I will speak in the anguish of my spirit.' He looked for comforters; but, behold, there were none to comfort him. Not on earth. The psalmist had the same experience: 'I complained, and my spirit was overwhelmed within me. Hear me speedily, O Lord, my spirit faileth.' There was poverty of spirit there, you see, it faileth; he was conscious of that. For by sorrow of heart the spirit is broken. And a wounded spirit who can bear?

Yet this is the very condition which Jesus blesses. He pronounces bliss on all those that are of a contrite and humble spirit, that tremble at his word. Messiah comes, in fact, 'to revive the spirit of the poor.'

He is anointed specifically 'to preach the gospel to the

poor.' It was reported of the poor that they had 'the gospel preached unto them.' These are the ones whom God hath chosen to be rich in faith, and to them is the word of this salvation sent.

But is their poverty also a natural one? Not of absolute necessity. Yet to a great extent it must be so, before the soul can enter the kingdom. How hardly shall a rich man enter into the kingdom. How few there are who can be entrusted with riches, without trusting in them. The confidence of the rich man rests in his wealth. Until that is taken away, it is impossible that he should trust in the Lord. 'And he went away sorrowful, for he had great possessions.'

The twentieth century has been characterised by the rectification of injustices done by the rich to the poor and needy. But this rectification has not been done on the basis of individual judgment and correction by the judiciary. It has been done through a social revolution upsetting the whole established order of things, and done by experimenting politicians not directly concerned with justice at all. One of the consequences of this process for the souls of the poorer classes is that the gospel has faded into their distant past and mammon has been brought within their easy reach. Much suffering has ceased; much deprivation has been eliminated. But what of the kingdom of heaven? To whom now shall we cry 'Blessed are ye poor'?

It is impossible to set the heart upon worldly advance-ment, a future career of greater wealth and leisure demanding all one's drive and ambition through the youthful years, or the struggle to maintain and advance what has been gained through single-minded worldly devotion, without laying the kingdom of heaven to one side. Many false prophets shall tell you otherwise, but they are liars. Hear Christ: 'Ye cannot serve God and mammon.'

Ye cannot become poor in spirit, whilst pursuing worldly riches. These things are mutually exclusive. One or the other must be given up. Make no mistake; in the seventies nothing has changed. 'Blessed be ye poor.' Not because of any inherent virtue in that estate: but such is the deceitfulness of riches that there is a certain indissoluble affinity between poverty in material possessions and poverty of spirit.

The gospel rule is this: 'After all these things do the Gentiles seek.' And, 'Seek ye first the kingdom of God and his righteousness, and all these things shall be added unto you.'

Then does the voluntary renunciation of worldly wealth and ambitious desire in and of itself bring poverty of spirit? How does one achieve poverty of spirit? Not by the bare rejection of worldly goods and opportunities. That alone cannot make one poor in spirit. It may do the very opposite, and fill one with rich self-satisfaction.

Poverty of spirit finds its dawning within the interior soul. It is not caused through a work of power by which God creates new life in the soul. Rather its origin is found in a divine illumination through which the soul is made aware of its true condition. It is lit up: the soul is conscious of its real state because it can see that state. So then, this is not a change wrought by God: it is a realisation given by him.

Hitherto — in the natural darkness of the mind — from a

child there existed all manner of egotistical dreams and woven fantasies of self-conceit. With overweening interest the youthful soul discoursed to itself of its basic virtue, intelligence, hidden strength, and spiritual richness. In maturity it pictured itself with gross distortions upon the mirror of the imagination. The image appeared so pleasant to the inner sight that upon reflection the soul became quite infatuated with this preposterous self-deception.

But these shadowy fantasies flee with the darkness when once the convincing light of God's Spirit illuminates the inner man. With the coming of the light there floods the soul a shocked awareness of its real and awful poverty.

How blind one had been! Where before blossomed dreams like a fruitful garden, now appears the barren harshness of bitter ashes. Where once diffused that misty glow in which real shapes dissolve and desired ones materialise, now the cold light of realism disperses the lying medium and with icy glare exposes the miserable penury of the soul's true bankruptcy.

Realism perforce causes the soul to admit its emptiness and deadness. The hollow sham of lying pretence — that was once the mind's defence against the truth of one's real condition — is now entirely deflated and debunked. Now is seen the reality behind the facade of a lifetime, and the sight is horrible.

The soul would never have come to this awareness and consequent admission were it not for the providence of God without, and his piercing illumination within.

Providentially, by long pressures and seeming catastrophes, God brings the soul to a halt in which it is made to consider its latter end. Simultaneously, an increasing divine illumination brings the soul at last to a shattering realisation of its true interior condition.

This realisation is magnified by the awareness of the total blindness and willing evasion that existed before. Not now. Now the inescapable consciousness of the state of soul before the all-seeing eye of the Almighty crushes the arrogant spirit and smites the soul with remorse.

God has not put something there, adding to the soul: he has taken away its false deceits and refuges, showing the soul what is there in fact.

This is the work of conviction. It causes the soul to begin its first trembling step towards God, the first sighing of the journey into the kingdom. This initiation is described as poverty of spirit.

Oh, cries the soul within itself, How deluded I was, how blind, how destitute of real inward religion! How void of God I am, sighs the broken heart, O, when shall I come and appear before God, can it ever be possible? This from the soul that was before so alive, so full of laughter, so warm towards the world, so rich in self-conceit, so sure of virtue and of God. But how cursed I was, weeps the now-afflicted soul. Now, he cries, now I know my real poverty, my true destitution, my bankruptcy of all virtue, and void of the least communication with heaven and with God.

From this new-found awareness of one's own poverty of spirit, comes the cry for the Spirit. From the consciousness of deep poverty in all things spiritual is gendered the contrite plea of the poor in spirit. From the awareness of the total absence of any affinity with God comes the state which is now pronounced blessed.

Out of the awful frustration arising from any sure means of communicating with the Almighty, arises the pathetic inward yearning for the Spirit that through him a communion might be established.

The poor soul beseeches God for his Holy Spirit. Poverty of spirit is the soul's most heartfelt awareness precisely because the Spirit is the medium of communication with God. But there is no communication. The lamentation of the soul therefore becomes that of the poor in spirit.

': for theirs is the kingdom of heaven.'

Blessed state! Although for the present such a state seems not to be blessed but rather grievous and accursed. Nevertheless the brightest promise attends, and afterwards sorrow shall give place to the sweetest possible relief.

Poverty of spirit seems so awful, such a casting away, so far beyond redemption. The soul is prostrate, groaning with despair. O my leanness, my leanness, it cries, Woe is unto me.

Covering the upper lip, crying 'Unclean, unclean,' in bitter poverty the soul wanders alone up and down the desert lands of a spiritual wilderness. How cursed every prospect appears. But in fact the very opposite is true, though the realisation of this is far beyond the remotest expectation. Yet it is the poor soul's very condition which brings to pass that most moving of benedictions: 'Blessed are the poor in spirit.'

'For theirs is the kingdom of heaven.' It is not said, Theirs will be the kingdom of heaven. But, theirs is the kingdom of heaven. It is present. Let the poor in spirit know and be advertised of this certain assurance from the mouth of the Lord Jesus.

It is not for other than the poor, though multitudes of the rich in spirit take it so easily to themselves. But it is for the contrite that tremble at God's word, though they find it so hard to believe of their own case. They feel so destitute and void of any hope of ever finding relief. Yet let it be settled deep within their souls, for it is a faithful and true saying: 'theirs *is* the kingdom of heaven.'

This present kingdom is not of earthly Israel, it is of heavenly Jerusalem. It is not temporal, it is eternal. It cometh not with observation, it is spiritual. It is not of time, it is everlasting. It is not exterior, it is interior. It is not of the Jews, it is of God. It is not of Palestine, it is of heaven. 'The kingdom of an inward heaven' brings days of heaven on earth, elevates the soul to God, brings down the Spirit from on high, and lights up with glory within.

And — all unbeknown, completely unbeknown, to himself — the poor broken-hearted soul who seems so far, afar off, has just walked right through its gates. His is the kingdom of heaven.

2nd. 'Blessed are they that mourn:'

Two questions immediately spring to mind. First, What is mourning? And, Mourning over what?

What is mourning? The Oxford dictionary states 'Feel sorrow or regret (*for, over*, dead person, lost thing, loss, misfortune, etc.) show conventional signs of grief for period after person's death; sorrow for (dead person, thing).' What more piercing sorrow or destitution than this?

Second; Mourn over what, then? How can this definition apply to the beatitudes? If the most intense pining, the most bitter anguish of which the human breast is capable — to feel that undiminished but unbearable ache for those irretrievably lost to one — I say, if that word is used here: then to what is it applicable?

Surely, to that about which one feels an equivalent spiritual desolation. So great must be this feeling, that any lesser word would have been inadequate. The Lord Jesus used the word for a pining emptiness; a sense of loss at times unendurable. The hollowness, the consequent *poverty* felt, is utter. Then if so, the second beatitude must derive its genesis from the first.

It is poverty of spirit that makes the heart to ache and keen as in bereavement. It is the absence of the Holy Spirit that causes the bitter soul to lament so pathetically. It is for the Spirit of God that loneliness mourns. It is for another Comforter that the mourner cries.

The soul cries like Rachel weeping for her children. She lifts her tear-stained and swollen face from her hands to

165

heaven, for no comfort on earth will suffice for this kind of sorrow.

It is like the desolate lamentation of Rizpah the daughter of Aiah who took the black sackcloth of mourning to bewail her departed. She bare the unendurable loss with silent anguish. In the burning sun by day and the cutting cold by night she sat still as a stone, the spread sackcloth beneath her, as she kept her long and lonely vigil upon the bald mountain. Among the children of men, behold and see if there be any sorrow like unto this sorrow. She looked for comforters, but there were none. Not on earth. Not among men.

This word, mourning, is the word used by the Lord Jesus to describe the intensity of the spiritual exercise which arises from real poverty of spirit. How this shames every kind of verbose, tawdry and superficial religion. How few can honestly say that they have come this way, and can see eye to eye in experience with this doctrine. But verily, it is the way into the kingdom, and the only way. Yet few there be that find it.

The mourning of the second beatitude is that of grief over what has separated the soul from God. Hence it includes the lament that is sounded at the felt absence of the inward witness of the Spirit. It follows that the grief referred to has both a negative and a positive aspect.

Negatively therefore one grieves and is sorry for past sin. 'But your iniquities have separated between you and your God, and your sins have hid his face from you, that he will not hear.' One really feels one was estranged from the womb — yea, that by one man sin entered into the world — that one was shapen in iniquity, and went astray

166

as soon as one was born; a son of disobedience, a child of wrath. One is aware of one's willing concurrence in the lawlessness, within and without, and of heinous and defiant sins without number. But now is the time of the soul's reckoning, and the consequences are spread before the mourner's face.

Positively one mourns one's barrenness of spirit. It is all so empty; there is nothing there. There is no means of communication with God. One pines and yearns for the Spirit to come and fill up the void, so giving plenitude to all the empty depths of the soul's poverty. The cry of the poor ascends, and the plea of the needy arises therewith. This is the mourning that follows naturally and of course from poverty of spirit.

His absence they mourn. Not simply Christ's absence: they know that Christ is present in heaven outwardly. Many are content with this, whose experience this beatitude is not. They do not mourn because they are content with an outward unexperimental Christianity. But it is *inwardly* that Christ is to be revealed. Hence the mourners mourn the absence of the inward Spirit.

One mourns one's unspirituality. The soul is mourning its interior desolation. The absence of communion causes yearning for union. It is for this, for the inward witness that union has been wrought between God and one's soul, that one mourns.

Luke contrasts the mourner's cry to God for spiritual relief, with the flippant and airy laughter of those who relieve themselves of all burdens by conducting their own way in scripture. Usurping the place and prerogative of the Holy Ghost the latter arrogate to themselves whatever texts they please. With numb complacency they finger every promise as their private property, though they are devoid of every interior mark of title, and empty of the least experience of the beatitudes. Self-styled champions of the truth, they have the temerity to call this audacious impertinence 'faith'.

These people — and they are in excess of the mourners as much as the wide gate exceeds the strait, the broad way the narrow — genuinely pity those that weep now. They cannot understand how such miserable souls still profess to follow Jesus! They themselves are effervescently happy; surely that is the criterion? How could these introspective mourners possibly be so obtuse?

Such bright and sparkling souls cannot understand the mourners, because they themselves feel so terribly happy. They are impatient with those who weep, because for themselves they are so full of laughter. They are unable to apprehend the weeping vigil and mournful waiting for relief within — within? — because they are bubbling with joy without. To them, all you have to do is come right forward and trust Jesus now, then accept that he has taken you at your word: feelings are nothing to do with it.

As to the saying of the Lord Jesus 'Blessed are ye that weep now: for ye shall laugh,' they have a dispensational scheme to dispose of that. If it matters. Anyway, they expect it is Jewish.

About that place where it says 'Woe unto you that laugh now! for ye shall mourn and weep,' well, you see, it is no longer relevant and meaningful to this day and age. The fact that they *do* laugh now; the fact that they have *never* wept: well, that has nothing to do with it, and nothing to do with them either. Because, you see, they took God at his word without all this morbid interior nonsense and all these unhealthy introspective feelings. Look, please don't mention it, because it is irritating, and besides, that would spoil their testimony.

How different are those who mourn their way into the kingdom. Totally different. What a contrast is seen in their sevenfold and twofold testimony of beatification and persecution. Let us listen to their cry. It is born of the Spirit. It is endorsed by the Son. And at the last its answer is received from the Father.

But not in haste. Attending the powerful preaching of the word, the mourner is wounded sore. Far from taking offence at such great plainness of speech, he is as one struck dumb, and trembles in the fear of God.

His demeanour alters completely. A voice from heaven thunders rebuke into his soul: 'Let your laughter be turned into mourning; be afflicted, and mourn, and weep.' For in that day doth the Lord of hosts call the people to weeping, and to mourning, and to baldness, and to girding with sackcloth. 'Behold,' saith the prophet, looking to the right hand and to the left to see the response of the people to this solemn call for repentance, Behold; 'joy and gladness.' And so it is today: no response, no penitence. 'Evangelical' joy and gladness. Then hath the word of God taken none effect? Have they not heard? The mourners have heard, though the rest were blinded. Yea, his people whom he foreknew have heard.

A remnant shall return and say, It is better to go to the house of mourning than to go to the house of feasting: for that is the end of all men; and the living will lay it to his heart. Sorrow is better than laughter: for by sadness of the countenance the heart is made better. The heart of the wise is in the house of mourning; but the heart of fools is in the house of mirth. It is better to hear the rebuke of the wise, than for a man to hear the song of fools.

Hearing wisdom's voice, the utterance of the mourner is the voice of the heart: 'I am troubled, I go mourning all the day. I am bowed down heavily as one that mourneth.' And what saith the Spirit? Calling for a deep work upon the ground of the soul, that it be neither stony nor shallow, the voice of the Spirit soundeth 'Break up your fallow ground, and sow not among thorns; take away the foreskins of your heart. Turn ye with weeping and with mourning, rend your heart and not your garments. Gird thee with sackcloth and mourn; make thee mourning as for an only son.'

The answering testimony of the responsive soul is this: 'I did mourn as a dove, mine eyes did fail. I mourn in my complaint and make a noise. We roared all like bears and mourned sore. Yea, we mourned, and wept, and fasted.'

What a testimony, a real testimony, to the truth! For it is the language of the penitent heart, and the way into the kingdom. And it answers to all the scripture, not to a few objective texts isolated from the truth, carried over to the world of entertainment, and mass-evangelised to blind and infatuated multitudes of worldly impenitents.

Hear the penitent. 'I wept and chastened my soul. I am weary, I water my couch with my tears. O, O hold not thy peace at my tears, for my tears have been my meat day and night.'

And here is the final cause: 'The sorrows of death

compassed me. The pains of hell gat hold upon me. The sorrows of hell compassed me about.' At last. This is the true fear, and the true sorrow, and the truth of the case. At last; this brings the soul without defence down to the depths of ultimate conviction.

'Then — *then* — said I, I will declare mine iniquity; I will be sorry for my sin. My sorrow is continually before me.'

But now, the work is done! It is all out. *Now* the soul is set free. Now the ground cleared, broken up, ploughed deep, and full of softened good rich soil.

One begins to feel the beams of blessedness. Faintly at first. The first intimations of calm after the storm: a strange tranquillity. Hardly daring to lift up the head, hardly daring to whisper, yet a song, sighing, escapes upon the mourner's breath

> Ah, Lord! if thou art in that sigh,
> Then hear thyself within me pray;
> Hear in my heart thy Spirit's cry,
> Mark what my labouring soul would say;
> Answer the deep unuttered groan,
> And show that thou and I are one.

> Shine on thy work, disperse the gloom,
> Light in thy light I then shall see;
> Say to my soul, Thy light is come,
> Glory divine is risen on thee,
> Thy warfare's past, thy mourning's o'er;
> Look up, for thou shalt weep no more.

And so it comes to pass. Blessed are they that mourn. Now

arises the day of our God to comfort all that mourn; to appoint unto them that mourn in Zion. Blessed are they that mourn.

'': for they shall be comforted.'

The mourner has been brought to the place of self-knowledge and humility where the merciful disposition which God bare from the very first can now safely be made known. Broken and penitent, the mourner has come to himself, and, weeping, blinded by tears, stumbles home. But the Father sees this afar off, and runs to meet him.

The Father of mercies and God of all comfort sends forth a sure word to all in his house, saying, Comfort ye, comfort ye my people. The Lord shall comfort his people. The Lord shall comfort Zion: he will comfort all her waste places; and make her desert like the garden of the Lord. He saith, I, even I, am he that comforteth you.

I know, saith the trembling soul, I know that thou dost speak comfortably unto Jerusalem. But what is thy servant? Who is blind as thy servant? Thy servant is but a dead dog; should the Lord look upon him?

And Jesus stood still, and commanded him to be called. And they call the blind man, saying unto him, Be of good comfort. Rise. He calleth for thee. And Jesus said, What wilt thou that I should do unto thee?
Lord, that I might receive my sight.
And Jesus said, Go thy way; thy faith hath made thee whole. And immediately he received his sight, and followed Jesus in the way.

But what is thy handmaid, that thou shouldest look upon her? Saith the Lord, As a mother comforteth so will I comfort thee: Daughter, be of good comfort. Thy faith hath made thee whole.

Now saith the soul, This is my comfort in my affliction. Thy merciful kindness be for my comfort. Lord, thou hast holpen me, and comforted me. Thy rod and thy staff they comfort me. Thou shalt comfort me on every side.

And not only so, for soon the company of them with like precious faith is found, those with whom the soul can see eye to eye in experience, who have also passed through fire and water to obtain this large place. And this must be so. They seek each other out: from the solitary place they are led together, that they might go unto a city which the Lord hath prepared for them in the land that is very far off, where they shall see the King in his beauty.

But now they are led together. Blessed are *they* that mourn: for *they* shall be comforted. Together. God's few, true, servants are directed to them 'To comfort you concerning your faith.' And they, too, 'Comfort one another with these words.'

They find that Jesus has given them — it is plural: 'I will send him unto *you'* — another Comforter, to be with them always. He doth not leave them comfortless. By this other Comforter — in the Spirit — he comes again to us, and, where two or three are gathered together in his name, there is he in the midst.

He manifests himself to them, and not unto the world. Nor to the worldly in religion. But as united in one, the erstwhile mourners experience the Comforter in a way superior to any singular experience known heretofore. And so they walk together and are edified; walking in the comfort of the Holy Ghost hand in hand, with their faces toward Zion.

Though they have come from the valley of weeping. Now they go from strength to strength. Every one of them in Zion appeareth before God.

3rd. 'Blessed are the meek:'

However before the sensation of this promised comfort to those who mourn, there are further steps in the soul's experience of entering into the kingdom of heaven. The mourners, awaiting now their Comforter, proceed to this next stage in the interior journey through the portals of the spiritual house of God.

Poor and mourning, nevertheless they awaken with a strange remembrance of the gates of pearl, the flashing turrets, the bulwarks of gold like glass. This spiritual dream of the holy city is but vague and cloudy. Yet the image persists upon the retina of the mind and, if unseen as yet, the vision is believed.

Though none is felt, already the soul is aware of coming comfort. It is hoped for. Still in the mists of gloom yet there is an unquenchable spark of consciousness that relief is on its way. The soul has a deep-laid certainty, like the hidden manna, that the Comforter will come, and will not tarry.

174

Firmly and yet meekly one is strengthened to ascend towards Jerusalem above, strengthened for the inward journey. Emulating her Master the soul approaches 'Meek and lowly, and riding upon an ass, and upon a colt the foal of an ass.'

But like Mephibosheth when descending, the soul stumbles at the sheer daring of such a wretch hoping to enter the thrice holy city. Made lame at the very gates by piercing thoughts of one's own unworthy wretchedness, the soul dare not actually enter in: And he bowed himself and said, What is thy servant, that thou shouldest look upon such a dead dog as I am?

The lameness of self-abomination makes the soul to halt even at the very doorposts. Head hanging like a bulrush, this hatred of self becomes too great for the soul to take another step. But although crippled by the bitter rising bile of self-loathing, nothing else prevents the penitent. One would rather die a thousand deaths than go back an inch. Like Joab at the horns of the altar — 'Nay, but I will die here' — nothing on earth will tear that soul from her post.

Sinking to the ground upon lame feet, still the soul determines within herself 'I had rather be a doorkeeper in the house of my God, than to dwell in the tents of wickedness.'

If the soul cannot move further forward, it will not go backward. Maybe for the time one is unable to take another step; but still, one has come to rest at the very portals of the holy city. Is it possible that such progress should prove in vain? Surely we are not of those that draw back unto perdition? On the contrary. The soul waits, as it were, lame and meek at the beautiful gate of the temple, hoping against hope that her salvation shall draw near, her expectation shall not perish, and that the day of her deliverance will prove to be at hand.

Meekness is now the trait most apparent. It is a lowly self-condemnation. As Job put it 'I abhor myself in dust and ashes.' It is a quality which springs from a poor opinion of one's self and one's importance. But because it is spiritually wrought, it goes very deep. It is not natural. It is wrought by a penetrating insight into the foulness of one's own interior.

'There is no soundness in my flesh because of thine anger. My wounds stink and are corrupt because of my foolishness. My loins are filled with a loathsome disease: and there is no soundness in my flesh.' When the experience — as a settled state — that brought forth these words becomes ours, then, and not till then, are we meek within the meaning of this beatitude.

Spiritual meekness is born of self-disgust. Its language is, I am a sinful man, O Lord. It springs from hatred of self. One feels oneself to be utterly, incurably vile. With the prophet one cries, Why is my wound incurable, which refuseth to be healed? One echoes with the apostle, I am carnal, sold under sin.

This is quite different from a natural, or constitutional meekness. The origin is different. Some persons are born with a meek disposition, a natural kindness, seen in their dealing with and attitude to their fellows. They are naturally yielding, self-effacing and humble. That has nothing to do with this beatitude. The meekness referred to here is not natural nor is it constitutional in any way; neither can it be isolated from the previous stages of poverty of spirit and mourning. Its origin is entirely spiritual, has to do with one's state before God and not man, and comes to light the nearer one approaches the gates of the kingdom.

When the Spirit of God works meekness into the soul, whether that soul is naturally meek or altogether arrogant, an entirely *new* meekness comes to light. It is not that one's worldly abilities have changed at all. But the conscious absence of any spiritual ability whatsoever becomes so all-absorbing, that the worldly things one boasted in before, or of which one was so proud hitherto, now become dust and gravel. They mean nothing.

Lowly, the meek judge and condemn themselves. Their whole attitude to others and to the world alters. Their demeanour, speech and dress changes. The ones whose company they once loved, whose boisterous jesting and popular conversation they once enjoyed, now become abhorrent to them. Such worldly company is shunned. But those whom before they despised, ridiculed as narrow, out of date, old-fashioned, whom they pitied as beneath contempt: why, these are now sought. Nothing but such serious earnest company will do for the meek.

Now one finds that the reason for this seriousness was not what one supposed. They were not such fools after all. The reason for their condition was not weak-mindedness, ignorance, over-compensation, escapism, or the inability to make money and get on in the world. The reason was that they feared being damned, they determined to be saved, and, following Christ, they were on their way to a heavenly country. Meanwhile they desired that Christ might be all and in all. This made them meek, and made their company desirable, nay irresistible, to the one in whose soul the Spirit of God was working meekness.

The English word Meek comes from the Old Norse *mjukr*, meaning soft, pliant, gentle. Free from self-will, submissive, patient and unresentful. The New Testament Greek *praus* means much the same thing: mild, soft, gentle, whether of things — such as sound — or of persons and actions. It is used of taming, or making mild, as with a bridle. Of animals it refers to being tame, not fierce or wild.

But as with the English, so the Greek describes the effect rather than the cause. There is no hint in the word itself as to *why* one is meek. Only that one appears so. Neither does the word in itself show whether that meekness is spiritual, before God, or natural, as seen among men. However these are things which must be discriminated to understand aright.

The Hebrew of the Old Testament is more specific and original. It is to the meek within this Hebrew sense, and with the spiritual interpretation of that sense, that the Lord Jesus refers in the third beatitude. Indeed, Psalm 37 itself declares, 'The meek shall inherit the earth.'

The Hebrew word for meek is both specific and original. The root of the word *Anav* finds its source originally in the toil and labour of an agricultural people: it is rooted in the soil. 'To bestow labour on anything; to exercise oneself in anything: specially, as it appears, *to till the ground, or, cultivate the earth, furrow.*'

This humble toil produces a natural meekness, and behind the Hebrew word describing the humility, lies the natural, labouring, cause. But in a chosen people of God everything, down to the humblest, is taken and transferred to the divine realm, given a double meaning by allusion from the natural to the spiritual realm. Things are spiritualised to refer to the work of God. And the word Anav, *meek*, is no exception. It is in this sense that it is used in Psalm 37:11, to which the beatitude refers. The interpretation of context must determine when the word is intended to be read spiritually, and usually this presents no difficulty.

So it is that the meaning 'to be afflicted, subdued by labour, tamed by toil, ploughed under, furrowed' developed a spiritual connotation when it was transferred to apply to the work of God on the soul as producing this effect in the character. When the Lord convicts the sinful soul, and slays the stout arrogant spirit by ploughing the furrows of his word within, there you have the meek in the spiritual sense.

When God ploughs up the fallow ground of the heart, when the word of the Lord is as fire and a hammer that breaketh the rock in pieces, then a sound work and a good foundation is inwrought within the soul. Not a swift work. It takes time, like clearing, uprooting, ploughing and harrowing.

This interior work of God is the sole and exclusive cause of the meekness upon which the Lord Jesus pronounces blessing. It is *that* kind of meekness. Such meekness springs from the resultant self-abomination: the hidden depths of the soul lie all exposed in unfolded rows like furrows, all the dark creeping things brought to light by this work. With this ploughing of the Lord, the soul thereby loathes what it sees of itself, hitherto quiescent beneath the surface.

One feels oneself utterly vile, beyond insult. The interior work of God by the word wrought this soul exposure. And its consequent meekness. Three things: the inward ploughing of God; the resultant uncovering and exposure; finally, the consequent humility and meekness effected in the soul.

The expression of this meekness was personified in Moses. He was very meek, the meekest man on the face of the earth. And not surprisingly, since, from being chiefest among the chosen princes of the earth — in the mightiest nation of the world — he was reduced to fleeing like a common criminal into the howling wilderness, pursued by the avenging Egyptians. Despised and betrayed by his own Hebrew brethren, Moses was driven into lonely exile whilst in the prime of his days at forty years old.

He loved God's people, and longed to speak for their deliverance. Treacherously spurned by them, he wandered destitute and isolated for forty years, up and down he went in the barren desert wastes under the baking sun of perhaps the most inhospitable climate in the world.

Apparently cast off, shut out, and despised by God as by his people, the lament of the poor man must often have echoed off the burning rocks:

> 'Wherefore their days in vanity
> he did consume and waste;
> And by his wrath their wretched years
> away in trouble passed.'

Outcast by his people for doing them good; forgotten by God for obeying his Spirit: for four decades — as his life trickled away into the sand — so it must have seemed. Befriended only by a few heathen and vagrants, Moses saw his strength ebb into old age, all those tremendous talents unused, all that latent power wasted, all those untapped resources useless. O bitterness of bitterness. Well might he cry, an old man of eighty, solitary as a hermit: 'I have laboured in vain, I have spent my strength for nought, and in vain.'

But it was not in vain. He became — mark that, he *became* — the meekest man on the face of the earth. But by that time he was eighty. And for all the hard, unending, heart-breaking providence of his pathway, it was the interior furrows ploughed into his soul that brought the deepest affliction, and which resulted in the meekest of characters. It was then that all his years came back; then that his lifework finally began.

Anav has often been translated 'humble'. As in 'He forgetteth not the cry of the humble,' and 'Arise, O Lord, forget not the humble.' 'Thou hast heard the desire of the humble.' You observe how their breathing, feeling, and desiring is all to heaven, all to Godward, always upward. And God responds downward: The Lord lifteth up the meek.

Blessed are the meek. For the meek will he guide in judgment, he will beautify the meek with salvation, the meek shall eat and be satisfied.

God hath sent his Son, who saith 'He hath sent me to preach good tidings to the meek.' So then; seek righteousness, seek meekness, for because of truth, meekness and righteousness, Christ rides forth. He reproveth with equity for the meek.

Yea, of a truth, it is but a little while, and the wicked shall not be; yea, thou shalt diligently consider his place, and it shall not be. But the meek shall inherit the earth; and shall delight themselves in the abundance of peace. The meek also shall increase their joy in the Lord, and the poor among men shall rejoice in the Holy One of Israel.

'; for they shall inherit the earth.'

This is not the portion of the wicked, though their estates spread at present. 'I have seen the wicked in great power, and spreading himself like a green bay tree. Yet he passed away, and, lo, he was not: yea, I sought him, but he could not be found.' No, for it is the meek that shall inherit the earth, whatever it may seem like at present.

A certain rich man thought that — in this present life, which was all that he considered practical — it profited a man to gain the whole world, if he could. But he could not. In retrospect, he gained very little. For, evidently having strained heart or health in the process of acquisition, abruptly he died. Thus the autopsy. But the truth was, God had decreed that his time was up: 'This night thy soul shall be required of thee.' Then whose shall those things be?

But the meek shall inherit the earth. Only not yet, not in this present life. Not even as did Noah, who in a certain sense inherited the earth prematurely during his lifetime when he emerged from the ark. But then afterwards he died.

However the inheritance of the meek is seen in Abraham. He was promised the earth, the world was to be his, and yet he passed away not having the slightest inheritance in it, no, not so much as to set his foot on. But God had promised that he would give it to him for a possession, and to his seed after him. But Abraham and his seed died, not having received the promises.

Nevertheless this was to be expected, since the promises incorporate the word 'Inherit'. For an inheritance postulates death. Certainly, not the death of the heirs, rather that of the testator, the donor. But, since *he* rose from the dead himself to dispose of the inheritance, then it is in this respect also that 'the meek shall inherit the earth.' By way of resurrection.

And not only we, but the earth also must be changed. 'The earth also and the works that are therein shall be burned up.' This must be so, for it has a curse within its matter, a groaning weight of ancient wickedness upon its surface, and a deep-soiled stain from the accumulated filth of innumerable generations spreading darkly through its texture.

Under this obscene pollution the whole creation groans and travails in pain until now, and will go on doing so until the Day of Redemption. Patiently turning through the seasons and ages, the earth labours for deliverance from the womb of this present evil age. And be delivered it will, for after the fiery dissolution in the end of the world, Behold! 'I saw a new heaven and a new earth.' This is that which the meek shall inherit.

Therefore the inheritance of the meek is not to be looked for in this present life, in time, or in the world as now constituted. This inheritance is in the world to come, when time shall be no more.

Thus it follows that if in this life only we have hope, we are of all men most miserable. Our portion in this present world is one of trials, denials, chastenings, buffetings, betrayals, false accusations. We are in peril of our own countrymen; in peril of 'Christians', in peril of Catholics, in peril of Protestants.

Here on earth we have the sword, the prison, and the

general contempt of all below. We are ostracised, we are the
sect everywhere spoken against, we are confounded with
the heretics. We suffer mortifications, a daily cross, oft
afflictions, persecutions. We are cast out of the synagogue,
and they laugh that we should suppose ourselves Christians.

They laugh. We weep. But woe unto you that laugh now,
for ye shall not laugh then. And blessed are we who weep
now, for then we shall rejoice. Then, after death, when
this world is no more, we shall inherit the earth. Then the
worldly shall have perished from off the face of the earth.
It will be vacant. And the meek are the heirs.

What blessedness, to know of life after death, of
consolation after affliction, of laughter after weeping, of
comfort after mourning. What bliss, to know of resurrection
after death: of physical, bodily resurrection. How blessed
are they who know of earth after death. Blessed are the
meek, for they shall inherit the earth.

4th. 'Blessed are they which do hunger and thirst after
righteousness:'

Not spirituality. It is not, Hunger and thirst after the Holy
Ghost. Nor, after a deeper spiritual life. That is what such
hungry souls *were* doing. They were longing and yearning
for the life of the Spirit throughout the past stages of the
first three beatitudes.

And yet it remains true at this present stage of the

fourth beatitude that they are *still* mourning and *still* panting for the fulness of the Spirit. But the new appetites now predominate completely. Then why the change? What has made the difference? Like the first probing fingers of dawn creeping across the dark eastern sky, strangely, a new realisation has risen upon the meek. Now it has burst upon them, as the light from heaven shining round about them, that their old longing is really only secondary to their real and chief need.

At this stage of their experience something breaks in upon them like the dawning glory: they had no idea. They never saw it on this wise. This is a new thing. They enter a new dimension by realising the real crux of their case. They see that their primary need never was subjective — within themselves — as they had always thought and assumed. Now they have discovered that their true need is objective — before God — a thing unrealised hitherto.

With this revelation their spiritual appetites focus. They 'hunger and thirst after righteousness.' Not, to be righteous. After righteousness itself. Here is reached that stage which is the turning point in the soul's history.

For all the deep consciousness of poverty of spirit, for all the long mourning for the coming of the Spirit, for all the resigned meekness in waiting on the Spirit, *at last the soul realises that the basic, foundational need is not for the Spirit at all.*

Lack of the Spirit, absence of spirituality — for which one had mourned so deeply; and, if proceeding no further, for which one might have waited forever! — were no more than the effect of the soul's ultimate dilemma. With the fourth beatitude, the real cause is found out.

That cause is righteousness. God's righteousness must be satisfied. That is the problem. That is the uttermost root of every possible human need. The need is for righteousness. It does not appear so — it never appears so — what appears is the subjective symptom. But the objective diagnosis is: *man needs righteousness.* So hunger. And thirst. After righteousness.

The need of righteousness. Not before man. Not within man. Not primarily. But before God. That is the crux for all mankind.

At last the meek are brought to this true valuation. But how long it takes! The idea of works is so ingrained. The conception of making oneself fit for God, or at least of God making one fit for himself, is so innate. But it is all hopeless. That way, that old instinctive way, every direction of it, is impossible. It is the old legal way and it works wrath, brings down a curse, and ends in death. It must do, because 'I am carnal, sold under sin.' Born in sin.

There is no path of approach by way of works: what the soul can do for God or what God can do within the soul. Sin taints it. Righteousness forbids it. The great white throne will reject it. And vengeance shall requite it. Withal the poverty of spirit, for all the mourning, notwithstanding the meekness, albeit that this is the interior effect of God's own work: the soul is still not holy enough to get past those gates.

There is a flaming sword of righteousness revolving in every direction to shut up all the paths of this way to the tree of life. Despite the heartbreaking yearnings after God, in spite of all the interior influences of the Spirit, inbred sin is still in the flesh and righteousness forbids the approach.

Such a soul is not clean enough for God's house. Then it is not spiritual life within that is needed, it is another way of approach altogether. Another way of obtaining righteousness of which righteousness itself shall approve, and approve to such a degree that the sword shall be sheathed.

All the previous exercises and stages have been to shut up the soul to this truth. To another way than can ever be wrought by man, or in man. The poor mourning Jew came at last to this when he discovered the end of the law for righteousness, crying 'O wretched man that I am! who shall deliver me from the body of this death?' Deliver me, you see, from it. Not within it. Within it, whatever was wrought was nullified by the corruption of the flesh.

Then is there no way? Not in the old way, the legal way, the old way of works, the way of improving and approving oneself before God, no. Not though one mourn till one dies. But is there no other way? Yes there is: '*Now* the righteousness of God *without the law* is manifested.' That is what the fourth beatitude is about. The soul has found another way. And happy is he that hungers and thirsts after it; for he shall be filled.

So the meek discover that righteousness is the question, and the question that must be settled before any other consideration can even remotely be entertained. All the spiritual exercises hitherto — poverty of spirit, mourning, meekness — were but to bring the soul to this profound consciousness. The testimony of the Spirit within sounds like the high note of the silver trumpet: *it is righteousness you need.*

Right to the gates of the kingdom came the labouring soul by these most tried, certain and experimental steps.

But through those gates no soul will ever pass till brought to the appreciation: *it is righteousness you need.*

They are gates of righteousness. It is a way of righteousness. Righteousness is the key to unlock the gates, and righteousness the title of admission through them. Without righteousness, none shall enter. With it, entrance is already gained.

At the gates of the kingdom the meek, now hungering and thirsting after righteousness, must be brought to cry — and of a truth they certainly shall be brought to cry — with a loud voice from the depths

> Open to me the gates of righteousness:
> I will go into them,
> and I will praise the Lord:
> This gate of the Lord,
> into which the righteous shall enter.

Yet righteousness has been openly dropped from modern evangelicalism. It is no longer the contemporary issue. Yet it was the burning issue of the Reformation and it remains the central question before God to this very hour. However, the heirs of Protestant Christendom have adroitly turned it to a forgotten issue and hence appears the dreadful treachery of the church against the souls of men today. But because the burning issue of righteousness has been currently and politely diminished to irrelevance, the sheer enormity of the modern apostasy is barely realised. No measure, no apostasy.

Thus, 'Hungering and thirsting after righteousness' has all but disappeared. And with it, the criteria which it creates.

'Coming to Jesus', 'Loving the Lord', these are not the issues. Which Jesus? There was more than one Jesus preached, even in the Apostles' day. We have been warned of many more 'Jesus' and false Christs yet to come. How are we to know which is the true? By faith? In what? And — quite apart from 'coming to Jesus' — what of being brought to Almighty God? Therefore we must have the Lord Jesus known by the doctrine; the way known by the truth; the faith known by the word. What word? *Righteousness.* If he, and it, answer that issue before God — as bringing in everlasting righteousness — then this is Jesus Christ indeed, and that is the gospel of a truth.

'Committal' is not the issue. What can we commit? I will tell you: we can commit sins. What can the exhibitionist false-promise of 'coming to the front' do? Is God at the front? The problems are above, and the issue must be joined and met there in righteousness. 'Love' one says, is the issue. With such people, love is no more than a solvent which they use to dissolve all righteousness.

Forgiveness of sins is not the issue. What are sins? What is forgiveness? Why does it matter? Who has power to forgive sins? What if sins are unforgiven? Only righteousness gives the correct answers. Because righteousness is the true issue.

The Holy Spirit is not the issue. Why is one poor of spirit? Why has the Spirit come? What are the marks of his coming? Why am I not filled with the Spirit? What is the baptism of the Spirit? What are the gifts? I tell you of a truth, righteousness is still the real issue, and righteousness provides the only balanced answer.

Righteousness is the centre of the gospel. Righteousness

is the issue in the gospel. Righteousness is the reason for the gospel. A gospel which does not radiate to and from righteousness as the constant, and the constantly recurring theme, is no gospel at all. The proclamation of righteousness is the mark of the gospel ministry. A ministry which is not supremely occupied in proclaiming righteousness is no gospel ministry whatsoever.

Saith Christ in spirit, prophetically declaring his risen ministry from heaven, throughout this present age

'I have preached righteousness in the great congregation:
lo, I have not refrained my lips,
O LORD, thou knowest.

'I have not hid thy righteousness
within my heart;
I have declared thy faithfulness
and thy salvation:
I have not concealed thy lovingkindness
and thy truth
from the great congregation.'

This preaching and declaration of righteousness tells us of the continuous occupation of Christ in his priestly ministry through this era. Albeit invisibly, through the Spirit he preaches in his servants, and likewise he preaches to the hearts of the hearers. By their being filled with the Spirit of the Lord, so as to conform exactly to his heavenly activity, you may tell his true servants. For they should reflect Christ from on high. Preaching righteousness is Christ's constant spiritual activity at this moment. Is it the Pope's? Is it the Archbishop of Canterbury's? Is it the Moderator's? Is it the constant activity of their church?

Or the 'free' churches? Or most of the 'gospel' halls? No it is not. It is irrelevant to their activities. Christ is doing one thing, and they are doing another. But we are answering to Christ, and faithfully telling you the truth.

The truth is that they have let the gospel slip through their fingers. They have what they call a gospel, but it is not about righteousness. Up and down the land we have wandered desolate into this place and that, and time out of number have been sent away hungry and thirsty. You know in your hearts that this is true. You know it, if, like us, you have hungered and thirsted after righteousness.

We have gone to hear the famous evangelicals, the well-known evangelists, the renowned Convention speakers. We have sought them out, yes, we have found them out. Existing as they do like tolerated charity cuckoos in the nest built and populated by the numerically superior brood of modernistic and unclean birds with whom they jointly feed from the same organisational and monetary dish.

Their song charms the ear a little, but to survive where they do at all, these cuckoos have necessarily to master the art of camouflage. Perforce they must imitate and mimic to perfection those birds of that feather belonging to the nest in which they themselves have made their real home. Flying abroad they are bolder. On the wing, their arminian 'Doo-Doo' is a real challenge, brother. That is to say, promising relief from the winter of discontent, it creates by the ever-anticipatory pangs, an anguish for the springtime of the soul far worse than before. But the spring never comes. Then shall we follow them home, till we cease to hunger because we can endure the pangs no longer, or, continuing, starve to death in a nest neither theirs nor ours?

191

Righteousness is the issue; let them face it. Face it in their ministry, face it in their churches, face it in their denominations, face it in their associations, face it in their communion, face it in their church. These are the people who by their sly surrender — pretending still to sound the gospel trumpet — have sold the Reformation down the river, more so than the modernists under whose denominational aegis they enjoy their living and influence.

Any Christian, Ministry, Church or Gospel that fails to find its cause of existence in the proclamation of righteousness is both false and deceitful. Any such thing without righteousness as its *raison d'être* is automatically invalid, no matter that all the world and all of Christendom pretend to authenticate it. Shall rivers of the blood of faithful protestants be shed for nothing? Will the godliest of men have been burned alive for nothing? Doth useless compromising mediocrity today think to put out Latimer and Ridley's candle? By God, not while I live.

Without the exalting, proclaiming and trumpeting of righteousness, any professed gospel is no gospel whatsoever. It is a false gospel, another gospel, a soft transatlantic frivolity, a spirit-centred excursion, a charismatic delusion, a loose easy-believist lie. But though I, or an angel from heaven, preach any other gospel than that which centrally proclaims righteousness, then let me, or that angel, be thrice-damned and double-accursed world without end.

Hearken to the holy apostle: *Therein* — he saith. That is, in the gospel — *is the righteousness of God revealed*. Listen to the gospel, cries Paul, and righteousness is what you hear. Open the gospel, and righteousness is what appears. Unfold it, and righteousness is revealed. It is the absolute heart, kernel, centre and substance of the gospel, giving to

192

every part its real character and true savour. It is the salt without which the wholesome body of the faith would breed worms and stink. Whoso preaches what he calls a gospel, or gospel-grace, or love, or a cross, or sacrifice, or blood: but in preaching neglects to give each and all these things their real character — because he fails to relate them to righteousness — he is a liar and a deceiver. He has chosen the heretics' lot. Let him be Anathema Maran-atha. That is how serious it is: as serious as Paul demonstrates in the Galatian and Corinthian epistles.

It is not the bare words grace, love, cross, calvary, sacrifice, blood, that make the gospel. It is the sound doctrine that gives them their savour that makes the gospel. All these words are in 'another gospel' as Paul calls it, II Cor. 11. 'Feigned words', as it is called by the apostles. Yes, all the words are there: but none of the doctrine. In a word, no righteousness. 'Jesus' is there: but it is 'another Jesus' than he who came to bring in everlasting righteousness. The 'Spirit' is there: but it is 'another spirit' than he who came to reprove the world of righteousness.

'Apostles' and 'ministers' are there, but they are 'deceitful workers'. They pretend to a gospel but it is no gospel. They pretend to a righteousness but it is no righteousness. They 'transform themselves into the ministers of righteousness' just as 'Satan himself is transformed into an angel of light'. But it is all transformation, all deceit; they are not real, and they neither preach nor do they know either righteousness or gospel. Now we have found them out for you; and how you may try them that say they are apostles, and are not, but are liars. Righteousness is the issue.

It is a tragic fact that modern congregations, conventions,

and evangelistic crowds no longer obey the injunctions of the Lord Jesus to take heed what they hear; how they hear; or whom they hear. Because they no longer judge by, look for, or demand to hear about, righteousness. Indeed, so conditioned are they by the sentimental 'devotional' opiate that they think that 'love' has superseded righteousness, and, of course, that 'judgment' is unloving.

As if there could be 'love' worth the name without righteousness. And as if there could be righteousness without judgment or discrimination. As well might there be a body without any bones. Well, I tell you plainly, awake to righteousness now; or you shall awake to judgment then, too late to rectify the everlasting error.

Blessed are they which do hunger and thirst after righteousness.

Hunger and thirst?

But there is only one way to assuage that. Food and drink. That is what the pangs are related to: being fed and watered. They are not related to righteousness; how could they be?

Then why are these appetites mentioned? Because of their painful, demanding and nagging acuteness. Because life depends upon their being satisfied — and not just by one act of eating, either. Because of the increasing desperation if these gnawing pangs remain unfulfilled.

These appetites are employed here to show the over-whelming urgency which 'hungering and thirsting' conveys. Their use is the only way to demonstrate the spiritual yearning and intensity of the true seeker after righteousness.

If so, how many can measure up to that intensity, who *claim* to have what that intensity alone can bring?

Again. If so, then how many evangelists, preachers, and ministers have deceived souls by deliberately ignoring the fact that such intensity is essential to salvation? And pretending that it is not? And then going on treacherously to promise righteousness to little more than mere stirred feelings — or even downright apathy — bearing absolutely no relationship to 'hungering and thirsting'? But bearing every relationship to gaining numbers by winking at the indulgence of the age.

We have heard tell of Samson arising at midnight to carry away the doors, posts and bar of the gates of Gaza, bearing them on his shoulders to the top of the hill by the Spirit of the Lord. But — tell it not in Gath — what is this? Who shall declare by what spirit these modern Philistines have arisen at noonday and borne away the strait gate — bolts, bars, lintel, posts and all — and cast them wholesale down into the maw of time?

No, no: these piercing appetites are used just because they convey the life-and-death anguish of soul, revealing the very intensity with which righteousness is to be sought. They are used just because they convey the pangs and gnawings of heart that sound the prayer to which righteousness is freely given. 'Hungering and thirsting' occurs precisely for the reason that this interior craving demonstrates that level beneath which righteousness will not be given, because it is not yet sought with all the heart and all the mind and all the strength.

I know that many will object to my saying it — not that I am used to permitting that to deter me — but I must declare with regret that I find both C.H. Spurgeon and J.N. Darby seriously deficient at this point. They both neglected — in my judgment — the early Methodist emphasis on the interior work of the Spirit necessary to and commensurate with the simplicity of faith. Of course it was a very different age, with a much better type, and so much more wholeheartedness could be taken for granted. Maybe. But that was also true, and even more true, when the Lord Jesus spoke the beatitudes. But he still spoke them.

I detect in these Victorian preachers — Philpot was the notable exception — an appeal to the superficially popular as to becoming a Christian. I believe both men avoided preaching the Spirit's work prior to and in regeneration, in favour of 'simple faith' — objective profession — alone. Hence I perceive with these early brethren and baptists the ground swell which led to the rising tide of 'easy-believism', now a nauseous flood in our own day.

But observe how intense — so the Lord Jesus instructs us — is the pitch to which rises the craving after righteousness in all who really seek it. No less intense than the pangs of hunger and thirst in the starving soul and in one dying for lack of water. This is the Spirit's way in and with the soul that is after righteousness, and there is nothing temporary or passing about it, nothing merely emotional. So teaches the Lord Jesus.

Any other way, any mitigation of this way, any dismissing this way as irrelevant to faith, is false. Let no man set aside the words of the Lord Jesus. Blessed are they that *do hunger and thirst* after righteousness: for *they* shall be filled.

Although 'hungering and thirsting' are interior pangs

satisfied only by interior filling, notwithstanding we are to notice carefully that it does not say 'hunger and thirst *to be righteous.*' That would imply a craving that one might be changed by the Spirit within oneself. That one might be newly formed within as righteous, actually and personally. But that is not the wording. Neither is it the predominant craving.

'Hunger and thirst *after righteousness*' is different. Although the hunger and thirst are still interior, the righteousness is not. It is exterior. Righteousness is a quality and as such to be regarded as objective: it is the quality itself to which the word points. Not the quality in oneself: the quality in itself. Not that one should be made it: but that one should have it.

But if it — the righteousness — is exterior, how will that satisfy the appetites? After all, the famished and parched soul is to be 'filled'. Yes, but not with its own righteousness, or with a righteousness created in the soul by the Spirit: filled with the certainty of possession of God's own righteousness. Because these spiritual appetites are the craving to know assuredly that one has divine righteousness, that it is reckoned to one, as one's own, and that *God himself* has done the reckoning. That is what the pangs and agony are about.

The 'hungering and thirsting' is the craving to know and feel in the interior the certain satisfaction from the witness of the Spirit, from God himself, that righteousness has been imputed to one. That the righteousness of God has been put to one's account, so that one has it in credit.

This gives a profound easement, a fulfilment and release from all pangs of hunger, all the gasping of thirst. The

Spirit witnesseth with our spirits that we have a real title to the quality of righteousness before God. It is there on our own account, put before him as our own, registered as being ours.

And that was what one was in such a craving agony about. Given that, one is full. And, of course, Blessed are they which do hunger and thirst after righteousness, for they *shall* be filled.

'; for they shall be filled.'

Filled with what? Righteousness? That was what they were hungering and thirsting after: therefore the assumption would be, it is that with which they are to be filled.

But we have before shown that what they are filled with is not the righteousness itself, it is the assurance that this righteousness is reckoned to them. It is the satisfying witness that righteousness of God is imputed to them, or put to their credit: that is what fulfils their craving.

The *title* to divine righteousness is meat and drink to their hungry and thirsty souls, because of that to which it bears record. They have the *title* within to their righteousness on high.

Well, what *form* does this title take, that to it the inward witness should testify so satisfactorily?

What is the title so assuring to the soul that God really has imputed righteousness to its account?

The title? It is this: *The body and blood of the Lord.*

Nothing else at once brings in divine righteousness to the account of the ungodly, and at the same time perfectly satisfies the pangs of hunger and cravings of thirst.

> 'For my flesh is meat
> indeed,
> and my blood is drink
> indeed.'

When God views this to faith's account, righteousness is imputed.

When the soul takes this into the inward parts, all hunger is assuaged and all thirst quenched.

It is righteousness before God that brings life to the trusting soul. Because righteousness earns life: it *deserves* life. And that is what Christ has brought in for the believer. 'Even so might grace reign *through righteousness* unto eternal life by Jesus Christ our Lord.'

The broken body and shed blood of Jesus presented before God not only appease his offended righteousness: so effectively does it do this, that the quality of righteousness in God positively radiates to and upon the trusting soul because of that wonderful sacrifice.

Because God reckons his own righteousness to such a soul, commensurate life is poured out in plenitude immediately. As soon as righteousness is imputed, life must follow. And that takes place when the sinner first believes. This outpouring is called the baptism of the Holy Ghost — no matter what Pentecostals may tell you — and it floods down forthwith upon the penitent. As he believes, righteousness is imputed, and the Spirit is outpoured.

If I am asked, What kind of life is it that is poured out upon the believer? I reply, the kind of life that answers to the sort of righteousness deserving it. Well then, what sort of righteousness is that? Righteousness of God. Then what kind of life does that demand? Everlasting life. Because the broken body and shed blood of Jesus satisfied God's righteousness for the trusting soul, therefore it must bring life to him also.

> 'Whoso eateth my flesh
> And drinketh my blood
> hath eternal life.'

And for this reason: because that flesh and blood brought in everlasting — or divine — righteousness. Therefore whoso trusts truly *must* have everlasting life.

When faith assimilates that flesh: yielded vicariously in death. When faith drinks in that blood: poured out on one's behalf at Calvary. Then, then everlasting righteousness rests satisfied, transferred to the believer's account. And not only so, but the inevitable consequence of righteousness follows, according to the quality of that righteousness. The consequence is this: one now deserves to live. The quality is divine: then one shall live eternally.

Therefore when the sinner is cast utterly upon that sacrifice alone for righteousness, the strife is over. All craving ceases. All heaven rejoices. Divine righteousness reposes. And, straightway, everlasting life is poured out in abundance.

Having made trial, that is my experience. From total ungodliness and absolute irreligion, to walking with God these twenty-five years past. The hand of God arrested me in West Africa and led on to a conversion no less dramatic than that of John Newton, whose seafaring life and whose place of awakening I also shared.

It is the written and testified experience — I have the letters and many living epistles are with me — of hundreds of converts to whom, as sent, I have preached this same gospel over many years. The word was mixed with faith in those that heard it. It is the foundation upon which the empty and derelict one-time Methodist Chapel at Tylers Green has been built up to overflowing. It is the foundation upon which I live and on which I shall die.

I do not merely think that this my doctrine agrees absolutely and precisely with the apostolic gospel as preached in the New Testament Church: *I know it. I have proved it. I have experienced it.* And so have a multitude of faithful witnesses.

Soli Deo gloria. Amen.

Now it will be asked, How does one eat and drink of Jesus' body and blood? Seeing that he says, 'he that eateth my flesh and drinketh my blood,' how is this done?

The Papal hierarchy and Roman Catholic church have always insisted that it is done through what they call the Mass. Clearly it follows — from the consummate importance of 'eating my flesh and drinking my blood' — once given the Roman Catholic dogma, the Mass must be at the very heart of the church.

But the word 'Mass' — or any word remotely like it — does not occur in the New Testament. Then the church during that foundational era never partook of it. If not, neither did Peter, for he never mentions it any more than any other of the New Testament writers. But would he not, had it been as central as the Roman Catholic church dictates and requires? And if not, am I to believe that he never 'ate my flesh and drank my blood'? Clearly the apostles and early church did so. Consequently, it was not through the 'Mass'. Therefore the 'Mass' is a complete misrepresentation of these words of Jesus, and falsely interprets how to 'eat my flesh and drink my blood'.

The Roman Catholic will say to me, 'What of the Eucharist? Do not make a man an offender for a word. If the actual word 'Mass' is not in the New Testament then certainly 'Eucharist' is; and the two words amount to the same thing: the sacrament which Peter gave to the Roman church.'

First of all, the word 'Eucharist' was never used by the Lord Jesus or his apostles to denote any ordinance or feast in the New Testament. It is true that as part of what is called 'The Lord's Supper', Jesus gave thanks. This was but one of many of his actions during that ordinance. But only a part, only one action. The Greek word for 'thanks' happens to be εὐχαριστέω, eucharist(eo).

Now why choose out only one of Jesus' acts during the Supper? Why call the Supper by the name of a part of it? Especially when there is no scriptural authority for doing so? In any event, why not translate the word 'eucharisteo' into English the same as any other word? Why the Greek mystery? Why change it from a verb — the action — into a noun — falsely designated to the whole ordinance? The Lord's Supper is no more 'The Eucharist' than it is 'The Breaking of Bread'. It is the Lord's Supper, during which as parts of the whole both these actions were performed.

As to 'Eucharist' the same word is used by the hypocrite in the temple who prayed thus with himself: 'God, I *thank* thee, that I am not as other men.' There is as much justification for *that* to be called the Eucharist, as the Supper. Neither has the least authority for it; no one has the right not to translate the Greek, much less change the part of speech to make it denominative. And finally, the same flimsy basis exists as strongly in the one case as in the other.

So that if it is claimed that the 'Mass' and the 'Eucharist' are one and the same: then since the one has as little scriptural authority as the other, it is not helpful to persuade the reasonable. Whatever it may do for the prejudiced.

In any event, by what exegetical right are the words, 'Eat my flesh and drink my blood', connected with the Lord's Supper? They were written by John who wrote nothing whatsoever about the Lord's Supper. He does not mention it in any of his writings. It is not his purpose to expound the doctrine, fellowship, worship and order of the church: apart from the special vision of the Revelation he hardly *uses* the word 'church'. John's purpose is *interior* to show the life — the divinity and inwardness of it — that is in the Father and the Son. Hence 'Whoso eateth my flesh, and drinketh my blood, hath eternal life.' But that is nothing at all to do with the Ministry, the Church, the Lord's Supper, or any particular Meeting whatsoever. It is to do with the heart, and the Son of God, irrespective of all these things.

But it was objected 'Peter gave the sacrament to the Roman church.' Sacrament? This word is derived from the ecclesiastical Latin for 'Mystery'. But the New Testament was written in Greek, not Latin. The Greek for 'mystery'

— or, if you will, sacrament — μυστήριον, *musterion*, is applied by the holy apostles *to the preaching of the gospel and the gospel fellowship which this brings in:* 'the mystery of the gospel', 'the fellowship of the mystery'. *It is never, never applied to any ordinance at all, least of all the Lord's Supper.* Therefore the Lord's Supper is neither Latin sacrament nor New Testament Greek mystery.

Incidentally the Greek word 'mystery' — Latin, Sacrament — is applied in prophecy to a terrible latter-day apostasy affecting the vast part of the church. The 'Mystery (sacrament) of iniquity' summed up as 'Mystery (sacrament) Babylon the great, the mother of harlots.' Does anyone question what this means? It refers to a vast and unified company distinguished by the Sacrament.

Now, did Peter give anything to the Roman church? He is never recorded as having been anywhere near Rome, in the only reliable and authentic sources of his activities: the books of the New Testament. Peter did *not* go to Rome. He did not write to Rome. Paul wrote 'to all that be in Rome, beloved of God, called saints,' and the epistle is called 'The Epistle of Paul the Apostle to the Romans'. There is no other. Neither from Peter nor anyone else. Paul went to Rome. He preached at Rome. But Peter did not. Never, according to the scriptures.

As to the Lord's Supper itself, Matthew records it, and so does Mark. The latter, of course, is supposed to have written under Peter's direction. However in Matthew and Mark nothing but the bare historical facts of the Last Supper are recorded. It took place, and this is what took place. Just as, for example, John tells us Jesus met the woman at the well, and this is how he met the woman at the well. But there is no more suggestion in Matthew and

Mark that the church should *re-enact* that Last Supper than there is in John that the church should re-enact the meeting at the well. Both are recorded as past events, which would have slipped into oblivion were they not frozen for us on the pages of the gospels. But there is no question of repetition.

Until Luke. For the first time the words are added, 'This do in remembrance of me.' Not, notice, in *partaking* of me. 'In remembrance.'

What was remembered, was the incident recorded in Matthew and Mark. It was to be recalled by the act of breaking bread and drinking the cup among the disciples. No question of Sunday. Much less, of supper for breakfast. None of 'priesthood'. Or of the ministry. It was an act involving a common meal taken together in the evening.

However this was not revealed until the ministry of Paul — assuming Luke wrote for Paul. It is by him that the early church is specifically instructed to 'remember' the Lord's death by an ordinance in which the Last Supper is re-enacted.

There was, of course — long before Paul was called — the incident on the Emmaus road. 'He was known of them in breaking of bread.' There are also other references to 'breaking bread' as such in the Acts. But I would point out that, far from being confined to the Lord's Supper, 'breaking of bread' was common to every ordinary mealtime. The fact that men *also* broke bread during the Lord's Supper is no ground for saying that such an act must necessarily indicate the ordinance. The reverse is actually true. Because the event was so very common, without some distinct qualification, it must be taken as read that the words 'breaking of bread' indicate nothing more significant than taking a meal together.

So then, let a man assume what he will as to the practice of the early church in respect of the Lord's Supper: nothing whatsoever is recorded until Paul's ministry. Anything to the contrary is mere speculation. The fact is, as an ordinance for the church the first Corinthian epistle and Luke *are the first and only clear references* to the subject! And whatever a man may conjecture, the truth remains that the Spirit of the Lord did not give the word of the Lord on the subject until doing so by Paul's ministry.

Now then, Paul was converted upon the Damascus road. This was years after the Church had been founded. Not until some twenty years again *after that* did the Word of the Lord first come to be recorded, recalling the saints to 'do this in remembrance of me.' And that word came by Paul.

Now one may say to me, But the Lord Jesus *did* say these words at the Last Supper, and therefore the church at Jerusalem at least must have re-enacted the ordinance. Such an one may say what he likes but his conjecture remains what it is. Not until Luke — and therefore Paul's ministry — was the word 'remembrance' added. There is nothing of it in Matthew and Mark. Nothing at all about anything in John. Despite wishful thinking as regards 'breaking bread', there is no reference to the Lord's Supper in Acts. And the *only* record of any church in which the Lord's Supper is recorded as having taken place is the Corinthian church. Founded through Paul's preaching.

Therefore as far as the doctrine is concerned in the epistles, and the history of the early church in the Acts, the scriptures show that not until Paul's ministry was the Supper instituted as a repetitive ordinance. Now, *until then* did the early church never 'eat my flesh and drink my blood'? Because it was not until then, some quarter of a century after the church was founded, that the ordinance was formally required by written revelation, and historically stated to have taken place. 'For I have received of the Lord that which also I delivered unto you,' saith Paul. He received it himself. Not the eleven. In his own ministry, not from their tradition: 'from the Lord.' If so, then as ascended.

Well, does someone tell me that for the intervening twenty-five years Peter, John, James, Stephen the martyr, with all the saints, were not constantly 'eating my flesh and drinking my blood'? We know they were. But it was not in 'The Lord's Supper' as we know it. Otherwise what further need was there for *another* revelation to the apostle 'I received of the Lord' all those years later? Were it in practice before, there would have been no further need to 'receive' it. Paul would have seen it for himself at Jerusalem. Years later Barnabas or Silas could have reminded him. But they did not, because both they and we learned the ordinance directly through Paul's ministry by revelation from the Lord. Then on this ground alone, how can anybody possibly equate 'eating my flesh and drinking my blood' with the Lord's Supper? How can they, even though they change its name to Mass, Eucharist, or whatever?

Then why does anybody do so? Partly by the unwarranted association of ideas from John. In John, Jesus is speaking of the mode by which eternal life is received. Referring to the manna from heaven, he points out that those who ate still died. What is needed is a kind of bread from heaven of which one may eat and never die. That is, live eternally. This leads to the question of what brings in eternal life. It is everlasting righteousness. But that cannot come in until Jesus' body is broken and his blood shed. Assimilate that. In the figure spiritually eat and drink of it as food for the hungry soul and as drink for the thirsting spirit. Rightly done, so as wholly to imbibe it within by faith, this will bring life. But the passage is absolutely nothing to do with the Last Supper. Nothing at all. John never even mentions either the bread or the cup.

As to the Last Supper, in the first instance — as Matthew and Mark demonstrate — that is what it was: a supper. Although eaten during the Passover, still it was an evening meal in which was utilised a figure for the time then present, a single event afterwards recorded in order that it might be soundly interpreted in and of itself. In the second case, as Paul teaches us, with Luke, the Supper is to be re-enacted in the communal evening meal of the saints. 'This do in remembrance of me.'

'For as often as ye eat this bread, and drink this cup, ye do show the Lord's death till he come.' If so, then the re-enactment of the Last Supper shows his death. For that to be valid, in turn the Last Supper itself must have shown his death. Not convey his life, remark; show his death.

The Supper took place on the night in which he was betrayed. In the integrity of his human flesh — his body intact — Jesus first of all took bread into his hands. Not before then, but only then did he bless what he had taken. He 'eulogised' that bread. That was the second thing.

The third thing Jesus did was this: gripping that bread with his own hands he tore it open and exposed the heart of it. He broke the bread.

208

Only then came the fourth and last action. He gave it to his disciples.

Finally he explained what he had done — about which they must have wondered — with these words, in order to clarify and give lucidity to his fourfold demonstration. The words, spoken about the bread, were uttered in the unbroken wholeness of his own actual body. They were these: 'This is my body.'

Not this *will be* my body. This *is* my body. Then and there; present tense. This *is* my body. But it was not his body. Yet he said that it was. Well, it was certainly not in reality his body at that time: then not at any other, for the words are in the present tense.

How could it be his body at the time? It was his body doing those things to that loaf. They could see plainly, it was a loaf of bread: it was impossible for that to be his body in fact. Then it must have been his body in a figure.

Having wrought the otherwise incomprehensible sequence with the loaf without a word, now at last he says, looking at it and them, 'This is my body.' These words therefore convey light to the four actions previously wrought over the bread. At each stage the disciples are to take back these words and use them to illuminate every step of the whole sequence.

'He took bread.' *This is my body*. When he cometh into the world he saith, Sacrifice and offering thou wouldest not, but a body hast thou prepared me. This speaks of the pre-existent and eternal Son of God entering the world and becoming incarnate.

Though equal with God, the Son was found in fashion as a man. By the Father's preparation, through the Spirit's creation, there was prepared for the Son of God that holy seed which he should assume and take into union with himself in the womb of the virgin. In doing this he saith to the Father: A body hast thou prepared me. 'This is my body.' That tiny seed in the virgin's womb. Yes, God was manifest in the flesh. He took bread. This is what Jesus is showing the disciples. *

'And blessed it.' *This is my body.* Our word is Eulogy: to extol the worth of. Why? Because of what the Son of God could do within that body. Without it, the work could never be done. With it, it could. Forasmuch then as the children are partakers of flesh and blood, he — the divine and eternal Son of God — also himself likewise took part of the same. For verily he took not on him the nature of angels; but he took on him the seed of Abraham. It behoved him to be made like unto his brethren.

Thus God and man in the unity of his person, he becomes the one, the only mediator between God and man. The mediator must be God. He must become man. He must then provide a suited atonement. With that last in view, the Son of God and Son of man, having taken 'bread', then 'blesses it', because of what it enabled him to achieve.

'And brake it.' *This is my body.* This is something Jesus did of himself. He took the bread into his own hands and brake it. No man took his life from him: 'No man taketh it

---

* See 'The Birth of Jesus Christ', Chapter One *'The Apostolic Foundation of the Christian Church'*, a separate volume in this series. It is imperative that this series be taken as a whole.

from me, but I lay it down of myself.' He had power to lay down his life, and power to take it. What he did was voluntary, and under his own control, and although he passively submitted, that was his decision, not his necessity.

'He gave himself for our sins.' The faith of Jesus Christ saw in the Jewish malice and the Gentile brutality, the instruments of God's providence by which, submitting himself, he would be broken. So, for his disciples' sakes, by faith in God, he submitted himself. 'I lay down my life for the sheep.' He brake it. It was not really men at all.

'And gave it.' *This is my body.* That is, gave the life-imparting nourishment of his body once broken. If so, then between the prior third act and this present fourth act, we are to see implied Jesus' burial, resurrection, and ascension. From that place on high he gives the fruits of his travail below.

Evidently he should not give his body to his disciples before it was broken on the cross. He could not give it from the tomb. He did not give it in the resurrection. Therefore he actually gave it from the ascension.

He gives it himself. Not the priest. Not the church. *He* gave it to his disciples; personally. Not for them to dispense to others, but for them to eat for themselves. All the life-giving benefits of his death he himself dispenses from heaven in a spiritual way to the interior heart of his disciples. It is his present, heavenly, spiritual activity. 'The words that I speak unto you, they are spirit, and they are life.'

This spiritual imparting of the reality and truth of his body broken is what is meant by 'he gave it.' Thus the atonement is ministered inwardly to the disciple by the Son of God from heaven.

Through the Spirit now he conveys the righteousness which he earned for us in the breaking of his body. This imparting is nothing to do with eating broken bread.

Eating broken bread is an external figure showing what Christ does perpetually in Spirit throughout the age for those on whose behalf he died. He takes the spiritual fruits of that death and invisibly but very really feeds the souls therewith, that hunger and thirst after righteousness. Thus convinced by him that his body was broken for *them*, they are fed, they are filled.

That is what the Supper signifies. An exterior material sign of an interior spiritual reality, which reality neither takes place in or with the sign. It takes place irrespective of it. From time to time, 'as oft as ye do this', the disciples show externally by this sign a graphic figure of just what continually takes place in the Spirit. And so it will, until he come.

The same principle applies to the cup. Jesus did three things, without explanation. He took the cup. He gave thanks. And he gave it to the disciples. The explanation follows, illuminating each of the otherwise inexplicable actions. 'Drink ye all of it; for this is my blood of the new testament, which is shed for many for the remission of sins.'

He took the cup. *This is my blood of the new testament.* Now carefully notice how aptly Jesus uses the figure, and how that with equal care the Spirit gives the record. It does not say, He took the wine. Not even the cup of wine. 'He took the cup.' Then at the time at which first he took it — in terms of the figure — it could not yet have been filled with 'my blood of the new testament'. Why not? Because that blood had not then been shed.

Hence the wording demands that we consider the cup: the container and not the contents.

So, when was the exact fulfilment of this figure, at which first he 'took the cup'? And what was in that 'cup' when he took it? Moreover, what is meant figuratively by 'cup' in any event?

The contents are not mentioned. The container is mentioned. Because of course when Jesus first took the cup — at Calvary — his blood had not yet been shed. The cup *he* took was the cup which *caused* his blood to be shed. In fact it was his drinking that cup which *enabled him* — through the consequent shedding of his blood — thereafter to hand that cup to his disciples, only now filled with something very far different from what he had had to drink from it to the bitter dregs.

Then just what is meant by 'cup'? When used figuratively in scripture a 'Cup' conveys the idea of emotional content. It is what one must drink, or will drink, which causes interior sensations of pain or pleasure commensurate with the content. For example 'Cup of trembling', 'Cup of my fury', 'My cup runneth over,' 'Portion of mine inheritance and of my cup.' These cases illustrate a measure, a content, meted out to the subject, which when he takes it into his inward parts, gives either pain or pleasure. An emotional content.

So then, what was in the 'cup' which Jesus took, which

was signified at the Last Supper when 'he took the cup'?
It was the 'cup' about which he spoke when he fell in an
agony to the ground and sweat as it were great drops of
blood *at the bare contemplation of it*. That cup.

'Father, if it be possible, let this cup pass from me.'
'O my Father, if this cup may not pass away from me,
except I drink it, thy will be done.' This cup refers to such
a vast measure of shocking and unendurable anguish that
the very anticipation of receiving it from the hand of God,
brought down to the ground the Lord Jesus with strong
crying and tears. First that if possible it might pass, and
next, since that was impossible, for fortitude to endure the
dread affliction. He was heard in that he feared.

At Calvary, Jesus drank to the dregs a cup poured out
without mixture of the wrath, fury and indignation of
Almighty God, against the sin which the sinbearer had been
made for the world, and the sins which he was then bearing
in his own body on the tree. That cup. He drained it to the
last drop.

When his head dropped in death, and his body drooped
lifeless on the cross, then, and only then, did the cup fall
bone-dry and empty from his lips.

But having drained it in death, rising he fills it in life. In
a figure, he fills it with what exhausted God's indignation
and wrath against the sinners for whom he died. Since he
drained that wrath, by doing so, he refills the cup with
the blissful certainty of remission of sins witnessed by the
blood shed to cancel them. Not oft to be repeated: he
suffered once. He bled once.

It is the new testament in his blood. For by one offering

he hath perfected for ever them that are sanctified. That is the character of his new testament oblation, made once for all at Calvary's cross.

For this he gives thanks. *This cup is the new testament in my blood.* Yes, now it is; now that his blood had been shed. But it was not that before: before, it was all that stood between God and the disciples measured in terms of the wrath thus generated. This he drank, and showed it by the shedding of his blood, which then he presents first to God, and subsequently to the interior faith of those for whom it was shed.

The word 'thanks' is 'Eucharistos' and simply means to give thanks. There is nothing exclusive in its use, nothing 'holy' about the word, nothing mysterious about it. In the common Greek from which it is taken, it is 'thanks' as one would say to another.

He gave thanks for all that he had been enabled to achieve for God by the shedding of his blood. He brought in God's eternal purpose in Sonship, and it filled him with joy that he had done it. He brought many sons to glory, he redeemed a vast multitude whom no man can number, out of every kindred, and tongue, and people, and nation, not just in one generation, but out of every generation since the beginning to the end of time. By blood alone he did it. 'For thou wast slain, and hast redeemed us to God by thy blood.'

So he gave thanks.

And gave it to his disciples. *This is my blood of the new testament.* Once again we are to look past the grave and resurrection to the ascension. From heaven it is that Christ

215

comes in the Spirit to preach peace to them that are afar off, proclaiming liberty to the captives, remission of sins in his name, and declaring that sinners are made nigh by the blood of Christ. Drinking all this in, they are filled with joy.

A cup filled with the truth of all that his blood accomplished, drunk in by the Spirit to the inward parts, fills the soul with emotions of 'joy unspeakable and full of glory'. The disciples' language now speaketh on this wise: 'The cup of blessing which we bless, is it not the communion of the blood of Christ?' They feel that it has 'preached atonement to their hearts'. That their hearts are sprinkled by blood. Once hungering and thirsting, now they are filled.

Of this experience a bare, inadequate figure is the cup at the Last Supper. But it is a sweet reminder, coming as it does from the thoughtful kindness of the Lord Jesus before as yet his blood was shed.

At the Supper not a drop of his blood was spilt. Notwithstanding he said of the cup 'This is my blood.' Of course it was not. Neither ever would it be: he does not say 'will be' but 'is'. Then why did he say it?

To demonstrate to his disciples in a figure why it was that he should be torn from them so rudely and treacherously. To prepare them against the event which must have seemed to them the end of all their hopes. To show them beforehand the true meaning of what would happen when he died and his blood was shed.

That is what he is showing them beforehand: it must be shed. Otherwise how afterwards could he minister from heaven all the assurance of remission of sins; all the benefits of the new testament; all that he had won for them in death? It was all by his blood.

In Spirit, as he ministers to the inner man this doctrine, let them drink it in. And be reminded of the figure. Have it in memorial.

Not that his ministering the sprinkled application of his blood to the heart takes place during or has anything directly to do with, the memorial feast. That ministration was done through preaching, not ordinances. Nevertheless the ordinance, rightly taken, is a wonderful figure of the reality, a sweet memorial of the event.

Now therefore — perhaps at greater length because of its great importance — I hope that I have adequately interpreted to the honest reader the true meaning of these words: 'Blessed are they which do hunger and thirst after righteousness: for they shall be filled.'

5th. 'Blessed are the merciful:'

Here we find a complete change in the character of the beatitudes. Hitherto the blessed quality has been that produced by the alarming, awakening, and convicting work of the Spirit in the soul. This brought in a true seeking after God and with it a profound humility and self-distrust.

All the previous qualities were to Godward. It is true that men could see the poor mourners, meekly seeking after righteousness; but then this was so because such qualities were both heartfelt and transparent. But they were not directed towards men, albeit they affected the seekers' whole attitude to their fellows. They were directed towards God.

This is not the case with mercy. Mercy is directed solely towards men. It has no direction towards God whatsoever. It is not that men see a quality which has its origin in the soul's seeking after God. Mercy is a quality which seeks after men, it has its origin in the intention and desire to relieve their condition. This is a complete change from the previous beatitudes.

If so, it is the result of righteousness. And since the change is so complete — and it is — one is not surprised to find that it is constant. All the beatitudes alter after the turning point of 'Blessed are they which do hunger and thirst after righteousness.'

Therefore the seekers must now be regarded as having found that righteousness which they sought. And found it by 'eating Jesus' flesh, and drinking his blood'. After the fourth beatitude they are filled. Filled with relief and satisfaction in Christ Jesus. Now righteousness is upon them and life is within them. Not only does partaking of Christ give them righteousness: it imparts life. 'Hath eternal life'.

As such the first and most immediate characteristic of that life to appear is *mercy towards others*.

Hence it is a change wrought by union. They are in union with the Father and the Son. Having 'eaten his flesh and drunk his blood' the spiritual power of the truth of his death has been conveyed to their inward parts by the Holy Ghost. Two things follow of necessity. Righteousness, I say, is imputed. And life is imparted.

This is not a change in their life: though their life does change altogether. But not of itself. It is a being filled with the Father and the Son. With eternal life their life is now sweetly blended. To it, their life is meekly yielded. Flowing through them—for 'they were all filled with the Holy Ghost' — it is manifested by them. And what appears is: Mercy.

It is not just that they are being merciful; though they are, profoundly. But the reason they are, is that the love of God which showed mercy to them, now dwells within them. And if so, shows mercy through them. From the inward parts, in union and communion, their ready lives melt in sweet agreement with the love of God shed abroad in their hearts by the Holy Ghost given unto them.

Here is a warm, interior and experimental religion the heart of which is love, the medium of which is faith, and the outlook of which is hope. It was gained alone through long personal and inward dealings with Christ, in bitter trials in the wilderness, secret meetings of the heart, lonely vigils in the night, assignations and trystings in the garden of the soul. But that soul had persevered, and persevered in a way that is spiritual, agreeable to the beatitudes. Asking; and thus the faintest directions were heard. Listening; and at last, the heart wakeneth. Seeking; and at length, the spiritual door was discovered. Knocking; and behold! the gate opened of its own accord.

This interior spiritual reality is in contrast with the more common way. The natural choice of man is one in which the bare doctrine will be taken up with relish, but the inward spirituality which goes with the doctrine, spurned and repudiated. Whilst text and notion drive in state carriage through the grand portals of the intellect accompanied by a proud escort, heralded by the fanfare of rational prowess, lo! Lo, the poor humble way of interior humility, of spiritual meekness, shamefully hangs her head without. She is shut out unrequited. Unwanted. She is scorned and in rags at the servants' entrance.

It is passing strange that what amounts to a natural choice for the wide gate and easy way in religion, is taken up by some who then appoint themselves champions of a narrow system of negatives denying the free-will which they themselves have exercised in practice! A system upholding unconditional election, asserting total depravity, limiting the atonement, and nasally declaring for divine sovereignty in everything.

Wilfully rejecting the path of prayer — that inward and spiritual way of the heart taught by Jesus — such people freely elect for the cold intellectualism of censorship on behalf of their own party system of doctrine. In practice this becomes the whole of their religion, and they have the quaint aptitude to think of this as 'soundness'.

Although being self-appointed nevertheless they would regard themselves as having a veritable divine vocation to safeguard what they suppose to be 'the truth'. They would certainly consider themselves as the sole custodians and interpreters of imputed righteousness.

Mercy is irrelevant to this system of theology; except it be the theory of the mercy of God. All the emphasis is placed upon doctrine. But the advocates of it are cold and barren. Dry as dust and as dead, all they have is 'the traditions of the fathers' handed down in books. Nothing sent down from heaven through the Spirit from Christ. They are distinguished by the 'correct' views with which they are at once without kindness and completely merciless.

Of this sort are those who would rejoice in the name of Calvin, and in that name form their party. However, Calvin's fastidious French eyebrows would have met his leather cap in puzzled astonishment had he heard of the miserably attenuated negatives, the cramped theology of narrow circumscription thus being perpetrated in his name. It is nothing but systematic constipation. The ancient Frenchman would soon have dipped his pen to censure such audacious trifling.

On the other hand in complete contrast stands large-hearted John Wesley. If as to certain theology too loose, Wesley might well be excused on the ground of over-compensation for the relentless hounding of the merciless.

But how warm-hearted and experimental was the heavenly-minded Wesley: how merciful! The largeness of his heart was ably hymned by his brother:

> Thou, Jesus, thou my breast inspire,
> And touch my lips with hallowed fire,
> And loose a stammering infant's tongue;
> Prepare the vessel of thy grace,
> Adorn me with the robes of praise,
> And mercy shall be all my song:
> Mercy for all who know not God,
> Mercy for all in Jesus' blood,
> Mercy, that earth and heaven transcends;
> Love, that o'erwhelms the saints in light,
> The length, and breadth, and depth, and height
> Of love divine which never ends.

Blessed are the merciful: for they shall obtain mercy. Even had one perfect knowledge, it is not, Blessed are the knowledgeable. 'Though I have the gift of prophecy, and understand all mysteries, and all knowledge ... and have not charity, I am nothing.' Even had one all doctrine to perfection, it is not, Blessed are the doctrinal. It is, Blessed are the merciful. That is the test.

Someone may say to me, But must you be so scathing about others? Yes, I believe that mercy to all demands it. Thus far in the fifth beatitude I have answered the question: 'Why is mercy put here in the natural sequence of the beatitudes?' And the answer is this: Precisely because carnal men in religion *do not* put it there, or anywhere else after righteousness. They substitute instead the doctrinal schemes of head-knowledge on which their religious pride and self-esteem depend. And is it love to shut one's mouth at that? What of immortal souls? Salvation *depends* upon being merciful, not doctrinal. Blessed are the merciful: for *they* shall obtain mercy.

Without becoming merciful, no mercy shall be obtained of God. Without retaining mercy, no mercy shall remain from God. Without abiding merciful, mercy shall be withdrawn by God. Mercy denied to man — any one man, all men — and God will deny his mercy at the last.

If imputed righteousness is claimed but does not issue in mercy, the claim is false. If the righteousness claimed is distinct from mercy, the claim is false. If imputed righteousness continues to be claimed, but mercy withers and dies: the false claim is found out at the last. Blessed are the merciful: for they *shall* — it is future — obtain mercy.

But what is mercy?

Mercy is a quality which may be exercised by God or man, but only towards men. However, not any men indiscriminately: only those in a certain condition. Mercy may be

— must be — *felt* for all; but the condition of many prevents the voluntary exercise of it consistent with this feeling.

Mercy is defined by the Oxford dictionary as 'Compassion shown by one to another who is in his power and has no claim to kindness.'

Strictly the exercise of mercy is towards those who are under obligation to one, but fail in that obligation and sue for pity. But there is no doubt that the merciful man is possessed of that disposition in which the quality of mercy colours all his attitudes and tempers all his judgments. The quality of mercy is not strained.

But it is not blind. Neither is it stupid. Nor is mercy lawless. Mercy does not flaunt law, just so that it may be exercised at the expense of everything else, or at the risk of undermining moral government.

So then, the merciful man longs for mercy to all. And he exercises it to whomsoever he may. But not to the detriment of law or at the risk of character. The merciful man in the exercise of mercy will be sure to recompense the broken law, redress any proper grievance, and make good all expense, at his own cost. The merciful man will watch alertly for the hypocrite, the pretend penitent, and the habitual scrounger. Mercy gives no bread to able-bodied loafers! She cries with a sternness fully equal to brother Justice: If any man will not work, neither let him eat.

Nevertheless, mercy's restless spirit searches diligently by day and by night to see whether — in company with her sister, Sorrow — she may bring about the state she cannot discover. To find if, by the precedent infliction of pain, shame, bereavement, chastisement or disgrace, souls now intransigent might in consequence be brought to that penitent state in which it shall be safe to pour out mercy's healing balm.

Mercy is one of several attributes of love, the combination of which answers to the character seen in the thirteenth chapter of first Corinthians. Mercy is not love; I repeat, mercy is one of the attributes of love. All of these attributes must be respected, held in balance to each other, and exercised in concert to sound the harmony of perfect love. Each attribute will study the other. None breaks away in self-will. Else were the fragile vessel shattered. Holiness must be regarded. Justice must be respected. Rectitude must not be slighted. Efficiency is not to be neglected. Pity must sound her bowels of compassion. Veracity must have her say. Intelligence must cast her bright and lucid gaze over all and review with wisdom the order of the day. Impartiality must never be ignored. And industry too must occupy the energies. Kindness views with gentle gaze each new circumstance calling for her exercise.

It is the balanced order and wise arrangement of these various attributes in their exercise that produces the restraint and reliability of the unique Christian character of love. And in that balance and order none is more to the foremost, more apparent in the demeanour, or more attendant upon the exercise of every other attribute, than mercy. She cannot help herself. It is in her nature. She even stands by shocked, wide-eyed, and hand to mouth as at last she is forced to give place to the stern vengeance of outraged rectitude. Mercy. As the gentle rain from heaven.

Mercy is not so much the opposite of judgment, as an attitude of kindness which defers judgment. If such a way can be found, mercy will step forward and satisfy judgment by that other way, to her own detriment. Only that hope may be realised and deliverance wrought for the poor, needy, condemned and helpless.

But wisdom might counsel that mercy should not be shown, until true penitence is wrought. Yet how often the sight of mercy's radiant figure, aglow with love, works penitence where every other plea falls to the ground and the lash but hardens the heart!

This is that divine quality which, above all, the justified man must reflect. It is extraordinary that with all the other attributes of love — immediately following upon justifying righteousness — this is the one insisted upon more than any other.

Why not the Christian characteristic of faith? Blessed are the faithful; the believers; the hopeful; the sanctified, for example. Or, as the doctrinal would love it, Blessed are they that have obtained mercy. But it is not. It is, Blessed are they that *show* it!

Yet the experimental might surely be excused for thinking, Why not 'Blessed are they that love'? Why not the whole quality of the life: love? Why only an attribute of love? And if an attribute, why select mercy in particular as the pre-eminent evidence of truly being the Lord's, of being a real Christian? Immediately after righteousness is imputed, mercy is most manifest. Why?

I think it is because mercy is so demonstrative. Mercy is that attribute in which love — in its very nature — is most demonstrably manifest. You can *see* it. You cannot talk it. You cannot pretend to it. Either you are merciful or you are not; but if you are it shows everywhere.

225

You can see mercy, because you can see the *cost*. Mercy *pays*. Mercy crosses the street. Mercy gets out the wallet. Mercy cries, 'If he hath wronged thee, or oweth thee ought, put that on mine account; I Paul have written it with mine own hand, I will repay it.' Mercy pays. Mercy does not say, 'Depart in peace, be ye warmed and filled; notwithstanding giving not those things which are needful to the body.' Hypocrisy says that.

Mercy cannot be hid. In God, mercy gives his Son to save lost sinners, his Spirit to awaken them. In men, for a recompense, mercy waives natural rights, sets aside natural authority, girds herself with a towel, and gladly suffers the loss of that material substance whereby she might have been profited.

Any other attribute might or might not be copied. Love is so general it might be confused with emotions and sentiment. Doctrine, knowledge, at the last, is talk. But mercy is deeds. And deeds that cost. Mercy demands loss of face and diminishing of property. Mercy *demonstrates* love and demonstrates it materially. Therefore it is chosen first by the Lord Jesus. Because it cannot be hid. Blessed are the merciful.

> ': for they shall obtain mercy.'

I have only one thing to say about this.

Therefore is the kingdom of heaven likened unto a certain king, which would take account of his servants. And when he had begun to reckon, one was brought unto him, which owed him ten thousand talents. But forasmuch as he had not to pay, his lord commanded him to be sold, and his wife, and children, and all that he had, and payment to be made. The servant therefore fell down, and worshipped him, saying, Lord, have patience with me, and I will pay thee all. Then the lord of that servant was moved with compassion, and loosed him, and forgave him the debt.

But the same servant went out, and found one of his fellowservants, which owed him an hundred pence: and he laid hands on him, and took him by the throat, saying, Pay me that thou owest. And his fellowservant fell down at his feet, and besought him, saying, Have patience with me, and I will pay thee all. And he would not: but went and cast him into prison, till he should pay the debt.

So when his fellowservants saw what was done, they were very sorry, and came and told unto their lord all that was done.

Then his lord, after that he had called him, said unto him, O thou wicked servant, I forgave thee all that debt, because thou desiredst me: shouldest not thou also have had compassion on thy fellowservant, even as I had pity on thee? And his lord was wroth, and delivered him to the tormentors, till he should pay all that was due unto him.

So likewise shall my heavenly Father do also unto you, if ye from your hearts forgive not every one his brother their trespasses.

For if ye forgive men their trespasses, your heavenly Father will also forgive you: but if ye forgive not men their trespasses, neither will your Father forgive your trespasses.

Blessed are the merciful: for they shall obtain mercy.

6th. 'Blessed are the pure in heart:'

The mere existence of this beatitude is remarkable. When one views the vast distance covered by the soul since 'Blessed are the poor in spirit;' when considering the tremendous blessings of 'Blessed are they which do hunger and thirst after righteousness;' when one contemplates that the whole disposition — as partaking of the divine nature — is now suffused with mercy: well might one ask, What remaineth?

Purity of heart remaineth. For all the progress, still, there remaineth a rest for the people of God. Even now, there remaineth yet very much land to be possessed.

Remarkable. The merciful soul is as yet but over the river dryshod. The land lies still before the feet. The word is, Go up, and possess the land. Go in, enter the inheritance. Blessed are the pure in heart. I say, purity of heart remaineth. Then, the pilgrimage must be continued.

This continuance, and the consequent refusal to be content with former experience, progress, victories, and achievements, is taught by the apostle Peter. Not only does he bid us add one thing to another, but he expects growth in the process. 'Grow in grace, and in the knowledge of our Lord and Saviour Jesus Christ.'

James likewise exhorts to patience — and hence indicates the passage of time — that at the last 'ye may be perfect and entire, wanting nothing.' Time would fail to draw examples from the epistle to the Hebrews, to mark the track of those exhorted to 'run with patience the race that is set before' them. Look how many carcasses perished in the wilderness;

what numbers turned aside to strew the verges. No wonder that we are told elsewhere not to stop short but 'so run, that ye may obtain' the prize.

Neither is John behind with this doctrine. Writing to his children in Christ, he designates them fathers, young men, and infants respectively. But not on account of age or relationships as men measure them in the world. These titles were nothing to do with their actual years: none of the converts was really an infant!

'I have written unto you, young men, because ye are strong, and the word of God abideth in you, and ye have overcome the wicked one.' Spiritual progress gave the definitive maturity: nothing else. It was age *in Christ*. And if so, progress. That is what brought them from spiritual infancy to heavenly manhood. The growth is not measured in natural years, nor is it due to earthly causes. Like the beatitudes, it is due to spiritual increase and heavenly pilgrimage. John's children have gone forward. That is the point: there is no stopping short. There remaineth yet very much land to be possessed.

It was the failure to continue, on the part of many who had begun well, that inspired Jude to write his epistle and utter its solemn warnings and examples. The Israelites were once saved out of the land of Egypt. They ate of the passover lamb, trusted in its blood, and made exodus in the strength of that meat many days. They were baptised in the Red Sea, steadfastly followed the pillar of cloud and fire, ate of the heavenly manna and drank of the Rock which followed them, which Rock was Christ. But afterwards the Lord destroyed them which believed not, though they had once believed. Nevertheless later they fell through unbelief. Howbeit not all that came out of Egypt; for Joshua and

Caleb pressed on to perfection and entered into the land of their inheritance.

The apostle Paul is famous in the ministry for his labouring day and night with tears, not now to save souls, but to keep, further, and bring on those who had once been saved. To them he preached Christ not without but with warning. To those who were in Christ, and in whom Christ was, he saith 'Christ in you, the hope of glory: whom we preach, warning every man.' So it is not just that stopping short of perfection is undesirable. It is dangerous. '*Warning* every man, and teaching every man in all wisdom; that we may present every man perfect in Christ Jesus: whereunto I also labour, striving according to his working, which worketh in me mightily.'

Mark that, Paul strove with many tears not only to save souls, but keep them. Not only to see converts, but see them sanctified. Not only to see men blessed, but to see them worshippers. They must go on unto perfection, or wither on the vine and go back to destruction. Howbeit many cautioned souls could say 'We are not of them who draw back unto perdition; but of them that believe to the saving of the soul.'

Saith Paul 'God hath from the beginning chosen you to salvation through sanctification of the Spirit and belief of the truth' — through it, not without it — 'Whereunto he called you by our gospel, to the obtaining of the glory of our Lord Jesus Christ.' But many then, and many now, attempt schemes to circumvent the necessity of spiritual sanctification. They profess to believe in Christ, but they ignore the Holy Ghost. In practice, they do not believe in Christ himself, only on those bare historical and doctrinal facts relating to his death. These dead souls keep repeating 'finished work' but this repetition is the whole of their religion. Words. They do not go on unto perfection. Rather they attempt to entangle those who would, catching them in the net of their schemes of petrified objective stultification.

It may have been, and it was, one act of Christ that procured salvation. That was a finished work. But it was not, and it never will be, one act of ours that secures salvation. Faith is not a finished work.

One act of Christ procured salvation, but one act of ours is not enough to retain it. It is not one act of faith, but faith *itself* that is needed. Faith is present, active and alive. It increases by growing, spreading and enlarging. Its object, the Son of God, must become clearer, more embracing and all-absorbing. There is progress, when things are real.

It is from faith *to* faith. The just are not only justified but they positively live by faith. And if so, they grow by it. Saving faith is not a bare belief in the forgiveness of sins; not even solely a trust in justifying righteousness; faith lays hold upon Christ himself and all in him is hers.

Faith ranges through the whole of experience. She pursues and searches out to perfection each ascending beatitude. Faith traverses the whole country of the soul, she climbs the heavenly heights of the spirit. Faith overcomes the world, laughs at impossibilities, triumphs over every area of the life. Faith faces every issue, searches out the secret depths, comes in with the shout of a king, goes up with the roar of a lion, bursts through with the chariot of Israel and the horsemen thereof. Faith looks the king of terrors in the eye, faith gazes into the grave with a smile, faith cries defiantly at the last enemy, faith goes up with a shout that rings round the vault of heaven, and at the last, swallowed up in sight, faith falls prostrate before the throne of God and of the Lamb. Oh, she continues all right: and increases: right to the end.

And to this end the apostles, taking nothing for granted, knowing nothing before the time, wept, prayed, laboured, strove, cried, besought, warned, preached, taught and exhorted. Oh, cries Paul 'I would that ye knew what great conflict I have for you.' Here is the ministry: preventing the dawning praying, fasting, supplicating. A ministry on the knees, on the face; a ministry of the warm heart, a ministry of great spiritual conflict. A ministry for the perfecting of the saints.

This was true of the godly ministers who laboured under the apostolic direction and counsel. 'Epaphras, who is one of you, a servant of Christ, saluteth you, always labouring fervently for you in prayers, that ye may stand perfect and complete in all the will of God.' 'We sent Timotheus, our brother, and minister of God, and our fellowlabourer in the gospel of Christ, to establish you, and to comfort you concerning your faith ... for this cause, when I could no longer forbear, I sent to know your faith.' Had they gone on? Or back? How these ministers' warm hearts glowed, their knees bowed, as they laboured with tears, wrestling in spiritual conflict for the perfecting of the saints.

Observe how the apostle continues: 'I sent to know your faith, lest by some means the tempter have tempted you, and our labour be in vain.' Mark that, for this possibility demonstrates the reason for the apostle's anxiety. Hence 'night and day praying exceedingly that we might see your face, and might perfect that which is lacking in your faith.'

A most striking instance of this perfecting is seen in the first of Paul's two prayers for the Ephesians.

Here are the Ephesian saints — yes, saints they are called — full of faith in the Lord Jesus, full of love unto all the saints, the word of God abounding in them, and the testimony of the gospel spreading from them. However the apostle — having heard all that of them — whilst thankful enough for what had been wrought, still drops to his knees and cries to God on their behalf.

And not without reason. For, at last rising from his intercession on their behalf, he is inspired by the Spirit of God to write this epistle exhorting and leading them up into the spiritual house of the Lord upon heavenly mount Zion. Thus Paul goes on to pray and labour mightily that the saints at Ephesus should at length make real progress in Christ by the knowledge of God both as God and Father, and in the relative disposition of his ways in respect of the body of Christ and of the house of God.

Paul prays for them. Not about their 'telling others' but about his telling them. Not that they may do something, but that God may do it to them according to Paul's doctrine.

Therefore we are to observe that the evidence of the saints being in Christ was but the stimulus to the true gospel minister for his leading them on unto perfection. When men think they have arrived at what is required, and are content so to leave their condition; when they say to themselves, 'Once-saved, Always-saved,' or think their salvation finished with and nothing remains for them but to 'tell it out', then I say, such men are fallen already.

The Ephesian saints, stretching every nerve, continuing

instant in prayer, full of faith and love, with a great
testimony in the world, might well have thought themselves
already to be the very exemplars of the church. Not to the
apostle. He ceases not to pray for them that they may now
receive — over and above all that which had previously been
given to them — a spirit of wisdom and revelation in the
knowledge of the Lord Jesus Christ; that the eyes of their
understanding might be illuminated; and that they might
have a penetrating prophetic vision into the future hope of
the God of hope. Not only of what they have from him;
but of what he has in them.

And, remark, this is only the first of the two prayers in
Ephesians. The second beseeches the Father for something
quite different, and brings the apostle right down to his
knees again.

Therefore we need not to be surprised upon finding
— for all the progress in the beatitudes since 'blessed are
the poor in spirit' — even after 'blessed are the merciful',
yet another step into the heavenly heights of glory: Blessed
are the pure in heart.

Now then, to the matter itself. The question that must
first be asked is this: What is meant by pure?

The word in the New Testament Greek is καθαρός,
katharos, and it has been translated variously Clean ten
times, Clear once, and Pure seventeen times. Also there
occur various other grammatical forms of the same basic
word, in which the stem *kathar* is retained and only the
ending alters.

As it happens the latter give a far better conception of
the meaning to the English reader. For example *kathar-izo*

234

has been translated variously Cleanse, Purge, Purify. And *kathar-ismos*, Cleansing, Purification, Purifying, and Purged.

From this it follows that *katharos*, Purity — as in 'Blessed are the pure in heart' — is not to be regarded as a word indicating innocence, virginity, intrinsic cleanliness. Unlike the English word, the Greek does not carry the connotation of 'that which has never been sullied or defiled'.

To the contrary, *katharos* is used in connection with *cleansing*, and if so, then that which was before unclean. It is the New Testament word used to state the effect of having been cleansed, purged or purified. The English word answering to this is not 'pure' at all. The best we have is the medical term Catharsis, purgation. Or Cathartic, purgative. Now this refers to the purging of foul matter stagnant within the body or bowels. *Katharos*, from which it is derived, refers however to the foul matter stagnant within the soul, and hence totally offensive to the Holy One of Israel, the Most High God.

Matthew writes as a Jew to the Jews, and he alone records Messiah's 'blessed are the pure in heart' spoken to his Jewish disciples. It is really a Jewish word. That is why we have no clear English equivalent. Even the Greek was hard put to it, although the Jewish mind was immediately alerted to the meaning.

It is a ceremonial word. *Katharos* and its cognates are used in connection with ceremonial Jewish cleansing. Particularly from defilement. I say, to the Jew it was a religious word for the ceremony of purgation, of making clean for the house of God, purging the defiled for re-entry to the congregation of his people. It is the word used to answer to the ancient Mosaic conception of the absolute necessity of being *clean* individually and collectively, before worship could be entertained in the tabernacle of the Lord. It was not enough to be a people of God. Jehovah must have a *clean* people of God. And that is where this word comes in: 'cleansed'.

So then, when the Jewish Messiah said to his disciples 'Blessed are the καθαροὶ, *pure*, in heart,' immediately this would convey a world of intelligence to the Jews who listened. Straightway they recognised a ceremonial word deeply rooted in Hebrew lore.

This truth is confirmed and abundantly demonstrated by many passages. For example, there is a direct reference to the legal ceremony for the purification of women — Leviticus chapter twelve — found in Luke 2:22-23 'That which is said in the law of the Lord.' Mary offers a sacrifice for her purification, 'καθαρ-ισμοῦ, *katharismou*', 'according to the law of Moses.' This shows that the *katharos* group of words is chosen to indicate the Old Testament ceremonial cleansing. Incidentally, were the peculiar error of 'the immaculate conception of Mary' valid, this offering would be totally unnecessary. It was not for Jesus: he was spotless and without sin. Then, since the blood of two birds was in fact shed, for whose cleansing was it shed? There remains Mary. And so it is said 'for *her* purification'. Therefore by nature and birth she herself could not have been pure. Jesus was; alone.

Further to demonstrating that *katharos* and its cognates indicate the Jewish ceremonial purifying, observe John 2:6. 'After the manner of the purifying — καθαρ-ισμὸν — of the Jews.' And again, Hebrews 9:22. 'Almost all things are by the law purged — καθαρ-ίζεται — with blood.' There it is: 'by the law'. For a final example observe Hebrews 9:13

236

'the blood of bulls and of goats, and the ashes of an heifer sprinkling the unclean, sanctifieth to the purifying — καθαρ-ότητα — of the flesh.'

These are but a few examples. Nevertheless they suffice to show that the word translated 'pure' in 'Blessed are the pure in heart' is deeply rooted in the ceremonial law of Moses and in the centuries-old tradition of Israel.

This ancient tradition, delivered to Moses upon mount Sinai and embodied in the laws of Israel, must be regarded as 'the shadow of good things to come'. Such purifying ceremonies were 'the figures of the true'. These traditions provided for the time then present a material type of future spiritual reality. 'The law having a shadow of good things to come.' But the reality having now come to pass does not obliterate the necessity of gospel purgation and cleanliness for worshippers: the reality proves to be the substance of which the old legal purifying was the mere shadow. It becomes not less, but all the more apparent. Not increasingly ephemeral but far more substantial. There never were, never are, and never will be any dirty worshippers. The New Testament does not alter that; it substantially confirms it with the solid rock of the gospel whose long shadow had been cast so many centuries before.

'Pure', as in *katharos* indicates the having been purged, purified, or cleansed, but not in the old shadowy figurative way of outward Jewish types and pictures. In a new profound substantial way of spiritual reality and inward permanence.

Purifying does not really respect actual sins. It is more the consequences of sin. A woman was 'cleansed' or 'purified' after childbirth. She had not sinned in bearing the infant. But the uncleanness of inbred sin came to light in the process, the innate corruption of the race was exposed in the blood, the original uncleanness of mankind was common to her. The leprosy was not a sin, a transgression. One did not do it. It happened to one. But it was unclean in the sight of God, its manifestation indicated the deep plague of the heart possessed by man in the fall, and no leper should worship in the congregation of the Lord forever.

So 'purity of heart' is not a matter of personal guilt resulting from moral, wilful, action. It is a result of pollution in consequence of what *man* has done. The corruption of the whole race as such, in which we share. 'Cleanse' or 'purify' might be termed a laundering word: not so much sin, as the stain left by it, the soiling that comes from being of a corrupt stock in the fall. 'Pure' is used in connection with cleansing from the dirt in man; the defilement of the race.

It was effected by blood, water, the ashes of an heifer *, cedar wood, scarlet and hyssop †, and also by fire. By fire the process is called purging. 'I will purely purge away thy dross, and take away all thy tin.' 'The Lord is like a refiner's fire.'

In a professing people of God, this process must take place, no matter which testament nor how high the doctrine believed. Men may come with the confession of Jesus' blood, the truth of his cross on their lips, but if their hearts are dirty the Lord will not hear them. This is seen in Cain and Abel. 'But unto Cain' — *first;* 'and to his offering' —

---

* † See 'The Red Heifer'. John Metcalfe Publishing Trust.

second; 'the Lord had not respect.' However with Abel —
first; the person and his heart first. And his offering —
second; the slain lamb, his fat and therefore blood second;
the Lord was well pleased. God is not worshipped by the
unclean. There must be *immediate present cleanliness*
before his presence can be entered in reality. Otherwise it is
all words, lies, and deceitfulness.

That is why it is said now, 'Blessed are the pure in heart.'

But it is 'in heart'. That is the characteristic of New
Testament purgation and cleansing, and the difference
between it and the old. 'For he is not a Jew, which is one
outwardly; neither is that circumcision, which is outward
in the flesh; but he is a Jew, which is one inwardly; and
circumcision is that of the heart, in the spirit, and not in
the letter; whose praise is not of men, but of God.'

Since Christ came, the purification is not of the flesh:
it is of the heart. It is no longer the type of the cleansing
of the body: it is now the reality of the pure in heart.
Forasmuch as Christ has come, the answer to the ancient
plea has arrived: 'Create in me a clean heart, O God; and
renew a right spirit within me.'

The Pharisees did then, and their counterparts do now,
make clean the outside of the cup and platter; but their
inward part is full of ravening and wickedness. They do not
wish to consider that 'There is nothing from without a
man, that entering into him can defile him: but the things
which come out of him, those are they that defile the man.'

'For from within, out of the heart of men, proceed
evil thoughts, adulteries, fornications, murders, thefts,
covetousness, wickedness, deceit, lasciviousness, an evil eye,

blasphemy, pride, foolishness: all these evil things come from within, and defile the man.'

Blessed are the pure in heart.

But 'Thou blind Pharisee, cleanse first that which is within the cup and platter, that the outside of them may be clean also. Woe unto you, scribes and Pharisees, hypocrites! for ye are like unto whited sepulchres, which indeed appear beautiful outward, but are within full of dead men's bones, and of all uncleanness. Even so ye also outwardly appear righteous unto men, but within ye are full of hypocrisy and iniquity.'

Blessed are the pure in heart.

In heart.

The end of the commandment is love out of a pure heart, and of a good conscience, and of faith unfeigned. Indeed, the true disciple holds the mystery of the faith in a pure conscience. This causes painful separation, in order that 'purging oneself' one may 'follow righteousness, faith, charity, peace, with them that call on the Lord out of a pure heart.'

They are not easy to find. But they can be found. One characteristic is this: they 'love one another with a pure heart fervently.' They separate from worldliness; pharisaical, outward, and dead-letter religion; luxurious sadducean and soft compromise. As separated, they ascend up inwardly into the hill of the Lord, spiritually entering his heavenly tabernacles, having 'clean hands and a pure heart.' They will gladly receive 'he that loveth pureness of heart, for the grace of his lips the king shall be his friend.'

'꞉ for they shall see God.'

What a statement this is! If one considered but the handful of the greatest of all men ever upon the earth; commanding at their will and ordering at their pleasure vast armies and nations. If one presumed only the potentates of the world, few and mighty, kings of kings, rulers over all the earth: a mere handful, as the gods among men. Did even they stand at the edge of the vast desert, and see the curve of the earth disappear in the haze of the horizon, and stop; and in thought transport themselves to that horizon, and look again, and lo! again the boundless plain in turn fading into illimitable distance: and on, and on. Well might they say, O that I knew where I might find him! That I might come even to his seat!

But where is it? Where dwellest thou? Come and see. Then let that handful of emperors, those few that have conquered the world, this small number that stand out from the dark mass of all mankind as the stars of Orion, or of the Plough against the night sky, for the awesome outshining they have made in the dark of human history. If any shall command the attention of the Unknown, surely it is they? If any shall draw His eye, must not these be the ones? Let them stand upon their palaces by night and gaze into the firmament of endless depth: let them arise in the evening watch and come forth to their turrets and consider the heavens, the work of His hands. Infinity above; infinity below; infinity around. Unreachable, innumerable stars mocking in cold light the impotence of the lost speck so far below. Eternity before; eternity behind; eternity around. And what is man? And this of the greatest. What of the swarming unknown nations, the teeming unnamed peoples living, breeding, dying all around the vast kingdoms? Who can find out the Almighty? If the kings are unknown dust in his sight, what is the humble labourer, what the shepherd beneath the sod roof, what the peasant in cave or tent?

Now hear the staggering condescension of God Almighty:

Thus saith the LORD, The heaven is my throne, and the earth is my footstool: where is the house that ye build unto me? and where is the place of my rest? For all those things hath mine hand made, and all those things have been, saith the LORD: but to this man will I look, even to him that is poor and of a contrite spirit, and trembleth at my word.

To this man will I look. Amazing. To *this* man will I look. Poor; contrite; trembling. Of a truth I perceive that God is no respecter of persons: but in every nation he that feareth him, and worketh righteousness, is accepted with him.

'For they shall see God.'

That is, in heart. How full the divine life that floods the soul! Christ dwells in the pure in heart by faith. They are strengthened with might by his Spirit in the inner man. By interior sensation and sight the pure in heart are able to comprehend the breadth, and length, and depth, and height, and to know the love of Christ, which passes knowledge. They are filled with all the fulness of God. Thus they see the Father, Son, and Holy Ghost in their experience. They see God in their hearts.

What a change hath been wrought in the heart, what purging, what purifying, what cleansing! How the blood, body, cross, death and life of Christ have answered all the Old Testament types and shadows of exterior cleansing. And, answering within, now the heart sees God. The purity is total. There is no mixture whatsoever. There cannot be, otherwise God could not be seen. The eye is single: the whole body full of light. The tree is good: all the fruit is good. The heart is pure: all the heart is purified. Pure. In the sense that there is nothing else there: everything else has been purged out, washed away.

They see God, for God it is that fills the being. And mercy was the key that obtained to open the door.

But one will say to me, Can the heart be so pure? Not in modern evangelism, no. Neither in current superficial evangelicalism, certainly not. But in true religion, yes, of course; it says so. This truth finds out false and shallow profession. The heart is totally pure, without mixture, when the work is real. Then, 'they shall see God.' But not without a pure heart, whatever the profession.

But one presses further, and says, Then what of inbred sin? I answer, Whatever may be in the members, it is not in the heart. Whatever may be in the flesh, it is not in the heart. Whatever may remain of the carnal mind, fleshly affections, concupiscent will — deeper yet — until the very citadel of the heart is reached: still, it is not in the heart.

Whatever daily and continuous mortification is needed as to the interior lusts, affections, passions, the corruptions of the sensibility as such: well, it is needed; and so often. But still it is not the heart. Whatever daily cross and crucifixion applied is needed as to the mind, the intelligence, the intellect, the memory, the reason, consciousness itself, in a word, the natural and carnal mentality: well, it is necessary; and very necessary at that, often and much. But still it is not the heart. Whatever is needed as to dying daily to the internal workings of the will, its devious intentions, its deceitful purposes, its immediate, proximate and ultimate resolutions: well, mortification is desperately important, it is utterly essential; and at every moment, too. Still, it is not the heart.

In all these, inbred sin does and will remain till the resurrection. In each of the cases mentioned, natural corruption retains its bias to the very end. Not that this is an excuse to let either inbred sin reign, or natural corruption have dominion. There is no excuse for that whatsoever. But that given, and mortification wrought: still, that is not the heart. None of the sensibility, mentality, voluntary faculties or the members, is the heart. The heart is something else again. And that is the subject of this beatitude.

The heart was purified completely, purged utterly, washed thoroughly. And it is free from sin, even though surrounded by it in the fleshly lusts, concupiscent will, and carnal mind of the soul. Not to mention the members. I say, all these last should be daily slain, as to what indwells them. But they cannot be purged. Not till the resurrection. It is too physical a thing. But the *heart* can be and in every true case of a real disciple is in fact purged. And purged to purity.

Otherwise purity is no more purity.

People argue, because it has not happened to them and they wish to justify what has, and rescue the shipwreck of a rotten profession. They are found out, but they wish to hide. They do not want to be found out. So they argue against purity of heart, and they do not see God. And they hate those who do. Rather than humble themselves — like the poor; contrite; trembling — these who are rich; these who vindicate a Christianity of platitudes, these who have never trembled at his word, well, they condemn the truth and deny real experience. Thus they justify superficial profession. But scripture stands out and condemns this hypocrisy to the teeth.

The truth is this: 'blessed are the pure in heart.'

And the consequence follows 'for they shall see God.'

7th. 'Blessed are the peacemakers:'
This is the seventh beatitude and the last to describe the inwrought characteristics of the true disciple or real Christian. It brings to perfection — as the number seven indicates — the Christian character.

Not surprisingly, since it indicates the priestly activity of the children of God. And priestliness is of the essence of sonship. Given sonship, there is priesthood. Given priesthood, there must be peacemakers. Hence it is said 'for they shall be called the children of God.' This is the ultimate in Christian maturity. Perfection. But it is very different from what both the world and worldly religion suppose, as I shall show you.

The compound Greek noun εἰρηνοποιός, *eirenopoios* — made up of the word for Peace and that for Maker — only occurs this once in the New Testament. There are no other references.

Also found once only in the Greek New Testament is

the verb form, εἰρηνοποιέω, *eirenopoieo* — made up of the word for Peace and that for Making — giving us the singular occurrences for both the noun 'Peacemaker' and the verb 'Peacemaking'. The noun occurs in the plural. The verb does not.

The fact that there are no other references to 'Peace-makers' might appear to the novice as presenting a difficulty in interpretation: especially since this one occurrence is a statement and not an explanation. But there is no difficulty once the golden rule of context is applied. As to the book, Matthew writes as a Jew to the Jews. As to the beatitudes, Jesus speaks as Messiah to the faithful remnant of Abraham's seed. Immediately they would perceive the connection. 'Peacemakers', to them, meant the priesthood.

Certainly the levitical priesthood, and that was without the veil. Here they are being told of another order, within the veil. It is of sonship.

Now I will be asked. How do I know that 'peacemakers' meant priesthood to the Jewish disciples?

The very first time the word Priest occurs in the Old Testament — and therefore in the Bible — is in Genesis 14:18. 'And Melchizedek king of Salem brought forth bread and wine: and he was the priest of the most high God.' One will say to me, Well; but what has that to do with peace? This: 'Salem' means Peace.

Therefore Melchizedek reigns in and over the place called Peace. His name indicates how he does so; Melchizedek is an elision combining *Melek: king* and *Tzedeq: righteousness*, hence it means by interpretation King of righteousness.

Melchizedek is a figure of Christ, as Hebrews seven teaches. He brings in righteousness and reigns in righteousness by satisfying divine righteousness through the offering up of his body — bread — and blood — wine. This brings in peace, and the Prince of peace, Lord of peace, and King of peace is established through the success of his priesthood and of his priestly offering. This reaches to satisfy the righteousness of the most high God. You cannot get higher than that. Hence absolute peace is brought in through perfect sacrifice in an eternal priesthood.

Every Jewish mind throughout the history of Israel has puzzled over the mysterious Melchizedek. Abruptly appearing without announcement, he seems without father, without mother. No descent is given neither beginning of days nor end of life. He disappears. Till he reappears in the Psalms of David the priestly king well over a thousand years later. In Abraham, all Israel did obeisance to Melchizedek.

No Jew has solved the mystery: and none can without turning to Christ. But in the manner of mysteries, it sticks in the mind. Therefore this the original peacemaker was first by interpretation King of righteousness — for it precedes peace — and then, on a basis of righteousness laid down, King of peace. This declared plainly that if peace was to be made it must be made in a priestly way between Abraham and his seed forever on the one hand; and the most high God, Jehovah of hosts, on the other. So to the Jewish mind, peacemaker and priesthood go together.

This was true of their own levitical priesthood, which presented figures for the time then present of the future priestly ministry of Messiah, the Prince of peace, who should be a priest forever after the order of Melchizedek.

That is, the order which was 'made like unto the Son of God; abiding a priest continually.'

In types and shadows I say, Levi foreshadowed this. And never more so than when it was commanded to Moses by the LORD 'Speak unto Aaron and unto his sons, saying, On this wise ye shall bless the children of Israel, saying unto them,

> The LORD bless thee, and keep thee:
> The LORD make his face shine upon thee,
> and be gracious unto thee:
> The LORD lift up his countenance upon thee,
> *and give thee peace.'*

So then, to the children of Israel, peace was made by priesthood, and if so, on the basis of priestly sacrifice; for example, the peace-offering. Hence peacemaker and priesthood go together. Indeed, God's covenant with Levi was of 'life and peace'.

David was the king who wore the ephod: behold! a king shall reign in righteousness. King David brought rest to Israel from all their enemies round about, and established the kingdom. As none before, the priest and king after God's own heart could say to all Israel: *'Shalom'*: *peace*. Howbeit, Solomon built him an house. This was of necessity. It is the *Son* of David that must typify the true peacemaker. David's son was named Solomon: that means, *peace*. He reigned in Ierou-salem, the priestly city of peace. Inevitably to the Jew this brought together priesthood and peace. Not to mention sonship.

All this prefigures Christ the Son of God, the true priest and the true peace offering. It is he who makes peace, and indeed he to whom the singular verb form of this word is applied: Christ Jesus 'made peace', *eirenopoieo*, the verb is singular — 'through the blood of his cross.' If that is not priestly, what is? Then peacemaking and priesthood are indissolubly united.

There is however a world of difference between Christ's making peace and the disciples' being peacemakers. He made peace because he made the sacrifice: 'having made peace through the blood of his cross.' This becomes the basis of the disciples' message of peace to the world. 'How beautiful are the feet of them that preach the gospel of peace, and bring glad tidings of good things!' So in turn they make peace by declaring the way of it in Christ Jesus.

This is not an automatic process as is so much of the forced and artificial 'witness' which pushes the bare letter of salvation texts, and indiscriminately thrusts the name 'Jesus' into the lips of carnal, worldly, and unconverted persons. This is something that comes from God. 'How can they preach except they be sent?' It is something that comes from being borne along by the Holy Ghost. It is something that comes from being controlled by the Holy Ghost. It is something that comes from being able to communicate the Holy Ghost. In a word it is something that comes from being — not just born but — grown into the maturity of sonship.

This is the heritage of all believers. But they must attain first to this perfect beatitude by much prayer, spiritual exercise, and heavenly progress. And they must do so in the face of the fact that most professing 'Christians' today simply will not learn patience neither will they suffer the discipline and pain of the school of Christ. Instead — refusing, like Saul, to wait — immediately with fleshly excitement they peddle the dead letter of scripture and never even approach the first let alone the seventh beatitude.

Consider the profound and spiritual way in which the Son of God made peace. Consider the cost to the Son of God of making peace. Consider that the fact of his eternal priesthood and the perfection of wondrous sacrifice, do not alter his condescension in sharing with us the unique kin description — peacemakers — to his singular work — making peace. Then shall we attain this honour without following in his steps? Without taking up our cross? Without ascending six beatitudes to a perfect man, unto the measure of the stature of the fulness of Christ? We shall not.

How wonderfully our great high priest made peace by the offering up of himself. He is peace. He personifies peace. 'For he is our peace,' Ephesians 2:14. And he 'makes peace', Ephesians 2:15. Moreover through the peacemakers, indwelling, filling, directing them by the Holy Ghost, he himself 'preaches peace', Ephesians 2:17.

When the disciples are full of the joyful spirit of this experience — and consequently empty of themselves and anything they have done or propose to do — completely and rapturously taken up with Christ, with what he has done, with what he is doing, with what he proposes to do — and not at all with themselves, or even of his making any use of them — then Christ is all and in all: then he has the pre-eminence. And then, then the disciples become true peacemakers. Priests available in the service. 'Ministering to the Lord and fasting' Acts 13:1-3. Blessed are the peacemakers.

We have seen that mercy is one of the attributes of love

divine. We have seen that purity of heart reflects the divine love. Love is of God, and God is love. The pure in heart do not merely know this, they experience it; they contain it; they reflect it. In consequence the fruits of it are ministered by them in priestly service. Peacemaking is not an attribute of divine love, not even the quality of divine love. It is the fruit of love's necessity; it is the efficiency of love faced with the necessity of priesthood. It is an activity towards men. Love must cry, and those who hear must echo, 'On earth peace, good will toward men.'

But what peace is this? And in respect of which war?

Between whom is this proposed peace?

'Blessed are the peacemakers' does not tell us. There is mention neither of the one from whom the peacemakers come, as ambassadors proposing peace by their ministrations; nor is there mention of the ones to whom they are sent, the ones at war, to whom the overtures of peace are made. Finally, nothing is said about the covenant, the foundation, the mediatorial work done, on the basis of which the peace proposals are put forward. It is merely the bald statement 'blessed are the peacemakers.'

Notwithstanding, we may interpret. The peacemakers make peace between whom? Why, first, between God and man. It is this alienation of man from God that is all the cause of men's malice one to another. It began with Cain. It is all the cause of war between nations and strife amongst peoples. None of them has peace with God. Had they, in so short a time they would be peacemakers one to another.

Then they would find that he maketh wars to cease unto

the end of the earth; he breaketh the bow, and cutteth the spear in sunder; he burneth the chariot in the fire. Then, for a recompense, nation should speak peaceably unto nation, and the people would dwell together with equity. They should beat their swords into ploughshares and their spears into pruninghooks. They would hang up the battle-trumpet. Nation would not lift up the sword against nation, neither should they learn war any more.

Then of a truth the earth would yield her increase. Righteousness and peace should kiss one another. Moreover, not only would all heaven echo the divine cry, but earth should answer it: 'On earth peace, good will toward men.'

Here is a cry from God to man, heaven to earth, the celestial host to the worldly multitude. The cry calls from above for a peace between earth and heaven, between men and God. The occupation of earthly humanity should agree with that of the heavenly host.

But what happened? Herod happened. The chief priests and elders of the people happened. Israel's indifference happened. For the light shined in the darkness, and the darkness comprehended it not. 'He was in the world, and the world was made by him, and the world knew him not. He came unto his own, and his own received him not.'

Nation battled against nation. Peoples warred against peoples. Country fought against country. Power and land were contested. Family strove with family over possession. Men coveted each others' gain. Careers must be forged. Plans made and laid. Brethren rose up indignant over the inheritance. To them, it was not a time for peace. 'His own received him not.'

Yet as to these human preoccupations, these material squabbles, the Prince of peace had a word. One saith to him, Master, speak to my brother, that he divide the inheritance with me. And he said unto him — him, notice — Man, who made me a judge or a divider over you? And he saith unto them — them, mark — Take heed, and beware of covetousness: for a man's life consisteth not in the abundance of the things which he possesseth.

So then, as to this present life, the world that now is, as to earthly distinctions, possessions, frictions, wars, squabbles, underdeveloped — or, as they used properly to be called, *heathen* — nations, worldly inequalities, the peacemaker saith 'Man, who made me a judge or a divider over you?' And advises his disciples, Take no thought for your life, what ye shall eat or what ye shall drink; nor yet for your body, what ye shall put on.

Wherefore, he did not come to bring peace in these things. Not at all.

Then what of broken families? Divorced relationships? Errant fathers and sons? Fallen daughters? Class distinctions? The social problem. Is that where he came to bring peace?

Well, he came to bring peace from heaven to earth. But he said 'Think not that I am come to send peace on earth: I came not to send peace, but a sword.' No, peace was between heaven and earth. He came from heaven to bring peace with heaven. Between God and men. And not to degrade that high office by making it a servile handmaid for human relationships. Let those relations, each one of them, ascend to gospel peace. Do not drag gospel peace into servitude to sordid human squabbles.

As to that, 'Suppose ye that I am come to give peace on earth? I tell you, Nay; but rather division.' He is not the coffee-bar social worker of whom the blind and foolish evangelicals fondly dream. He is not that great Robin Hood the greater-than-Marx, that the apostate churches vapidly suppose. No more is he the whining beggar outside the fast-closed door that sentimental liberals fatuously imagine. He is something quite different. And the peace he brings is something else again.

It is between heaven and earth, God and man, that the mediator, the peacemaker, comes. Here the war is found; and here peace must be made. Moreover, he who would make peace by him, must expect no better lot on earth for making it, than he himself received. They did not thank him, and they will not thank us.

Saith he 'Suppose ye that I am come to give peace on earth?' I tell you nay. It is peace with heaven. Peace with God. And for those who close with it, this causeth the contrary on earth. Not peace 'but a sword'. Not that they wish it; but that the world gives it.

Suppose ye that the peacemaker came to give peace on earth? 'I tell you nay, but rather division. For from henceforth there shall be five in one house divided, three against two, and two against three.' That is the earthly effect of the heavenly peace. The world scorns it. Man as a whole rejects it. But the few who receive it, pursue it, and urge it upon the house and family in which they were born. With what effect?

'The father shall be divided against the son, and the son against the father; the mother against the daughter, and the daughter against the mother; the mother-in-law against her daughter-in-law, and the daughter-in-law against her mother-in-law.'

No; as between worldly relations, he gives no peace at all. Rather a sword. Because his peace-making causes those relationships to divide on the issue. Just at this very point I have found virtually the whole of modern evangelicalism to shun the cross in favour of the flesh; aye, and the 'famous' names too. But I tell you and them, heaven is still heaven, God unchanged and eternal, Christ the same, the judgment unaltered, and the word of God abideth.

So then, the peacemaker makes peace between individuals, and God. It may — and often does — please him to save whole households. 'Thou shalt be saved and thy house.' But this can only be as each individual member separately and distinctly looks up alone and sues for peace by Jesus Christ. In and of itself it is not peace between families, groups, or nations.

Very, very often, in an unconverted household previously happy in alienation from God, or in a superficial 'evangelical' or worldly-religious household, a sound and spiritual conversion making genuine peace with God will cause a breach in the family. 'And a man's foes shall be they of his own household.' It is not sought — their peace is sought — but it is found.

The 'committals' and 'conversions' of modern evangelism are so shallow and trivial that hardly a ripple is felt upon the surface. Indeed the world welcomes them: they confirm worldliness. But the real thing from the true peacemaker causes a veritable sword. Make no mistake. I tell you the truth in Christ, and lie not.

Because it is resented when one is regenerated by the Holy Ghost and brought to genuine peace in Christ, this causes a rift in family relationships. The old alienation is shown up, the more so as the new convert sets to work with a will to see his family really saved. If they are 'evangelicals' the false 'peace-peace' of dead profession is rent asunder by the lively new convert. The lightly healed wound of old complacent 'Christian' parents broken open and the stink arises again from the unhealed wound of old nature. It is all far too much for those sleeping their way to hell, and, 'a man's foes shall be they of his own household.'

But if so, his friends are the household of God. True peace brings the new-born soul into unity with the children of God. Concord with the brethren brings in sweet heavenly relationships where before there were none. Nature is scattered but the disciples are united. That peace. Peace like a river. Perfect peace.

Of this peace, there shall be no end.

Is it any wonder that 'blessed are the peacemakers'?

'∴ for they shall be called the children of God.'

There is the usual translators' confusion over 'children' and 'sons'. Ignorant of the vast spiritual significance of 'sonship' as opposed to the important 'children', these Anglican churchmen often confounded the two together. Well; ignorance is one thing: though I would have thought it inexcusable in betitled, berobed, behonoured 'Masters in Israel'. But when one word means 'children' and another 'sons', to confound the two together out of caprice is another thing altogether. But what do you expect?

The Greek word for 'Son' is υἱός. It means Son. It has been translated Child, fifty times; Foal once; 'son', one hundred and twenty times; and Son, two hundred and ten times. The like confusion is in the cognate υἱοθεσία uniformly translated to mean the very thing it is absolutely essential to contradict. In that case, it is really dreadful, the way the ignorant carelessness results in completely undermining the purpose of God, grace of God, counsels of God, and work of Christ. Of that, I expect to speak elsewhere in my doctrine.

The Greek for 'Child' or 'Children' suffers the same confounded clerical arbitrary confusion. Why? Why be so perverse? It is in the nature of the cleric. Τέκνον means nothing but 'child'. So therefore our great doctors have translated it child, seventy-seven times; daughter once; and son, twenty-one times.

What ought to have happened, what the most elementary fidelity would have caused to happen, was this: υἱός, son, three hundred and eighty-one times. Τέκνον, child, ninety-nine times. Any fool can see that. It is the clergymen that have the problem. But if their sight were that straight, how could they remain hired clergymen? Hence the innate optical difficulty.

Here in the seventh beatitude — Matthew 5:9 — it is υἱός, therefore sons. It is not children at all in any respect whatsoever. Neither is there any article in the original. They are grown into the stature of sonship. They are not merely born with the right and title: they are grown into the measure and reality. A babe may be born a son. But

257

the responsibilities of that heirship in practice and fruitfulness to the father are another thing altogether. That maturity 'the measure of the stature' is indicated by 'sons'. So the translators put 'children'.

The blessing of the peacemakers is that they shall be called sons of God. Not 'the' sons; just 'sons'. As sons of God it is a question of likeness to *the* Son. Notice how the absence of the article — in the original — stresses this. They have grown into the maturity of real likeness to him as brethren. The life of the Father is no longer a tiny infant seed: it is now a mature adult growth. 'Sons of God.' As brethren they are now at length like the Son. As he is, so are they in the world.

By a sevenfold process of ascent, by a perfect degree of growth and maturity, the peacemakers have been brought into conformity with Christ. They live, but not them; it is Christ that liveth in them. Christ has been formed in their hearts by faith. This is evident. His life is their life. His work from the glory is their work on earth. And what is this but *making peace?*

Therefore the peacemakers are called sons of God, because by the Son of God they are exactly fulfilling his work, answering to his chief likeness as the peacemaker, and reflecting his primary activity. If so, doing that, what else should they be called but sons of God? They are doing what he does, by the life with which he does it. Wherefore the peacemakers must be called the sons of God, for none but these fulfil this function with that life.

How selfless they are: benevolent, disinterested, their own ministry is not their concern; their whole interest is in the accomplishment of a peaceful union between God and men.

A peacemaker is one who makes peace between two alienated parties. He is a disinterested and benevolent third party, a kind of mediator.

The best example of this is Jesus the Son of God. He is the one mediator between God and men. But the peacemakers now publish the basis of reconciliation which he wrought long ago at Calvary. They pray day and night with fervour as priests for the effect of union to be wrought at this very present. Moreover they cease not to preach and teach peace by Christ's blood and person as filled moment by moment with the life of the Son of God, who first loved them, and gave himself for them.

Blessed are the peacemakers: for they shall be called the sons of God.

Sons of God!

So then, the sevenfold character of the true disciple, the real Christian, has been opened to us in the first seven beatitudes by the only one qualified to speak upon the subject: The Master.

And I know that the Lord hath given me the tongue of the learned to teach his doctrine. I know that I have spoken a word in season by the word of the Lord. I can testify that he wakeneth morning by morning. My prayer and cry has prevented the dawning. I have ceased not to labour in the night seasons for the good of the soul of my reader. God is witness. The day will declare it. Truly I can say, he wakeneth mine ear to hear as the learned.

The Lord God hath opened mine ear, and I was not rebellious.

Now may he fulfil the ardent heart's desire of the reader's servant, and lead the reader by the same seven steps of ascent into a large place, for his holy name's sake. The Lord bless the reader.

In the next and final two beatitudes there follows a description of the lot of such disciples — who have ascended these seven degrees — in the world at large. This is their earthly portion. The eighth and ninth beatitudes show how the family, street, district, town, county, nation and world; how the brethren, hall, assembly, congregation, chapel and church, will be likely to treat them. Unless in the latter case they are found, as they ought to be found, cleanly separated from unregenerate and worldly religion and met together in unity. Even so worldly religion will continue to scandalise, tale-bear, tell lies, spread rumours and persecute in every way possible.

But this is the lot of the godly, as Christ tells you, and it is the truest mark by which they may be distinguished from the hypocrite. The true disciples of Jesus Christ, real Christians, will be persecuted to the exact measure in which they are manifest and apparent to the world and to false religion.

This is as inevitable as it is unmistakable. It marked the Lord Jesus. It marked the apostles. It marked the early Christians. And it will mark real Christians to the very last day. The absence of it is the mark of Cain, the mark of the beast, the six six six on the dead-letter hypocrite. Be warned, reader.

8th. 'Blessed are they which are persecuted for righteousness' sake: for theirs is the kingdom of heaven.'

This is the first of the two persecution beatitudes, distinct from each other not because of any difference in the kind of persecution, but because the cause of this opposition is different. Here the cause of persecution is 'righteousness' sake'.

In the eighth and ninth beatitudes the mood changes completely. Before it was active; the disciples were this, or were doing it. Now the mood is passive; the disciples are doing nothing, it is being done to them.

The first cause of persecution is 'righteousness' sake'. Therefore the result of the sevenfold perfection of the godly character is that righteousness is distinguished to such a degree that it becomes thoroughly offensive to the world and worldly religion.

This always has been the first cause of persecution. 'Cain brought of the fruit of the ground an offering unto the LORD. And Abel, he also brought of the firstlings of his flock and of the fat thereof. And the LORD had respect unto Abel and to his offering: but unto Cain and to his offering he had not respect.' Well, Cain was a worshipper wasn't he? He offered, didn't he? A proper offering, wasn't it? Well, what's with the favouritism, then? 'And Cain was very wroth, and his countenance fell.'

'And Cain talked with Abel his brother.' There is no doubt about that, and a very one-sided conversation it must have been too. But no doubt sufficient to elicit the fact of the spiritual perception of his brother as opposed to his own arrogant and blundering ineptitude. That is, as regards discerning the will of God about the mode of true worship. Once determined, Abel justified, Cain shamed, only one thing could happen. 'Cain rose up against Abel his brother, and slew him.'

Now, why did he slay him? The apostle John tells us: 'Cain was of that wicked one, and slew his brother.' Wicked one? But he was a worshipper, wasn't he? He offered didn't he? It was a proper offering, wasn't it? Therefore you see that these things alone are not enough.

But 'wherefore slew he him? Because his own works were evil' — mark that, his worship and offering, his works, were *evil* — 'and his brother's righteous.' That is it, Righteous. Therefore Cain slew Abel for *righteousness'* sake.

There you have the first and clearest instance of one being persecuted for righteousness' sake. If so, it stood in the difference between two worshippers, and their respective ways of worship. One was of human invention; and God calls it *evil*. The other was by divine revelation; and God calls it *righteous*. For these things' sake, for righteousness' sake, the one brother slew the other.

So you see that 'righteousness' sake' is not a question, here, of the religious and the irreligious. It is a question of the distinction between the religious. It is a matter of discerning the way of worship acceptable to God. And who cares about that today, to search it out?

But I wish to assure the reader, and, if I could, the whole professing church, and all the world besides, of the ultimate, basic, and most true way of acceptance with God. 'Who will render to every man according to his deeds: to

them who by patient continuance in well doing' — as Abel;
and Paul, who wrote these words by the Holy Ghost —
'seek for glory and honour and immortality, eternal life.'
You see that it is not the degree of written revelation and
profession irrespective of the state and purpose of heart
and life. Rather, it is the state and purpose of heart and life
no matter how little the revelation or how faint the gleam
of light.

So many trust in the magnitude of light they have
received. They trust that because they profess it, therefore
God is obliged to save them. But they no more continue
patiently in well-doing, seeking for glory and honour
and immortality, than did Jeremiah's rutting ass in the
wilderness.

Don't these Christian brethren read of what the apostle
warned the Jews? Thou art confident that thou thyself art
a guide of the blind, a light of them which are in darkness,
an instructor of the foolish, a teacher of babes ... thou
therefore that teachest another, teachest thou not thyself?
For he is not a Jew — neither a Christian — which is one
outwardly. Nor is true worship, professing Light. It is what
is *done* about that light from the heart, every moment,
with all the strength, throughout the life.

Now see; will they not persecute me for this righteous
saying?

The apostle Paul continues as to the true and false way
of worship from the beginning of the world to the end of
it, irrespective of the degree of revelation man possesses:

'But unto them that are contentious' — like Cain, who
'talked with' his brother; like carnal Israel, that contended

against the prophets; like some who were 'puffed up',
arguing against the apostle — 'and do not obey the truth,
but obey unrighteousness' ... they *hold* the truth of course.
They *profess* the faith, naturally. But what they *obey* is
unrighteousness. And they persecute the true servants of
the Lord for righteousness' sake.

Well, the Holy Ghost assures such people, brethren,
professing Christians, that, without repentance, they have
something coming to them: 'Indignation and wrath,
tribulation and anguish, upon every soul of man that doeth
evil' — like Cain when he worshipped — 'of the Jew first,
and also of the Gentile.' Not to mention the 'Christian'.

So then, that is the root of persecution for righteousness'
sake. It is the *righteousnesses* of the saints. Not their talk.
And righteousness in respect of their way of worship, of
their sheer unworldliness, and of the determination with
which they persevere as seeing him who is invisible and as
seeking a better country, that is, an heavenly.

They shame the hypocrite; the dead, cold confessor
of truth; they shame the carnal and worldly; the merely
intellectual and doctrinal; they shame the ceremonial and
formal; and also the merely sentimental and soft. That is
why all these in religion and the church — quite apart from
the world — persecute them.

For righteousness' sake.

Yet so much is this the distinguishing mark of the poor,
earnest, serious, God-fearing little flock of Christ, that it is
said:

'Theirs is the kingdom of heaven.'

9th. 'Blessed are ye, when men shall revile you, and persecute you, and shall say all manner of evil against you falsely, for my sake.'

Here the cause of persecution is expressly stated to be 'for my sake'. It is a question of what his disciples have to endure because of their association with him. Of the tenacity with which under shame and reproach they hold to and confess the name of Jesus Christ.

Many are found out by his name. Many will own a church, and speak of going to it. Many vociferously uphold the Bible. Many will confess a preacher, and openly declare their loyalty to him. Many will profess their favourite texts, droning them out *ad nauseam*. Many will declare their cherished theology, loudly proclaiming the system of grace, assembly truth, law, works, plan of salvation, or whatever. Many trumpet protestantism, yet others the Puritans, or else brethrenism. But ask them openly to confess that 'Jesus Christ is my Lord', and so many shuffle and blush with embarrassment, unable to declare their regeneration. Ask them when last they confessed the Saviour's actual name before strangers, acquaintances, neighbours, friends and relations and they are found out by the sheer awkwardness which they must force upon themselves. They cannot say 'Jesus is Lord' rightly or easily. They shuffle and stutter, much like to Ephraimites when made to say, Shibboleth.

But saith Jesus Christ, Whosoever therefore shall confess *me* before men, him will I confess also before my Father which is in heaven. But whosoever shall deny *me* before men, him will I also deny before my Father which is in heaven. And saith the Son of God, Whosoever therefore shall be ashamed of *me* and of *my* words in this adulterous and sinful generation; of him also shall the Son of man be ashamed, when he cometh in the glory of his Father with the holy angels.

It is he himself, directly; his own person, his own name, his own sake. Upon that rest the issues of eternity.

What revilings, what persecutions, what evil speech in times past fell upon those who faithfully confessed and upheld the Lord's name. One may read of such worthies in Fox's Book of Martyrs; once, with The Pilgrim's Progress, and the Authorised Version Bible above all, standard education — and a much superior one at that — for Britons worth the name. Hear the Name confessed in the rising waters of Bladnoch at the Solway; hear it from the blood of the Covenanters, blood that dyed the heather: 'the voice of thy brother's blood crieth unto me from the ground.'

Hear the Name croak from the throat of faithful old Tyndale, strangled by the Jesuits in the Belgian Castle to which they had beguiled him, afterwards to burn his dead body at the stake. Hear the Name solemnly intoned by George Fox and a thousand Quakers, rising from the noisome dark holes into which they had been thrust for refusing in Christ's Name to pay tithes to hired priests of the Church of England. Hear the Name sweetly arise upon a sigh from the dark dungeon into which the lordly bishops had cast the godly John Bunyan.

Hear the Name sung in ten hundred 'unlawful' conventicles upon field, in barns, beneath the trees, within the fens and marshes, in the wild places of England, as the last hope of the spark of the Reformation was snuffed out of Anglicanism and the doors of the Church of England were slammed shut upon the godly Nonconformists. Hear the Name cried the length and breadth of England by the great and godly John Wesley and his fellows, persecuted, abused, mobbed by the rabble raised by the parsons; nevertheless crying bruised but victorious: 'Jesus, the Name high over all!'

Hear the Name roar from a hundred thousand free English throats, sturdy independents all, no bishops, no popes, no episcopates, no presbyteries, no learned doctors, no human learning ruling over them! Hear the roar, I say: 'CHRIST IS ALL!' Hear the Name arise in later sweet meetings of the saints, the first 'Plymouth' brethren, guided by devout J.N. Darby and other of the early ministering brethren. But reviled, ostracised and despised by the clergy and nonconformist ministers alike. And socially — though earls, lords, viscounts, knights were common amongst them — quite, quite unacceptable. But they chose rather to suffer affliction with the poor and despised, but real and reviled, people of God.

And last, but never least; last, and, aye the brightest: — can you not discern the Name writ in wreathen columns of oily smoke, ascending from the shameful burning at Oxford? Discern THE NAME as a cry comes in holy defiance from the midst of the flames in the very teeth of the Papist murderers: 'FEAR NOT, MASTER RIDLEY! WE SHALL THIS DAY LIGHT A CANDLE IN ENGLAND WHICH SHALL NEVER BE PUT OUT.'

No more will it, Master Latimer, no more will it. For Englishmen still live who have caught the gleam and are worth the Name. WORTHY THE NAME. Worthy the Lamb.

Now, all these came out of great tribulation.

And all who live godly in Christ Jesus shall suffer persecution. It is inevitable. It is appointed. 'No man should be moved by these afflictions: for yourselves know that we are appointed thereunto. For verily, when we were with you, we told you before that we should suffer tribulation; even as it came to pass, and ye know.'

It is the clearest mark of the saints, of salvation, of the election of God. Therefore, be glad, and be grateful for it. It is the only way through the gates: for 'we must through much tribulation enter into the kingdom of God.'

Theirs is the kingdom of heaven.

One will say to me, 'No; but the modern world has become much more educated since those old times, the nation is Christianised, persecution has therefore ceased. The offence of the cross is over in these tolerant days. Who is persecuted today? The world has changed, you see.'

To the contrary. It is the church that has changed. It is the ministry that is corrupted. It is the truth that is obscured. Therefore the world tolerates the church, and does not dream of persecution. Because the character of the beatitudes is neither preached nor required.

If it were, they would.

'Rejoice, and be exceeding glad: for great is your reward in heaven: for so persecuted they the prophets which were before you.'

The prophets' function was to recall the people to the testimony of God, in a day when they had departed from it and gone a-whoring after other gods. Invariably they were persecuted for their plainness of speech and the sharpness of the rebukes with which they woke up the truculent and haughty nation. Their greatest persecutors were the false prophets and priests. Yet despite the cutting indictments of the prophets and their lion-like boldness they were at heart broken, melted, sensitive men. Men who wept sore at the departure of Israel, and whose lives were a living sacrifice of long-suffering as they cried and spread their hands all day long to a rebellious people.

They were seldom 'successful'. Never 'popular'. Usually slain.

The prophets were persecuted sore. One time, there were four hundred false prophets in Israel that prophesied before the king, and all their prophecy went one way: to please man and especially the great in the earth. But there was only one Micaiah. He stood alone. He prophesied clean different and clear contrary to every other prophet in Israel. His prophecy went another way altogether. He pleased God alone. He cared nothing for men, and less for the kings of the earth. He prophesied the truth from God, and the four hundred were in error. So they put him in prison.

Now says the Lord Jesus: as they did that to them before you, so they will do to you in turn. But today, in England, who looks even remotely like Micaiah? And what convention, platform, pulpit, assembly, hall, would want him, were there anyone like Micaiah in our own day?

Then there was Elijah. He stood alone on mount Carmel against eight hundred and fifty false prophets. All Israel stood silent to see which way the wind would blow. Elijah the mighty prophet of the LORD contested every one of the four hundred and fifty idolaters who corrupted the pure worship of Jehovah, and at the same time he contested every one of the four hundred worldly hirelings that begged their sustenance from that whore Jezebel's table. But God owned Elijah, and Elijah slew every last one of the false prophets and hirelings. Then he had to flee for his life.

Look how they persecuted the Forerunner, John the Baptist. The Jews sent priests and Levites from Jerusalem. Yes, in their gowns and with their titles, and with their academic degrees in the dead letter, those orthodox corpses sneered down their noses at the living prophet: 'Who are you?' Then to frighten him — they thought — 'That we may give an answer to them that sent us.' Some hope of frightening John. He gave them short shrift. But in the end, between them all, they had his head.

See how they persecuted the Lord Jesus himself! How they envied and hated him, fairly foaming with malice. Seven classes of enemies conspired to hound the Lord all that suffering way to Calvary. Here they are, mark them; for as the Spirit that was in Christ — which they persecuted — lives on in his true servants to this day, so the spirit that filled these sevenfold enemies lives on also, filling their modern counterparts. Can you recognise them?

First there are the haughty Pharisees, whose high doctrine, they consider, sets them apart from others whose intellects and holiness are hardly equal to this exclusive and theologically orthodox circle. Then there are the Scribes, the 'grammarians', the pedlars in the dead letter, their meat is old books. They are always reasoning, arguing, debating about the form and the letter, but they have neither life nor power. Thirdly we see the Chief Priests. Well, these are ceremonial sacramentalists. Their religion hangs upon priesthood, mystery, and repetitive sacrifice. One sacrifice once for all is their nemesis: they see that. Fourthly there are the Elders. What enemies these are! They gnash at Jesus and his disciples for transgressing the 'tradition of the elders', and Jesus 'suffered many things of the elders'. Fifth we find the Herodians, defined as 'A political Jewish party that favoured Greek customs'. How very familiar. Sixth, there are the Sadducees. Here are your liberal theologians, your rational modernists, your expedient moderates. So kind, modern, tolerant. So broad-minded that they came to John's baptism. John sees them and says 'Ye generation of vipers!' Finally there are the Doctors and Lawyers. 'One of them, which was a lawyer, tempted him.' 'A certain lawyer stood up' — certainly; people can see him better. Saith Jesus, Woe unto you! Reply the doctors of the law, *'Thou* reproachest *us?'* How ridiculous; stick to your carpentry. That was and is their diagnosis.

These seven, together, slew the Lord of glory. They represent the range and the various temperaments, classes, ideologies, sects, parties and preferences into which the variety of the flesh will develop in religion. But it is *all* flesh. None of it is of the Spirit, who brings in another thing altogether. Which these, all of them, then persecute as they persecuted Christ and the Spirit that was in him. So to the end of the world. 'As then he that was born after the flesh persecuted him that was born after the Spirit, even so it is now.'

This truth is abundantly illustrated in the life-giving ministry of the apostle Paul. So many false apostles, deceitful workers, Judaisers, legalists, legal gospelists, slandered the apostle and gnashed against him with their teeth. But why? Because God chose Paul and he did not choose them: they chose themselves. God prepared Paul but he did not prepare them: they prepared each other. God put Paul into the ministry but he did not put them into it: they put themselves into the ministry. And hence they persecuted Paul, and those of their spirit persecute those of the Spirit of Paul even unto this day. Why? Because they are so full of envy, and at heart feel that God must have had a case of mistaken identity. They are so much more suitable.

However, Paul's call was from God and not men. It was not from the Lord Bishop, nor from the venerable Presbytery, neither yet from the learned Assembly; it was not from the Conference neither was it from the Union, nor was it from any one Church or group of Churches. *It was from God alone.*

And so was his ministry. 'How that by revelation (it) was made known unto me.' 'I was made a minister, according to the gift of the grace of God.' 'The gospel which was preached of me is not after man. For I neither received it of man, *neither was I taught it*, but by the revelation of Jesus Christ.' Thus his ministry was in the administration and operation of the Holy Ghost. It was according to his own sweet spiritual experience, and his temptations, trials, afflictions and persecutions answered to this experience. So did his comforts and consolations.

Paul's ministry was to the hearts of his hearers, and answered to their poor, mourning, meek, and hungering experiences. He ministered righteousness, peace and joy in the Holy Ghost. His was a soul-establishing testimony, in rich doctrine opening and expounding the pure word of God as filled with the Spirit. The people plainly saw Jesus Christ evidently set forth crucified among them. Glory was about, as Paul set forth the Son of God by the Holy Ghost sent down from heaven.

Out of Paul's belly flowed rivers of living water, within was evidently a well springing up into everlasting life. And they glorified God in him. He gave wondrous accounts of his regeneration. He gave clear testimony of the souls saved under his ministry, now walking in the comfort of the Holy Ghost and in the fear of God.

But how different were the dry, letter-learned, legal preachers who learned from each other and old books. They beat up the dust of death. They flogged down the flail of the law. They moralised their forensic exactitudes. Theirs was a killing ministry, a ministry of stone tables, an administration of death. And at heart, at heart they knew it, and fumed furiously. And saw the life-giving fruitfulness of Paul and raged together, Away with such a fellow from the earth. And Paul ended in prison.

They might appeal to books, the authorities, their schools, degrees; in a word, to men. But Paul shows that his call came from God 'not of men, neither by man'. 'Immediately I conferred not with flesh and blood.' But such a conference is all the call that the poor scribes of men's ordination ever possess. So in their envy they persecute whom God calls, Christ prepares, and the Spirit sends.

Yet look at Moses at the bush. Where was man in that? Consider Samuel at Shiloh; who called Samuel, and put his Spirit upon him, by which he should be taught and in which he should minister? Did Isaiah read 'I saw the Lord high and lifted up, and his train filled the temple'? No, he saw it. And that is where his ministry came from.

Was Amos a student at the Tekoa Bible College when the Lord called him to be a prophet? No. He was a herdsman and a gatherer of sycamore fruit. But THE LORD took him, taught him, gave him vision to see, and sight to prophesy.

What 'varsity trained Jeremiah? 'Before I formed thee in the belly I knew thee; and before thou camest forth out of the womb I sanctified thee, and I ordained thee a prophet unto the nations.' But what of his theological preparation and education? 'Then the LORD put forth his hand, and touched my mouth. And the LORD said unto me, Behold, I have put my words in thy mouth.' But what about a proper library, where should he get his sermons? 'And the word of the Lord *came unto me.*' But, but, but, say the advocates for men's learning and men's looking after God's gospel for him. Now I have a 'but'. *But* God has sent the Holy Ghost to do what they take upon themselves. So Jeremiah says: 'The Lord said, Jeremiah, what seest thou? And I said, I see ...' He *saw* his ministry.

So the men that called, trained, and sent each other threw him into a pit.

Look at Ezekiel. Where did he get his ministry? From visions of Glory. From eating the book. Tell me what college, what book, even what *Bible* can give you that vision? Only God gives it, and he gives it when, where, how and to whom he will. And to the frustrated professional religious teacher who offers himself but is not accepted, this is infuriating. So he persecutes the prophet. Tell me, when Ezekiel ate the book, How did he do it? And how long did it take?

Consider the apostles. Fishermen, a taxgatherer. 'Unlearned and ignorant men'. But they had been with Jesus. Consider Jesus. 'Is not this the carpenter's son?' 'How knoweth this man letters, having never learned?' Well, the plain answer he gives is this 'My doctrine is not mine, but his that sent me.' So they crucified him.

Consider the canvas sewer. Paul. He made tents, not taught scholars. As to all he had learned from Gamaliel or anywhere else 'I count it but dung.' It was darkness. But now he had 'the ministry which I have received of the Lord Jesus'. He was an able minister of the New Testament, not of the letter but of the Spirit. What he dispensed was the dispensation he received from God. And despite his wonderful call, and gifts, for nearly fifteen years he was alone, waiting and learning from his Teacher. The flesh cannot wait. Hence it persecutes what shames its sham.

Enoch the prophet prophesied because he heard somewhat as he walked with God. Noah did the same, and as they took steps together he was warned of God of things not seen as yet. Moses was shown the pattern in the mount, and that was the content of his ministry. Daniel saw the visions of the Lord. Zechariah saw by night. The burden lay on Malachi. And the word of the Lord came to the prophets. But not the hirelings. So some prophets they entreated shamefully, and some they stoned, and some they slew.

What prophet ever stole his sermons from another? But they condemned the false prophets for so doing, and thus were persecuted. What prophet read up all the other prophets, copied bits out of other books, and added quotes from the contemporary academic scene? 'The word of the Lord came unto me,' and they wrote their books by that alone without a sight of another man's work. So saith Paul 'Not to boast in another man's line of things.'

Paul did not get his ministry off a shelf in the library. Nor did Timothy, nor Silas, nor Epaphras, nor Titus, nor Silvanus. But Paul's dry-bones persecutors would fill their sermons from other men's books as they do to this day. And since despite God they are determined to preach, from where else can they fetch their matter?

But what is that to one who received the gospel by revelation, in the power of a mighty salvation, who was led by the Holy Ghost into all truth, and taught within by the Spirit of Truth? What was that to one who turned and saw the Lord in the midst of the seven golden candlesticks, and was told to write what he saw in a book and send it to the angels of the seven churches? What is that to one whose gospel is not of men nor by man, neither is it grave-robbing from dry bones long dead, but marrow and fatness in the Lord? It is the overflowing cruse. It is waters to swim in.

Nevertheless, those were the prophets, and these are the men, that were before you. And that is the way that they were persecuted, and the reason for the persecution, and the kind that persecuted them, ere ever your time came. Now that it is come: REJOICE, AND BE EXCEEDING GLAD: FOR GREAT IS YOUR REWARD IN HEAVEN. 'For so persecuted they the prophets which were before you.'

After all, do *you* know of better company?

¶ Righteousness and the kingdom. Ch. 5:13-48

The remainder of chapter five is concerned with righteousness: the rule of rectitude or uprightness in the kingdom of heaven. A mere glance confirms this. 'The law' ... 'Except your righteousness' ... 'these least commandments' ... 'Thou shalt not kill' ... 'Thou shalt not commit adultery' ... 'Thou shalt not forswear thyself' ... 'Thou shalt love thy neighbour' ... 'The righteous and the unrighteous'. Right through the chapter it is all about the rule of righteousness.

Therefore the first question in the 'Sermon on the Mount' and the whole question of chapter five — after entrance has been made into the kingdom — is that of righteousness. It is the burning, the urgent, the primary question of real disciples, and therefore the one dealt with immediately by the Master: By what rule of righteousness should they walk?

I say, it is a question of the rule of righteousness for the disciple: What is it? Is it that of the scribes and Pharisees? No! 'Except your righteousness shall exceed the righteousness of the scribes and Pharisees, ye shall in no case enter into the kingdom of heaven.' But is it the same *rule* as the scribes and Pharisees only with a new *power* to keep it? No. O, reader, learn this all-essential negative. No! It is *not* the same rule — with a new power to obey — at all.

The vastly all-important truth is that the *rule* is changed for the disciple. Observe: 'It was said by them of old time ... *but* ... I say unto you.' It is not at all a question of new power for the old rule. It is a question of new power for a new rule of righteousness altogether. And on an entirely different basis. Now that Christ is our priest, not only does the power come forth but the rule of righteousness changes. 'For the priesthood being changed, there is made of necessity a change also of the law.' Not only the power, but the rule alters.

The essential thing to grasp is that before the 'Sermon on the Mount' was uttered, *there was already a rule of righteousness in existence.* It was that given by the law. That contained in the commandments. That said to them of old time. That taught by the scribes and Pharisees.

The fact that under the old legal rule of righteousness men failed, is no ground of supposing that Christ has come *merely* to give his people power to keep the old rule so that they should now no longer fail. That is just not true. It is in fact the 'other gospel' of Galatians which supposes that it is true. And to this day there are those who would bring us into bondage and under the rule of law, although they understand neither what they say nor whereof they affirm. I warn you in Christ's name of these people: unable even to put their own case, they use dead men's writings and cunning creeds behind which they hide, meanwhile stupidly screaming 'Antinomian' at us. *They* are the antinomians, who profess a rule of righteousness which neither they nor their fathers were able to keep.

Such a doctrinal error is contrary to the apostles. It is contrary to the Reformation. Such a doctrinal error sets Christ at nought. They make Christ a schoolmaster to bring us to Moses. But God makes Moses a schoolmaster to bring us to Christ. And then Christ becomes the end of the law — the end of it — for righteousness to every one that believeth. Such people assign Christ a task subservient to Moses, and when their Christ has done his work, and they have finished printing 'This is our beloved Moses, hear him,' then these foolish bond children see no man save Moses only.

So then, there was an old rule of righteousness — legal righteousness — given to Israel according to the law. No distinction is made in holy scripture within the integrity of this rule. Although subtle men make a difference between moral, ceremonial and judicial law, scripture knows nothing of this, it is nothing but the tradition of the elders to set at nought the word of God. They do this, so that obvious passages which speak of deliverance from law can be relegated to 'ceremonial' law: and slipping the 'moral' law past the cross, they can then bring us into bondage.

There is no such thing as 'moral' law in Old or New Testaments. There is just the law as such. It came from God by the disposition of angels. It was given by Moses. It is a rule of righteousness for men. It was delivered to Israel. It pertains to men, for this present life and it prescribed righteous works. Its reward was life — extended and blessed human lifetime on earth — and its uttermost curse was death. It had long been in the world in Israel, and when the Lord Jesus spake the Sermon on the Mount he referred to it: but it is quite distinct from the new and different rule of righteousness which is the main content of the sermon.

Therefore there are *two* entirely different rules of righteousness. One had long been written and was that of the law. The other Jesus now states. It is the righteousness of God by Jesus Christ. One was of men striving to please a hidden Jehovah behind the veil. Its works stood in the hopeless task of attaining to legal righteousness in order to be justified. The other rule is that of God dwelling in man and outworking his own character of righteousness from within. This can only occur when a man has been justified by faith and rests in having obtained the Spirit. One is a prescription for men to try to be righteous. The other is the life of God in its own character dwelling in the heart. One is what men ought to have been. The other is what God is. These are two entirely different rules. They cannot be mixed. The first is the proper rule of legal justification for men. It always will be and it cannot be anything else. The other is the outworking of the indwelling righteousness of God. The first is to earn justification with God. The other is because one has been justified by God.

Thus in Matthew chapter five we see that a new rule of righteousness, the law of the Spirit of life in Christ Jesus, a new rule of walk has come into the world by the Messiah. For the law came by Moses, but grace and truth came by Jesus Christ. Messiah's rule for his people is not the law. '*Your* law', saith he to the Jews. Messiah's rule for his people is the Gospel. 'But *I* say unto you.'

It is not legal it is evangelical. It is not the dead letter it is the living Spirit. It is not the ministration of death it is the administration of righteousness. It is not servitude it is sonship. It does not address a veiled Jehovah it proceeds from a revealed Father. It is not for children of Jacob it is for sons of God. It is not in the kingdom of Israel it is in the kingdom of heaven. It is not of the Old Testament at all it is of the New Testament entirely. It is not of law it is of grace. It is not by works it is through faith. It is not Mosaic commandments to them of old time but of Jesus' present pronouncement to his own disciples today. It is not for man in Adam it is for the elect in Christ. It is not for man in the flesh it is for man in the Spirit. It is not for this world it is for the world to come. It is not of time it is of eternity. It is not for this soiled city, Jerusalem below, it is for the holy city Jerusalem above. It is not the striving for the righteousness of the law: it is the consequence of the righteousness of God. It is not 'another gospel' it is *the* gospel. It is a new thing.

The flesh addressed the law and the law addressed the flesh and demanded righteousness on pain of condemnation and death. That is all the law ever can do: 'other gospel' antinomians who claim that it is a 'rule of walk for the Christian' are real heretics: they put the believer back under toiling works for salvation. Whatever they say, that is what the law is for, and that alone, so therefore that is what they do. If their hearers are sincere they groan under the hard yoke, and the harsh bitterness rises. If their hearers are hypocrites like them, they tone down the rule of law, and boast like Pharisees. One or the other. I tell you in the name of the Father, the Son and the Holy Ghost: it is either Christ or Law. In *no form* can you have both. Not without either abrogating law and contemptuously despising its sanctions — which is real antinomianism — or else overturning the cross and setting Christ at nought, which is truly making void the gospel.

It is either Christ or Moses. Either grace or law. Either faith or works. Either gospel or legality. The law in *its entirety* is one thing, and the gospel *entirely without law* is the other thing, and these two can never be mixed. 'I through the law am dead to the law.' 'We are not under the law but under grace.' 'But now we are delivered from the law, that being dead wherein we were held.' The flesh is dead. It is dead on the cross. The law can say no more. It cannot speak past the cross. And we *are* past the cross. Whoso brings the law past the cross to pretend that it speaks to Christians is a liar. He both undoes the death of Christ and overturns the crucifixion. He preaches 'another gospel' of the most pernicious and heretical sort.

Well then, Matthew 5:13-48 is about righteousness, and Messiah handles his doctrine on this wise: The Salt. The Light. The Law. The Contrast. The Conclusion. Now more particularly: —

The Salt and gospel righteousness	vv 13-16
The Light and gospel righteousness	
The Law and gospel righteousness	vv 17-20
The Contrast of gospel righteousness	vv 21-47
The Conclusion of gospel righteousness	v 48

In verses thirteen to sixteen certain are referred to as the Salt and then as the Light. The one is of the earth, the other of the world.

It is said to the disciples 'Ye are' the salt; and 'Ye are' the light. Not 'Ye will be' notice, but 'Ye are'. This to the Jewish disciples. Not exactly as Jews; rather as Jews taken up to be disciples. Still, they were Jews; as yet there was only the Jewish background; and therefore they are spoken to as Jewish disciples against that existent background, the only one comprehensible to their then knowledge. The truth is that *all* the Jews should have been disciples, 'beginning at Jerusalem'. This is part of the background. In a sense here there is through the Jewish disciples, as Jews, a reference to the failure of Israel.

As Jews the disciples represented 'his own' to whom Messiah came. The whole people of the Jews were Israelites; to whom pertained the adoption, and the glory, and the covenants, and the giving of the law, and the service of God, and the promises; whose are the fathers, and of whom as concerning the flesh Christ came. 'Ye' — all of ye, really, it should have been; still the poor, weak remnant before him, 'Ye' — are the salt ... *but.*

282

But the Jews had lost their savour. How was this? What savour was this? The sharp astringency found when true righteousness is the real issue in religion. That prevents corruption. But bring in false, self, righteousness, and there is no savour any longer. 'For they going about to establish their own righteousness, have not submitted themselves unto the righteousness of God. For Christ is the end of the law for righteousness to every one that believeth.' But they believed not, but worked, to have somewhat wherein to boast, and in their self-righteousness they lost their savour. Because they corrupted the true character of righteousness.

Then was there no savour of salt in Israel? Yes, in those few that 'hungered and thirsted after righteousness'. But the rest were blinded. Wherefore? Because they sought it not of faith but works. And so Israel was cut off. And for two thousand years have they not been trodden underfoot of men? And who has risen in their stead in the counsels of God? Real experimental believing Christians.

To change the metaphor to the olive tree of God: 'Boast not thyself against the — broken off — branches.' Why? 'Well; because of unbelief they — the Jews — were broken off, and thou — the Christians — stand by faith. Be not highminded, but fear. For if God spared not the natural branches, take heed lest he also spare not thee.' They thought, God was so obliged to them, it was such a long history, there could be no question of rejection. But they were cut off, the whole nation snapped off. Now, professing Christians, evangelicals are just like they were: *no savour* but audacious temerity mixed with high-minded self-righteousness. Just like them but without their connections. We Gentiles are at that point. Salt without savour. Save for a poor remnant. A remnant with the savour of righteousness. If the earth knew it, like righteous Lot in

Sodom, that remnant is the sole preservative from the threatened collapse.

And light. Salt is in the earth. Light is over the world, shining out like a city on a hill. What is lit up? Righteousness. The righteousness of God. Hear, O Israel, for it is written: 'Abraham believed God, and it was counted unto him for righteousness.' *Four hundred and thirty years before the law.* But you saw nothing, so busy were you corrupting that law — which was supposed to bring the knowledge of sin — into a warped form of tradition and doctrine for self-righteous Jews to boast in: you saw nothing. Not till Paul brought out the meaning. No light. Israel. No light. Under a bushel you put that sacred light, while you busied yourself with your traditions. And when Righteousness personified came, you put out the Light of the World. And for two thousand years you have paid for it, for your candlestick is utterly taken away.

Now, ye Gentiles, now where are you as to light on righteousness? Better? Or worse?

Verses seventeen to twenty, The law and gospel righteousness.

Here the operative words are Law, Prophets, Commandments, Righteousness; and over against these, 'I say unto you.' This raises the question of relationships between the two.

Does the fact that Messiah begins to 'say unto you', make the commandments obsolete? God forbid. It establishes the commandments. Then doth the coming of Messiah destroy the prophets? Certainly not. He did not come to destroy but to fulfil.

Then doth Christ abrogate the law, or — which is the same thing — remove its penalty and so reduce it to moral advice for Christians? Absolutely not: that would be illegal. To the contrary, while heaven and earth stand Christ magnifies the law and makes it honourable. Then how can his disciples be delivered from it?

Because its every word, its last word, is exhausted and stopped by that substitutionary broken body on the tree. Its last word, its final sting, its most vindictive curse, is death. Then it can say no more. *It can demand nothing from a dead man.* How can it? The law is there in all its majesty. But the dead man is not. The dead man is removed from view to the grave. And *law cannot speak beyond the grave.* But that is the Christian's position: beyond the grave. 'For ye are dead, and your life is hid with Christ in God': the Christian's position is beyond the grave. Thither, law cannot follow.

Thus the law is honoured. But so are the saints delivered.

Well then, what of the commandments? Shall we do evil that good may come? What? God forbid. Whoso saith it, his damnation is just. But if we are dead to the law, how do the commandments apply? *They* do not apply. Notwithstanding, the righteous requirement of the law can never be less than righteous. However, quite apart from law, there is righteousness and to spare when the Spirit of the Father fills heart and mind. Therefore since Christ brings in a righteousness far superior, far higher — through indwelling those whom God has justified — it follows: *that* righteousness will *include* the righteous requirement of the law, but far transcend it. And not in order to be justified. But because we are justified.

Therefore the righteous requirement of the law is fulfilled in us who walk not after the flesh, but after the Spirit. Fulfilled, not merely by coming up to the rule of the commandment. Rather going far beyond it, as indwelt by the love of God; that divine righteousness proper to the divine life infinitely transcends the commandment which God gave and soars to the heart of the God who gave it. The legal rule of righteousness is the bare prohibitive commandment: the Christian rule is 'Be ye therefore perfect, even as your Father which is in heaven is perfect.' Two different rules, one of death the other of life. But there is a righteous requirement in what condemns the transgressors to death, even though it is never fulfilled by those under law. And this is what is more than answered, far more, and more than fulfilled, it is utterly transcended in Christ, by way of the indwelling Spirit answering to the word of gospel righteousness.

Hence it is written, Except your righteousness shall *exceed* the righteousness of the scribes and Pharisees, ye shall in no case enter into the kingdom of heaven. Their righteousness was a legal rule which neither they nor anyone else under it ever kept. All who are under that rule are dead transgressors and nothing else, whether they are Jews or professing Christians. Whether they claim to be justified or not. The law is a rule of justification for the flesh that no flesh ever kept. If the 'justified' turn to it — though they claim its penalty was removed at the cross — then in fact they overturn that cross, necessarily walk past it, undo divine justification, and apply to the rule of self-justification. Meanwhile they get themselves under the curse. Still, this suits the pride of the flesh and agrees with the hauteur of the hypocrite. Sulphur suits his nose.

It is not what a man says neither what he theorises. It is what he is that counts. It must be said of many, 'What you are speaks louder than what you say.' Many trumpet total depravity, thunder divine sovereignty, trill limited atonement, and talk about unconditional election. But because they actually turn to the old dead letter, the law of a carnal commandment, the 'moral' law as they call it, they *show in fact* their boasting pride in their own righteousness and prowess. What they *are* speaks louder than what they say. Whereas, vice-versa, many *theoretic* Arminians show the very contrary to what they theorise. The wise have always recognised this.

The acid test is whether a man applies — whatever he claims — to that old legal rule which requires righteousness from him; and therefore is self-righteous. Or whether a man is filled with the Spirit of life in Christ Jesus, and walks by this rule of regeneration; in which case righteousness glows through him. The acid test, I say, is this: Except *your* righteousness shall exceed the righteousness of the scribes and Pharisees, ye shall in no case enter into the kingdom of heaven.

Now follow verses twenty-one to forty-seven. The contrast of gospel righteousness.

Three times over the Lord Jesus states 'Ye have heard that it was said by — or rather, to — them of old time.' This statement is followed respectively by 'Thou shalt not kill,' 'Thou shalt not commit adultery' (here there is an appendix on divorce) and 'Thou shalt not forswear thyself.' This takes from verses 21-37. After this — and between verses 38-47 — twice more Jesus states 'Ye have heard that it hath been said,' leaving out 'by them of old time'. A little less force, perhaps, than the preceding and fuller threefold statements. These last two are followed by, respectively, 'An eye for an eye, and a tooth for a tooth,' and 'Thou shalt love thy neighbour, and hate thine enemy.'

These statements — three major and two minor — are not the contrast of gospel righteousness. They are *that with which gospel righteousness is contrasted.*

How?

By this formula: 'But I say unto you.' That is the contrast. Six times over Jesus repeats these words, each time after stating what had been taught to the Jews concerning the law of God given by Moses. Immediately. following the three major statements 'Ye have heard that it hath been said to them of old time,' Jesus says, 'But I say unto you.' Additionally those words are spoken in the appendix on divorce. Again, twice over 'But I say unto you' follows after the minor 'Ye have heard that it hath been said.'

So then, six times in all Jesus asserts 'But I say unto you.' In the previous teaching on the law and gospel righteousness — at verse twenty — it may appear to the casual reader that there was a preliminary utterance of these words, but actually the Greek construction is quite different. In fact the words are stated six times only in this form 'But I say unto you.' Why six? The Lord from heaven reserves the last word to be spoken immediately from the glory. The 'you' to whom he speaks varies from time to time, and place to place, and from generation to generation. But when his living voice sounds personally to 'you' perfection will be brought in.

From what has been said it is crystal clear that this is *not* Jesus' new spiritual interpretation of the law, as opposed to the old outward interpretation of the scribes. Quite apart from overthrowing the New Testament, such a view is exegetically ridiculous.

It would presuppose a previous scribal interpretation which 'Ye have heard'. But, 'Thou shalt not kill' and 'Thou shalt not commit adultery' are not scribal interpretations.

'Ye have heard that it was said to them of old time, Thou shalt not kill; and whosoever shall kill shall be in danger of the judgment.' That is not an interpretation of the scribes. That is the law of God which the scribes and Pharisees then set about to interpret. But Jesus does not quote what they set about. Rather he quotes the thing itself, the law itself, the very commandment.

Now in contrast to that commandment — not an interpretation of the scribes about it: the very thing itself — I say, in contrast to that commandment the Lord Jesus says *'But ...'* If Jesus had quoted an *interpretation* of the commandment and said, They say that, but I say this, I would agree he might have been contrasting his true interpretation with that false one. However, this is not the case. He actually contrasts what Moses said — which he quotes — with what he, Jesus, now says in his New Testament doctrine. Had he contrasted his interpretation of the law with that of the scribes, he would have been correctly interpreting the law. But since he quotes the law

itself and then contrasts what he says with that, it follows
he is delivering an entirely NEW rule of righteousness.
Therefore we see two rules of righteousness. Not a new
spiritual interpretation of the one old rule.

Under the law Jehovah, utterly veiled in cloud and
smoke, said one thing. But in the gospel the Son of God,
plainly revealed, and the Father made known, saith another
thing altogether. The legal commandment saith *that* to
Israel. But. But Jesus says *this* to his disciples. Here is seen
the contrast of gospel righteousness with that of the legal
rule.

The integrity of the law faced with the value of human
life declares the specific commandment 'Thou shalt not
kill,' and appends to this the penal sanction 'Whosoever
shall kill shall be in danger of — or liable to — the
judgment.' What judgment? The judgment of the law upon
the murderer. It is death. The convicted murderer —
liability established — shall be put to death. That is what
the law required, and that is what the judges should exact,
for it is right. It is nothing whatsoever to do with the last
judgment.

'But I say unto you.' What? Let off the murderer with a
caution? Abrogate the law? Dismiss its sanction? Make
void its penalty? Show 'Christian compassion' and put the
convicted murderer in prison for a little while, or hospital
for psychiatric treatment, or under some probationary
scheme? God forbid! Who will make the Lord Jesus author
of such vile unrighteousness? Cursed be he, whosoever doth
this.

What then? The Son of God brings in a gospel rule of
righteousness infinitely beyond the mere 'Thou shalt not

kill.' He does not mitigate the sentence of the law. He deepens the character of the subject to a purity beyond what the law dreamed of or considered feasible for men. It is not feasible for men. It is feasible only for sons of God.

Howbeit, not one jot or tittle of the law alters, for all that. Nothing falls to the ground. What happens is that for the disciple the law is transcended by the gospel.

Still the flesh is there: suppose men should flaunt the gospel rule? Listen: 'He that despised Moses' law died without mercy under two or three witnesses. Of how much sorer punishment, suppose ye, shall he be thought worthy, who hath trodden under foot the Son of God, and hath counted the blood of the covenant, wherewith he was sanctified, an unholy thing, and hath done despite unto the Spirit of grace?'

Consider, Whosoever is angry with his brother without a cause — lightly — shall be in danger of the judgment. The same penalty as the law demanded for murder! That is how deep the gospel rule regulates and how solemn is its regulation. What the law demands against the red-handed murderer, the gospel proposes for the angrily contentious. It is not a question of whether it is exacted or not: it is a question of how much deeper the gospel goes than law and of how much more serious it is to flaunt the gospel word than the legal precept.

Mind you, it is not anger absolutely that is condemned. It is anger 'without a cause'. If Christian disciples are not angry 'with a cause' they are just as guilty as if they were angry without one. Soft, smarmy, jelly-like and characterless insipidity — supposedly the goal of the liberal evangelical — is just as innately satanic as the raging murderer. Therefore, in a just cause 'be ye angry'. Only, 'sin not'.

Now notice another complete contrast between the gospel rule and the law. Under the law, as the sin increased in seriousness, so the penalty became more severe, even unto death. But under the gospel, the reverse is true. As the sin decreases, so the penalty becomes more severe, even unto hell fire. 'Anger; Raca; Fool!' From implacable anger, the intensity tones down to spiteful vituperation. From that, to mere contemptuous dismissal. The assize varies also. Appear before the judges of your town; appear before the Sanhedrin of the nation; appear before the great assize at the Day of Judgment. Their respective penalties? The death penalty. Death in national ignominy and shame. Hell fire. The duration? With the first two, a short but painful departure out of this world. With the last one, everlasting torment world without end.

The passage is couched in terms which the Jewish disciples could comprehend. The judgment of the elders, sitting to judge in the gate. The Sanhedrin — no longer the wise elders of the town or area — the choice in wisdom out of the whole nation, gathered for judgment in council at Jerusalem.

This principle is seen in the case of the gift left at the altar, upon remembrance of a brother wronged. It was the Jewish altar, with a sacrificial gift brought according to the law. It may be a bullock, an ox, a lamb, or a goat. It might be a burnt offering, or a peace offering. It could be fine flour for a meat offering. Whatever 'I will have mercy and not sacrifice.' All relations with all brethren everywhere must be right — perfect — and absolutely clear, before God will entertain the presentation of the sacrifice.

292

And if this is true of the gifts and offerings typical of Calvary, it is doubly true of the sacrifice of Christ at Calvary. But if true, it is rarely believed. Two things have happened over the decades spanning the collapse of the true testimony into the decadence of modern evangelism and liberal evangelicalism.

First, repentance has been dispensed with as irrelevant to faith. 'Salvation by faith alone', originally stressed to guard the truth that it is 'without works', slowly came to mean — in the unspoken cant unique to the religious — salvation by faith alone; that is, 'without repentance being necessary'. The second thing that has happened is that faith has been divorced from The Faith. Doctrine, both as to the objective truth of Christ, and the subjective effects of that truth, has been shelved.

We are left with this sickly subjective decadence which most resembles the very worst kind of fatuous sentimentality. This is distinguished by nothing more conspicuous than a vacant loose grin supposed to convey 'joy'. A kind of mindless but limited self-indulgence. And what there is of will being fixed in the resolution to avoid every issue and controversy and agree with everything at once.

This 'evangelicalism' is convinced that everything will be all right. Hell is never mentioned. Because 'God' cannot really mean it, you know: it was a sort of vague threat for the middle-ages — before proper state-education, you see — to keep them in order before light dawned ... But you know, he would not really have actually *done* it. You see, God is not so much love, as universal forgiveness. And if you think Calvary is necessary, well, that's fine, just get your card stamped, 'decision taken'. Now, be careful not to put this stamp in the 'committal' box, instructions for which will follow later. That's: Later, Box 666, Blind Alley, Babylon.

Now, make no mistake. Repentance towards God is commensurate with faith in the Lord Jesus Christ. God will accept no man's presentation of the sacrifice of Christ at Calvary, until that man is *absolutely right with his fellows.* 'Faith' will never be accepted from the impenitent. Moreover if one that is called a brother think to hold the merits of Jesus' death by faith, but yet remains unjustly angry in his heart, or bitter and spiteful in his tongue, or contemptuous with his lips, let him think again. Let him take heed to Jesus' warnings, which take precedence over that man's fail-safe schemes. Let him plough up his fallow ground, and sow not among thorns. Whilst it remains in front of the face and feet, there is still a heaven to gain and a hell to lose. Keep the faith. And keep penitential.

Verses twenty-seven to thirty-two follow. This passage falls into two parts, marriage and divorce. First Jesus states what the Jews had been taught as to the law of God and doctrine of Moses. Next in contrast he teaches his own doctrine, not contradicting the righteousness in the commandment, but soaring way above and over its limitations: 'But I say unto you.' 'I', being the Apostle of the New Covenant; and 'You', being his own called disciples. And the things which he says, being the doctrine of that covenant.

The subject is adultery, and therefore the scope is prohibition in relation to another man's wife. That holds good throughout the passage.

Another thing. This was spoken against a Jewish back-ground. It is that which is taken up — not contradicted —

to become the stage upon which the Christian doctrine is then propounded.

It is vital to notice that this teaching is addressed to men, not women. It is men who are held responsible in these relations in this passage. They were not to blame the woman. Not that she might not be blame-worthy; but at any cost the man is responsible to keep himself clean.

The last general observation is this. There could be no question of divorce rights for women. The passage simply does not apply to this modern practice. Such a liberty was unthinkable. Divorce was for men and men only, and Christ had somewhat to say of their wicked abuse of it, and of the evils that followed from the malpractice.

The law of Jehovah forbad the committing of adultery. No Israelite was to defraud his brother by stealing his wife, or conniving secretly to lie with her. She was his brother's woman, not his, and all the majesty of Jehovah stood behind his brother's right. It was folly in Israel, and wickedness against the law of the Lord for a man to fornicate with the wife of another.

'But I say unto you, That whosoever looketh on a woman to lust after her hath committed adultery with her already in his heart.' Here again these deceitful clergymen have translated so as to misconstrue Christ's words, and give an impression which he never intended.

In passing, someone may say, Why do you stand up for the Authorised Version then? It is not primarily the Authorised Version for which I stand, but Tyndale — not a committee; a man — whom God raised up to give us the Bible in English, from whom the translators borrowed.

Moreover I do not see what that has got to do with the High and Mighty Prince James, either. But I honour pious and humble Tyndale, who died for God's work in him and God's word by him, for he provided the basis of the Authorised Version.

Quite apart from that, it is the *Greek text* that to me validates the Authorised Version above all. That text, the *Textus Receptus*, was the text of the Reformers, and God gave and mightily used it to raise up his word. That text, and the Authorised Version which is translated from it, was used of God in countless reformations and revivals. Nothing else has been. God has authorised it. That is why I uphold it. But God authorised the throne of David, yet wicked men afterwards filled it. So, up with the throne and out with the malicious occupants. So, up with the Authorised Version and out with the unauthorised clergymen's mistakes.

The Authorised Version is not perfect, but it is far and away the best we have, and the one which God has used for real conversions and true outpourings of the Spirit. It is the only widely available English version which is translated from the text God gave to the Reformers. It is the text the Holy Ghost used and uses. All the others are translated from the altered and erroneous Greek text of unbelieving academics who could show no regeneration and whom God did not use. Nor has he used the results of their strivings for fame in the academic world. Nor has he justified the financially-orientated constant republishing of various 'Bibles' ever since. When will the saints learn that 'modern scholarship' in biblical things is a euphemism for infidel speculation with a view to financial gain and academic ambition?

However I admit freely that the Authorised Version has

certain blemishes. When I see them revealed by the original, I explain them, and to the best of my ability, correct them, meanwhile warning of the traits in the translators that let slip the truth and brought in the error. So if I am wrong, reject it. But if I am right, why the argument?

Why have I stopped to say this here? Because it should not be translated 'whosoever looketh on a *woman* to lust after her hath committed adultery with her already in his heart.' Who has not looked on the girl he desires to marry, and desired — exactly the same Greek word as 'lusted' — her in his heart? Is that condemned then? What married man has not looked upon his own wife, and desired, lusted, after her in his heart? Is this wrong? No, it is not, and frustrated old dry-stick clergymen should not over-compensate for their deficiencies, sucking in their inhibited lips, and imply that it is. It is not a fair translation of what the text says, and it is certainly not what Jesus meant. Marriage is honourable in *all*, and *the bed* undefiled. If you can have a marriage-bed without desire — 'lust'; it is exactly the same — then I am sorry for your wife.

Consider. In verse twenty-seven, it is 'adultery' therefore with somebody's wife. In verse thirty-one it says 'wife'. But that is the same Greek word exactly as the one translated 'woman' in 'Whosoever looketh on a *woman* to lust.' The same word exactly in a context totally occupied with marriage and concerned with men and married women. If the passage is speaking about a 'wife' when it opens, and when it closes, and the same Greek word translated 'wife' is arbitrarily translated 'woman' so as to extend the case of adultery *to every occasion* upon which a man looks to desire, then it makes a man an adulterer over his fiancée or wife. Not only ridiculous, it is wicked. The word γυνή has been translated wife ninety-two times and woman one hundred and twenty-nine times. Here context and consistency demand the translation 'wife' not 'woman'. Besides if it were 'woman' it would not be adultery. It would be fornication. Since it is adultery, it must be 'wife'.

The word 'lust' too. Lust is not necessarily wrong. We read of Jesus, angels, apostles, and saints all 'lusting'. Only then the translators render *exactly the same Greek word* used for 'lust', as 'desiring'.

It is the forbidden character of the object desired that makes desire wrong. The desire itself is merely constitutional, having no moral character in itself. To desire a woman, lawfully, as one's wife, or to take her to wife, this is not wrong. But to desire a woman that belongs to another man, that is his wife, that is wrong. And saith Christ to his disciples, for you to keep the exterior commandment in your bodies, but desire another person's wife in your hearts, that is all one as if it were actual adultery.

Someone may say, Well, if Tyndale was the basis of the Authorised Version — and you think so much of him — why did he put 'Whosoever looketh upon a woman', then? He didn't.

Tyndale put this 'Whosoever looketh on a wyfe, lustinge after her, hath committed advoutrie with hyr alredy in his hert.' That was in 1525. In 1611 the king's hired clergymen put 'Whosoever looketh on a woman to lust after her hath committed adultery with her already in his heart.' A step right back from Tyndale, whom God raised up not far off a century before.

God gave us Tyndale, and the king took note, and

ordered his bishops to give us King James, taking cognisance of the great English Martyr. But, Your Majesty, God needed no help from you, and the poor saints among your subjects would have been well content, and done better, with godly Tyndale's translation alone.

One may ask, Why did the 1611 translators change from Tyndale's 'wyfe' to the incorrect 'woman'? In the King James' tradition the Great Bible (1539) comes next after Tyndale, and that is even stronger: 'But I say unto you that whosoever loketh on another man's wyfe to lust after her, hath commytted advoutrye with her all ready in hys hert.'

Then from whom did the change come, which caused the Authorised — by King James, incidentally — Version translators to reject Tyndale and the Great Bible, and put 'woman' for 'wyfe'? Calvin. It came from Calvin. He used to lean over the pulpit with dry French authoritarianism and a leather cap, and precisely deliver moralising strictures upon the people putting them under this yoke. The Frenchman in Switzerland changed it from 'wyfe' — the original English and correct translation — to 'woman' in the Geneva Bible in 1560. From then on the rest were whipped into line by various assemblies, councils and the like. Or if not, there were always the troops.

In verses twenty-seven to thirty, no penalty for adultery is mentioned. The 'but I say unto you' takes the gospel rule of righteousness to the heart, as opposed to the legal prohibition of the act. Adultery to the disciple becomes the threefold interior combination of imagination, passion, and intention. Given these three in wilful conjunction — albeit under the most pious, serious and restrained exterior, and with the most impeccable outward conduct — adultery is regarded as having taken place.

If such a practice — heart adultery — once should be found to have gained the grip of habit, it is better literally to maim oneself in this life, to cut off or pluck out a part of one's body for this short uncertain pilgrimage, than risk the hell of fire in the next life. The consequences of such a dreadful judgment stand in bodily resurrection world without end, as physically raised to last as long as the unquenchable fire, as long as the undying worm, as long as the endless ages of eternity. It is not 'thy whole soul should be cast into hell.' It is 'thy whole *body* be cast into hell.' Hence this demonstrates a physical resurrection. And if so, then an everlasting equivalent of a literal, material fire.

The disciples receive this terrible warning, for it is addressed to them. The heart must be clean. It must be purged. One dare not indulge its natural propensity for uncleanness. The ultimate prospect is too fearful even to contemplate. This applies to the Christian, the believer.

> 'But fornication, and all uncleanness, or covetousness, let it not be once named among you, as becometh saints;
> 'Neither filthiness, nor foolish talking, nor jesting, which are not convenient: but rather giving of thanks.
> 'For this ye know, that no whoremonger, nor unclean person, nor covetous man, who is an idolater, hath any inheritance in the kingdom of Christ and of God.
> 'Let no man deceive you with vain words: 'For because of *these things* cometh *the wrath of God* upon the children of disobedience.
> 'Be not *ye* therefore partakers with them.'

No plan of salvation, no assurance of redemption, no doctrine of justification, no profession of conversion, no reckoning on Calvary's cross, no presuming on Jesus' blood will save the man that wilfully continues in sin, who deliberately goes on committing adultery in his heart. Let the unclean and the adulterer be warned. For all his Christian insurance scheme, the lake of fire yawns beneath his feet. And unless he repent, thoroughly cleansing his impure heart for good, in the resurrection he will assuredly be cast into the everlasting fire. Then he will never see God: only outer darkness. Let him strive rather for the blessedness of the pure in heart. For they shall see God.

As to using a divorce paper to get around the technical problem of a man not being called an adulterer when he casts out his wife to take another woman: it is a rotten, evil thing to do to one's lawful spouse. Moses never meant that writing of divorcement for men's indulgence: he meant it rather for women's protection.

'But I say unto you.' If a disciple takes advantage of the law of Moses, and divorces his wife, he makes her an adulteress. The Lord will not hold that man guiltless, but will be a swift avenger of the poor woman. Moreover, despite the piece of paper declaring the divorce, she is still regarded by the Lord as her husband's. Anyone marrying her not only commits adultery himself but also causes her to commit adultery, so long as the true husband shall live. However, if she should commit fornication herself, then her husband is not obliged in such circumstances to tolerate her. He may put her away with the Lord's authority.

In verses thirty-three to thirty-seven the last of the three major contrasting statements appears: 'Again, ye have heard that it hath been said by them of old time, Thou shalt not forswear thyself, but shalt perform unto the Lord thine oaths.'

This is what David meant when he said, For thou, O God, hast heard my vows. He meant it, because having made a vow to the Lord, invariably he returned with an offering, an oblation, a peace offering, and performed the same. David never forswore himself by failing to fulfil what he had promised to the Lord. Having made his oath, he determined to keep it,

> 'I will go into thy house with burnt offerings:
> I will pay thee my vows,
> 'Which my lips have uttered, and my mouth
> hath spoken, when I was in trouble.
> 'I will offer unto thee burnt sacrifices of
> fatlings, with the incense of rams; I will offer
> bullocks with goats. Selah.'

He had not then done it; he had made vows, and sworn when he was in trouble, that if God should deliver him, he would render such-and-such to the Lord and in the presence of the people by way of thanksgiving. Now he has been delivered. Does he, like multitudes, straightway forget his adversity, his cry for help, and the Lord's wonderful deliverance? No. Not at all. He says, 'I will pay thee my vows.'

And even more so: I will sing praise unto thy name for ever, that I may daily perform my vows. He will never forget, do you see, never forget. He is determined: 'Unto thee shall the vow be performed.' Neither will David delay: I will pay my vows unto the Lord now. Now. David fulfilled what was said unto them of old time. He kept his promises to God. He fulfilled his vows in their times. He did not forswear himself. He performed unto the Lord his oaths.

That was David; but his like was rare. The more common amongst the people was the natural hypocrite, a man for all seasons, whose line has not been extinguished but even now flourishes as the green bay tree. Having the form of religion, he dare not go too far. But being a natural man, he will go as far as he can. He will not quite dare to swear by the Lord when he vows to stop this thing, or give up that, do the other, or perform something else. He dare not, because his treacherous heart tells him even whilst the oath is hot upon his lips, Well, what will you do when you want it again? Or, But if you give it up, look how much it will cost; give something else; something small, man, it's all the same.

How can he reconcile the word of his lips to the Lord, with the voice of his heart to himself? On the one hand, the religious image in which he preens himself demands a great sacrifice to the Lord. On the other, the snivelling selfish liar that skulks within his heart sniggers, You needn't think I am giving that up, old boy, because I am not. And the old boy's problem is this: he knows who is the stronger, who is going to win. Is it the hypocrite in the mirror, or the deceiver in his heart? You know.

A compromise is called for. A mediator, one pompous enough to keep up the charade, able to save the face of both parties within the one man. On whom shall he call? Is there anyone so qualified as himself? Thus the religious hypocrite dons yet another of his many hats, and acts the part of the grave and judicious sage.

The wisdom of this lesser-than-Solomon does not propose to divide the innocent child before the two whores. The child of disobedience dons robes not his, pretends to a wisdom not innate, and sits on the throne of the heart to divide the two whores that dwell there with him. To the one, the whitened sepulchre whore, he divides the right to keep up the sham and allows her an oath. To the other, the worldly covetous whore, he divides the right to break the oath rather than part with real money, or give up a darling lust.

But what for himself? Well, for himself he lies with both whores. He keeps his religion and retains his covetousness. He has invented new religious oaths, never dreamed of by Moses, or heard of by them of old time. Swear by heaven? Swear by earth? Swear by Jerusalem? Swear by one's head? Never heard of it. No, but by this invention the hypocrite keeps up the appearance of obeying Moses' law. Thus he satisfies his desire for outward whitening. Yet without — he hopes — incurring the wrath of God for a broken promise. After all, it was not made in the Lord's name. Why not? Because when he made it, he knew he would break it.

So then, on the one hand what he swears by does not involve the Lord's name — the only valid Mosaic oath — thus minimising the guilt of a broken promise. Yet on the other hand, it satisfies his desire to appear religious to himself and others. Therefore he trusts God will not be too angry when his treachery appears as, sooner or later, appear it must. Meanwhile both whores in the heart, and the presiding judge over all, are satisfied.

But the Lord is not. Thou hypocrite! Swear not at all. Just, Yes or No. And always mean it and always keep it. 'For whatsoever is more than these cometh of evil.'

Now follows the first of the two minor contrasting statements, verses thirty-eight to forty-two. 'Ye have heard that it hath been said, An eye for an eye, and a tooth for a tooth.'

'But I say unto you, that ye resist not evil: but whosoever shall smite thee on thy right cheek, turn to him the other also.' The same principle applies to anyone who would sue Christ's disciples for their coats: give him the cloak as well. And if another should forcibly compel the saints to go a mile, elect to keep him company freely on the next stretch of road.

'Give to him that asketh thee, and from him that would borrow of thee turn not thou away.'

Someone says to me, how are we to take this? What a state you people have got yourselves into, under your hired priests, that you have to ask this!

How do I take it? Literally of course. There is no question of taking it any other way. It is a matter of doing as one is told. Once that is settled 'intellectual' problems are non-existent. The 'intellectual' problem exists when people want to be thought Christian, but have no intention of going to the extremes that are necessarily implied in that absolute term.

Servants do not argue. They are not there to think. Slaves are there to do their duty, and do as they are told without answering back or dragging the feet. For my part, I am still amazed ever to have been let into his house, and grateful enough but to wash the feet of his servants. If people had been really saved, they would feel the same as that poor woman who washed his feet with her tears and dried them with her hair. She loved much.

In my experience people with intellectual difficulties create their problems by their own cold unexperimental hearts. Obedience, not understanding, is the problem. Love, not brains, is the deficiency. At the bottom of every intellectual problem lies an unbelieving heart gripped by the icy coldness of self-interest, unthawed by the love of Christ. Once that dissolves into willing obedience, all the 'problems' dissolve with it. Especially have I found this to be true in what is fondly imagined to be 'The Ministry', filled with people who seem to have more problems than anyone else.

When I was first saved, and left the sea, I went about sometimes whole nights — for I could not sleep for joy — laughing and crying at the same time, quite literally giving away to strangers all that I possessed, even to the shirt from off my back. I felt such a radiant warm glow flowing out from my heart that it seemed to bathe the very pavement on which I walked. I wanted to — and so far as I could, I did — pour out all that I had and all that I was, to my very life, for all mankind, that men might but know the stupendous, the unutterable, the overwhelming love of Christ that I had found.

Problems? What problems?

Of course I had much to learn. And if I have learned much, it is but the things which I have suffered, which I did not expect. Of course my enthusiasm needed to be tempered with the wisdom of experience. But where I had nothing to learn was in the attitude. That remains the same.

Half the problems come from people who are themselves so void of living experience and direct communion with the Lord, that they must spend all their time reading, recounting, and trumpeting the histories of others long dead. This always forms divisions, and creates a party spirit. Saith the Lord against this religious tendency, 'Your fathers, where are they? and the prophets, do they live for ever?' 'Be ye not as your fathers!'

Never mind about arguing over dead men's histories — grovelling in dead dust, and snarling over old bones is dogs' business, not men's — obey the living Christ! Never mind what they did; what are you going to do? What a way to spend a precious lifetime: dissecting history. Serve the living God for yourself! To live over the long-dead life of another; to think over the long-past thoughts of the dead: that is of a truth never to have lived at all.

But men will do it, and when they do it, they whitewash the faults of the dead men whose image they have elected themselves to uphold. For example the Reformers. Now, do they vindicate the fearful wars these men fought in the name of the Reformation? For example Calvin. Do they vindicate the 'Glass City', the force with which 'morality' was imposed, the burning of Servetus? For example the Covenanters. Will they justify the reeking claymore, the dripping dirk? For example the Puritans. Do they acquit the force of arms and the bloody slaughter at Dunbar? The burning alive at Drogheda? The forcing of Christian principles by the state power upon the whole populace? For example the state church of England or Scotland. Do they vindicate the alliance of church and state to further the advance of the faith by the state's authority and power?

If they do, they are utterly wrong. Whether their 'eye for eye or tooth for tooth' conformed to legal righteousness is not the point; whether their magisterial authority and use of force was legal or not is nothing to do with it. We are talking about the *gospel*. They are wholly at fault: they flaunt the words of Jesus by this resistance of evil with force, this using the law to dominate, this applying state

307

authority to the church. It is a clean contradiction of Matthew chapter five, verses thirty-eight to forty-two, and sets these words of the Lord Jesus at nought. It is obvious that this passage teaches to his separated disciples that the rule of gospel righteousness in respect of exterior power, legal imposition and state force is that of total passivity, non-resistance, and yieldedness on the one hand, and on the other willingly going far beyond, to win the heart of the oppressor with no other weapon than love divine.

No doubt, despite the faults that appear in the previous generations mentioned, there were those whose hearts were filled and overflowing with this divine love. But studying that will not fill our hearts! It is not, The love of God is shed abroad in *their* hearts by the Holy Ghost which is given unto *them*. It is immediate. It is God with *us*. 'The love of God is shed abroad in *our* hearts by the Holy Ghost which is given unto *us*.'

The second and last of the minor statements — 'Ye have heard that it hath been said' — revealing the righteousness of the gospel in relation to one's enemies, is found between verses forty-three and forty-seven.

Israel had been taught under the righteousness of the law 'Love thy neighbour and hate thine enemy.' The righteousness of the gospel speaketh on this wise 'Love your enemies, bless them that curse you, do good to them that hate you, and pray for them which despitefully use you, and persecute you.'

This may appear to conflict with Jesus whipping the moneychangers out of the temple and overturning their tables; with his denouncing Herod as an old fox; and with his sevenfold woes thundered against the scribes, Pharisees, doctors, lawyers, and suchlike. It may appear to conflict with the bitter denunciations of II Peter and of Jude. It may seem to contradict the apocalyptic revenge in John's book of the Revelation. It may seem contrary to Paul's curse upon Alexander the coppersmith, or his calling the Jewish high priest a whited wall, or his exposing by letter the fault of the apostle Peter to the Galatians.

But such objections are easily answered. When a person or class of persons — particularly those professing to be teachers of the people of God and leaders of the church — when they, I say, are in fact leading the people astray, then in the Lord's name the servant of God is bound to expose and denounce them. The Minister of the Gospel is not doing this for any personal reason, but for love of the people. Care for their souls demands the exposure and downright condemnation of those whose errors would lead to the damnation of many. The true Man of God will expose the false apostle, deceitful worker, false prophet, and blind guide, and expose them by name, and expose them thoroughly, and expose them with dread warnings ringing in their ears and the ears of all who follow them.

He will do this without the least personal ill-feeling or vindictiveness. His sole motive will be the salvation of the people. One will find nothing reactionary, or bitter, or by way of compensating for any failure or inadequacy on his part. Love inspires him, light exposes to him, and life fills him with vitality in his energetic and prophetic crying aloud and sparing not. By the Spirit of the Lord, void of personal feelings of sourness or choler, he lifts up his voice like a trumpet, showing God's people their transgressions, and the house of Jacob their sins.

The false apostle, the false prophet, the false minister:

these are the enemies of the Lord; they are not the Man of God's personal enemies. They are the enemies of the gospel: not enemies of the Servant of the Lord as such. They are the enemies of righteousness: it is not a question of the individual at all.

However, when the Man of God has declared the prophetic word against such enemies of the truth, and they claim — as they always do claim — that he is critical, vindictive, has a personality difficulty, is jealous, envious and so on; and moreover that which he says is not the word of the Lord but a perversion of it: then he falls on his knees and prays for them. They persecute him but he intercedes for them. Those persecutors that accuse him of having no love, he loves them on his knees.

See this with Stephen. With face full of glory he cries from his open, guileless heart 'Ye stiffnecked and uncircumcised in heart and ears, ye do always resist the Holy Ghost: as your fathers did, so do ye.

'Which of the prophets have not your fathers persecuted?'

And they who felt he had not loved them well enough — for the love they required was one which condoned their sin, prejudice, blindness, and traditional substitution for the word of God, and let them sleep their way to hell — then stoned Stephen. Was this then an example of the love they felt Stephen lacked? This 'love' of the persecutors?

But the same love which hurled denunciation at the high priest and leaders of Israel, then poured from the same lips, as Stephen fell upon his knees with the stones thudding into his head and body: 'Lord, lay not this sin to their charge.'

'Father, forgive them; for they know not what they do.' So saith he who had lately denounced every sect, party, and leader in Jerusalem, at last rejecting their temple like the barren fig tree 'Your house is left unto you desolate!' Nevertheless: 'Father, forgive them; for they know not what they do.'

And the Father, does he not bless the evil and the good with the same sun? Does not the same rain fall upon just and unjust? Is he not the Saviour of all men? Did he not so love the world? Was he not in Christ reconciling the world unto himself? Came not the Lamb of God to take away the sin of the world? Is he not the propitiation for the whole world?

If the love of God did this in and through the Father; if that, in and through the Son; and if the love of God dwell within our hearts, and Christ be formed in the inner man, how shall the Spirit of God do less in us, than is ever consistent with himself? His love is of that character. Therefore, so is gospel righteousness.

Legal righteousness is another thing, requiring love only to those who love oneself. But publicans and sinners have a like bond. What do ye legalists more than others? My experience of you, better the love of a publican.

But the love of God is altogether divine and heavenly and above human affection. It is free, generous, noble, large and universal; it lavishes, wastes, pours out itself upon the thankless, ungrateful and implacable enemy.

Go, and do thou likewise.

The last verse is verse forty-eight. It is itself the gospel rule of righteousness which we have seen applied in the examples — contrasted with the legal rule — of killing, adultery, divorce, speech, revenge, and love. The rule follows the indwelling love of God and is unqualified, unmitigated, and without compromise:

> 'Be ye therefore perfect, even as your Father
> which is in heaven is perfect.'

MATTHEW CHAPTER SIX

¶ Godliness and the kingdom. Ch. 6:1-34

We pass from the subject of righteousness, in chapter five, to that of godliness or holiness in chapter six.

We have seen that righteousness refers to the rule by which one lives and to which one conforms one's life. For the Christian, divine life becomes the life, and this is expressed in the word of the truth of the gospel. It is another thing altogether from the legal rule of rectitude, to which man must address himself unaided, and by his own supposed wisdom and strength, wrestle and mortify his being and existence into presumed conformity with its righteous precepts. But this cannot be done. Not that the law is not holy, just and good. It is. But that the interior heart of humanity is corrupt and carnal, fallen and sold under sin.

So therefore, by the deeds of the law no flesh could produce rectitude. If righteousness could have come by the law, the gospel would have been a mistake, and Christ erred in judgment. 'For if righteousness come by the law, then Christ is dead in vain.' But the Son of God came to bring in everlasting righteousness freely for all believers. Not just the righteousness of the law: his blood meets that, and his death delivers from it; but what he brings in is the everlasting righteousness of God. It comes in by faith in his blood. This in turn brings in the Spirit.

Walking by that indwelling Spirit, divine life becomes the Christian's rule of life. He can say 'I live; yet not I, but Christ liveth in me: and the life which I now live in the flesh I live by the faith of the Son of God, who loved me, and gave himself for me.' And as many as walk by this rule, peace be upon them, and upon the Israel of God.

Now, however, in the chapter under consideration we leave the rule of righteousness and come to the question of godliness. This reveals the degree to which God is to be regarded, and shows that, for the disciple, life before God comes first, infinitely before any regard to man even enters into the picture. A secret, interior, exclusive regard to, life with, and relationship towards God has long decided the heart and conduct, before any human being is even remotely considered.

This is called Godliness. To the disciple, God is more real than man. God is much closer than humanity. And so one walks in his fear, and with a single eye to pleasing him alone. The fear of man, the opinion of the brethren, the traditions of the assembly: all these carry no weight with the true Christian. The love of women, the comforts of wife and family, the affection of children: these take second place to the God-fearing disciple. Love to God is first.

The righteousness in the great commandment of the law — 'Thou shalt love the Lord thy God with all thy heart, and with all thy soul, and with all thy mind, and with all thy strength' — is fulfilled in us who walk not after the flesh but after the Spirit. So also is the imperative of the great gospel injunction: 'If any man come to me, and hate not his father, and mother, and wife, and children, and brethren, and sisters, yea, and his own life also, he cannot be my disciple.' No; he is no Christian at all, just a hollow sham. His hypocritical profession is all that he is. 'And whosoever doth not bear his cross, and come after me, cannot be my disciple.' How will you know one who does not bear his cross, yet falsely professes Christ's cross? Easily. He will make a distinction between disciple and Christian, so excusing himself from these words of Jesus. That liar is the hypocrite who draws near to God with his lips, but his heart is far from him.

Not so the godly. His heart dwells in God, and God dwelleth in him. God is that close to him. Godliness refers to the sanctification — saintliness — of the disciple or Christian, and reveals the measure of his separation. It means 'separated to God'. Godliness is the subject of chapter six.

In Matthew chapter six godliness is illustrated by four aspects. It is seen in relation to Alms, Prayer, Fasting and Worldliness. This completes the chapter.

The 'Sermon on the Mount' consists of three consecutive chapters, each decreasing in length. In the first and longest of these chapters the word 'Father' occurs three times. In the last and shortest, twice.

This word, 'Father', is that which speaks of the intimacy of the relationship between the Father and the Son, into which by the Spirit the disciples have now been born. This relationship with the Father is so overwhelming in its precedence over every human relationship that Jesus cautions his disciples 'Call no man your father upon the earth: for one is your Father, which is in heaven.'

As with the Son of God who did 'always those things that please the Father', who could 'do nothing of himself, but what he seeth the Father do: for what things soever he doeth, these also doeth the Son likewise', so also with those who 'live by the faith of the Son of God'. That becomes their rule also. Not because they have strength but because they are weak. Then they are strong, and they live by the life of the Son of God, so attentive and exclusive to the Father's good pleasure. Godliness.

From this it is obvious that godliness stands in sonship. Godliness and sonship go together. And sons are begotten by the Father. Therefore since Matthew chapter six deals with godliness, it need not surprise us to discover in this central chapter of the 'Sermon on the Mount' that the Father is referred to no less than twelve times.

If so, it is because sonship is being emphasised: what it is to be sons to the Father. It is to be godly. The relation and maintenance of living sonship between God and his people is thus stressed by the twelvefold emphasis on spiritual, heavenly, and divine Fatherhood. This teaches us that the new covenant relationship stands in sonship and that sonship is experimentally to know, revere, and love the Father totally and absolutely. In a word, to be godly and God-fearing, the most striking feature of the early church: 'And fear came upon every soul.' 'And great fear came upon all the church, and upon as many as heard these things.'

Yet nothing is more conspicuous in the denominations, the churches, assemblies, halls and groups of today than the shocking absence of the fear of God. 'There is no fear of God before their eyes.' Instead there is a spirit of worldliness, of levelling, of Jack's-as-good-as-his-master, of audacity, of lawlessness, of impertinent disrespect, of the destroying of distinction between child and adult, young and old, and male and female. And 'except ye repent, ye shall all likewise perish.'

Now, chapter six verses one to four lays stress upon the godliness of the secret interior heart necessary to the exterior observance of almsgiving. The passage concludes with the words which toll like a bell three times across the face of this chapter — in verses four, six and eighteen — 'Thy Father which seeth in secret.' 'Thy Father which is in secret.' 'Thy Father which seeth in secret.'

Think of that. It is the essence of godliness. It is the test of sonship. By the degree of awareness of this reality one may measure one's real progress. 'Thy Father which is in secret.' In secret. How many secrets, and secret ways and secret times, unknown to any man or woman, hast thou with the Father?

The word translated 'Alms' is derived from the word for Mercy, and actually means, Merciful Acts, Kindnesses, or Deeds of Pity. Such deeds are illustrated by those occasions referred to in the Acts, when, for example, Peter and John were accosted by the lame man at the Beautiful gate of the temple, asking an alms of them. Or of Cornelius who feared God, giving much alms to the people, and who prayed to God alway. To him it was said 'Thy prayer is heard, and thine alms are had in remembrance in the sight of God.'

These acts of pity or mercy called alms are not to be confused with Modern Professional Charities employing large staffs and spending fortunes upon newspaper and other advertising, in papers ranging from downright sceptical through nonconformist, protestant, catholic, and, if there be any prospect of money, no doubt outright heretic too. Add the name of a peer or two, a professional horror photograph, a good London address, and they are in business. This is definitely not what the Lord Jesus meant or early Christians practised by way of alms.

The alms of the early Christians were associated with the way that they worshipped. It was an act of worship. Such acts were never organised by other people, much less unbelievers, and certainly not on grounds of harrowing descriptions or emotional appeals. Alms were *purely personal acts*, in connection with *the whole doctrine and practice of worship*, and they were not originated from emotion, but the *fear of God*, and a serious, sober devotion.

As the Christian 'has opportunity' he is to 'do good unto all men, especially unto them who are of the household of faith.' This 'opportunity' will be personal, private, and from person to person. The very word 'show Deed of mercy, Act of kindness' demands that there is a personal and direct appeal from the needy to the worshipper. Never from a professional photograph or professional fundraising organisation's paid description calculated to needle conscience and excite pity; both the fundraiser and the advertisement being paid for out of the amount raised as a result of feelings stirred by the 'Tear Jerker'.

Nowadays most of the advertising Charities have no doctrinal, gospel, or even church basis. Their one purpose is to get people — any and all people — to give money. No Christian should support this in the delusion that this is 'alms' in the sense meant by the Lord Jesus and his apostles. It is not. Moreover, such Charities and Organisations are at best concerned with the relief of the body irrespective of the gospel for the salvation of the immortal soul. They do not even believe that the lost will be damned without Christ. It is not right for a Christian to be involved in such an unholy alliance.

In this connection we hear of appeals for the 'underdeveloped' nations. This is ridiculous terminology. They are called by Christ and his apostles, and have until recently been called by the churches and Christians, *heathen* nations. Their need is for *the gospel of God concerning his Son*. Furthermore, many of the terrible afflictions and 'natural' disasters common to the idolatrous and infidel lands occur as a partial judgment from God to alert the benighted heathen to the heinous sin of idolatry. The solution is the gospel, not a frantic attempt to undo the warning providences of God.

And in a day when heathen idols have been paraded on vast floats through the main streets of London by idolatrous foreign priests: in a day when idol temples are being erected throughout the parts of Great Britain: let the Sovereign, and her Ministers, and the Peers of the Realm and the people take notice: a great curse is brought on the land equal to that of the heathen. Worse. The heathen make no profession to be of Christendom.

How swift has been the terrible decline! Now with one accord they all begin to make excuse. This would never have happened in the days of the Queen's father. Nor for reign after reign before that, during which, for the tolerance and favour granted to the true saints in the land to worship freely, and for the proper application of the righteous requirement of the law to the realm as a whole, England prospered above all nations of the earth. And that was the reason: because it is the firm but kindly application of righteousness that exalteth the nation. But now, from the highest places in the land, there comes a cry for Peace, Peace, when there is no peace. There is no peace, saith my God, no peace to the wicked. The mouth of the Lord hath spoken it.

Alms, then, are an exterior act of worship in the name of the Lord Jesus and demonstrating his compassion, directly given to the poor and needy by those walking in the truth of the gospel. Such are to guard the secrecy of these acts, not permitting even the one hand to know what the other doeth. So far as it lies with the disciple, it is a secret between him, his God, and the person benefited.

Like every other act of worship it is to be done in the Spirit and in the name of the Lord Jesus, with a free and ingenuous admission of the heavenly origins of the kindness to the person receiving it; the meanwhile, as to all other persons, keeping the secret before the Father. Such shall be rewarded openly.

Next follows the passage on prayer, divided into two parts. Verses five and six warn against hypocrisy, much like to the previous warning of hypocritical almsgiving. Verses seven to fifteen are concerned with a further warning of

heathendom in prayer, an example of true prayer, followed
by a final warning directed against an unforgiving spirit.

The whole spring of the hypocrites' almsgiving and
praying is that men should notice how pious they are.
Before they give, they peer out at the windows, and peep
round the doorways to make certain the street and the
synagogue are full of people. Then, with modestly downcast
eyes, and nearly covered — but just not quite — purse, they
tread with humble steps, apparently too enrapt to notice
all the silly people whom they take in so easily.

I could never understand the uncouth practice of forcing
a plate upon a public congregation, anyway. They reckon
their 'churches' are the 'house of God', and promptly hold
up the guests to shame if they do not put something upon
a publicly exposed plate passed from hand to hand with
many a sidelong glance, from one massively standing figure
at one end of the row, to his looming counterpart at the
other. Miss out if you dare. Now, if this is done to guests in
'God's house' — as they call it — do they do the same thing
to guests in their own houses? And if alms are to be in
secret, why the public plate? Some secret.

Or how about a brass plaque to commemorate one's
charity? Or a graven stone? Or a stained-glass window? Or
a table and chairs? Or a publicly acknowledged donation
to, say, the Baptist Union? Verily I say unto you, they
have their reward.

But the hypocrites love to pray as well. Provided only
that it is where everyone can observe them. How can they
believe, which receive honour one of another? They are not
Jews — or Christians — that are outward; nor those whose
praise is of men and not God. Yet that which is highly

esteemed among men is abomination in the sight of God. They can pray at the Wailing Wall, or in the prayer-meeting, or in a public place. However when it comes to the closet, to the lonely vigil, to the long hours of wrestling alone with God, they know nothing of it. He does not answer the hypocrite. But then they never expected him to: he was just a convenience, an almighty sounding board for the sonorous intonation of their excessive ego before men. Well, men heard them, men praised them, and that is what they expected, wanted and attained. The account from God, however, in breaking the law by taking his name in vain, shall be rendered later.

The Christian — not the hypocrite — is the true disciple who disciplines himself to closet work. Daily. It is said of the lonely man by the angels of heaven 'Behold, he prayeth.' And he went out all night into a mountain alone to pray. Nobody knew. Nobody saw. But the Father. 'And thy Father which seeth in secret shall — shall! shall! — reward thee openly.' Believe it, man; for he telleth thee the truth.

Now follows a warning against heathen repetition and, in consequence, an example of what not to repeat, but view as a guide to the spirit of prayer.

The warning of verse seven — 'But when ye pray, use not vain repetitions, as the heathen do' — does not at all refer to the idols to which the heathen prayed. There could be no question of the disciples praying to plaster models, painted icons, wooden carvings, or stone effigies. Nor does this warning visualise their adopting heathen prayer-postures, or prayer-robes, or the terminology and form of words used by the idolaters. Such an apostasy simply was not envisaged.

What the Lord Jesus assumes here is that the disciples will pray to the Father; moreover that the form of their words will be acceptable. The warning is in respect of the spirit of prayer. Of quenching the living Spirit, and substituting heathen rotes and automatic repetitions from written prayer books to be repeated over and over and over again. That is what the Son of God is forbidding.

So what happens? Instead of a living, Spirit-inspired λειτουργία, *service*, on the part of all the brethren as led spontaneously, we have a singular priest-ridden imposition devoid of both Spirit and spontaneity. Clothed with the long robes which the Lord of glory expressly forbad, titled with the titles which he sternly rejected, refusing the spontaneity which he definitely required, the 'church' which claims to be Christ's then holds in its hands a written liturgy, a repetitious prayer book, so to do exactly what the Son of God emphatically prohibits his disciples from doing.

Others, such as the Baptists, reject the prayer book. But then they have excerpts from it printed in their hymn book! Not to mention a Roman hymn to transubstantiation. And without batting an eyelid these repeat with monotonous repetition on every possible congregational occasion the guide to spontaneous prayer which the Roman Catholics call the 'Pater Noster'. This immediately follows the words 'When ye pray use not vain repetitions as the heathen do.'

Of course once upon a time the 'Plymouth Brethren' judged the being gathered on the ground of baptism as a form of sectarianism. In fact they rejected every partial or dividing ground, in order to come together in the unity of the one body. No longer. Themselves divided and in

322

disarray, now the children build again the things which once their fathers destroyed. One of their chief organs goes under the name 'Paternoster'.

As to the character of this heathen repetition, it appears to be constant request and demand, with no thanksgiving and worship. Yet another case of the horseleech having two daughters, crying, Give, Give. But 'your Father knoweth what things ye have need of, before ye ask him.'

'After this manner *therefore'* — that is, so as not always to be clamouring Give, Give — 'pray ye.' And it is 'After this *manner.'* Not after this *form*, these very words or this rote of mere repetition. It is a mode or manner, a guide to the general tenor, or emphasis in prayer. Not to contradict what had just been said!

The general mode is to place the emphasis upon God, not men; upon the Father, not the children; upon the deity, not self; upon worship, not gain. Our Father; Thy Name; Thy Kingdom; Thy Will. As to us, daily bread is quite sufficient for faith, and for the rest to be forgiven, led and kept. It is not for us to design the manner of prayer, the Spirit leads into it: Thy Kingdom; Thy Power; Thy Glory.

As to forgiveness, we need expect none, without rendering it to all. The basis of the Father's relationship to us is forgiveness. Without that, he could have had neither initial nor continuing relationship. It is therefore one of his most conspicuous features. Since prayer proceeds from the indwelling Spirit of God, it is therefore impossible to pray in the Spirit without being in accord with the forgiveness of the Father. And accord means a merciful disposition. Lack of it, makes us impossible to fill: we are at complete variance with the Father of mercies. Therefore he who would pray must lay aside his beads and books, and be filled with the living Spirit. And he who would be filled with the Spirit must render mercy to his debtors, and forgiveness withal.

But primarily he must ascertain that he is a child of God. The entrance is through the beatitudes. Righteousness will be characteristic. 'Our Father'. But whose Father?

Not the world's. Not man's by nature. Not the merely biblical. Not the religious by circumstance of upbringing. Not that of the exterior church member or communicant. But the born of God, the regenerate, those who progress through the portals of Matthew five, verses three to twelve.

He is the Father of sons, of children, of saints. Of the brethren, the faithful, believers, disciples, friends. As united — and they are united — not with denominations or worldly congregations, but with each other, they are called: the church, the temple, the bride, the body, the kingdom, the house, the tabernacle. Now, if the description fits experimentally, the relationship is true actually.

When this is true, the name 'Father' is hallowed or sanctified. When it is confused or polluted, then the name is profaned by worldly mixture and by falsely trading it to the unclean and to impenitent sinners. The result of this is a moral chaos and darkness equal to that which preceded creation.

The section on fasting is next, verses sixteen to eighteen. We do not hear much about fasting nowadays, except it be from unbelieving Hindus, criminals, murderers, or social protesters. Then it is called 'hunger striking'. Well, that will not work with God. However the Lord Jesus expects us to fast and here are the directions for doing so aright.

First of all, not as the hypocrites. They have a cosmetic arrangement by which all concerned can see perfectly well what they are doing. And if anyone should still be so crass and stupid as not to notice, they are not above dropping a verbal hint or two between sighs.

Disciples are to fast without telling a soul; without dropping any hints whatsoever; and so as deliberately to hide the fact of what they are doing in order that no one could possibly guess in any circumstances. Then 'Thy Father, which seeth in secret, shall reward thee openly.'

From verse nineteen to the end of chapter six Jesus discourses upon godliness as it stands in relation to the world or worldliness.

Now the world, and worldliness, are fraught with danger for the disciple. Indeed, many who began as fine disciples, superior to others, at the last have been brought down by worldliness. One must overcome the world, or the world will do the overcoming. After so bright a beginning in youth, many have ended in middle and old age, choked and strangled with the deceitfulness of riches, the cares of this world, the love of other things entering in, the pleasures of this life: things not dreamed about when the auspicious beginning commenced.

The danger consists of two parts. The world. And worldliness, 'the things of the world'. What the Messiah is strictly admonishing his disciples in this place is absolute in respect of these two things. There are no half measures. Dallying will ensure defeat. It is 'love not the world, neither the things that are in the world.' Why? 'If any man love the world, the love of the Father is not in him.' That's it: it is just not in him.

Jesus commences his doctrine by stressing the imperative necessity for utter rejection of both the world and worldliness. This is done by a determined attitude of inmost will. An interior resolution that is at once absolutely single-minded, totally united in heart, and completely passionate in its intense rejection of worldliness.

This is revealed by three figures, or illustrations, of the truth.

First from that of the gnawing anxiety over the security, and mind-absorbing fixation about the value, of one's treasure-hoard. No two ways about that.

Secondly, the truth of this undivided heart-resolution necessary to reject the world and all its blandishments, is demonstrated by the way in which one uses the eye. The direction and focus of the eye. Can't look two ways at once.

Finally, the imperative of a clean cut decision and consequent fixed intention to reject the world and attain heaven, as being essential to salvation, is shown by the sheer fallacy of attempting to serve two masters. A servant with two masters? Hopeless. Cannot be done.

The Treasure. The Eye. The Master.

The illustration of the treasure is conveyed in verses nineteen to twenty-one. It is unfolded in the following manner: What not to do, and why not, verse nineteen. In contrast, verse twenty, What to do and why. In verse twenty-one, The overwhelming motive for hearing and doing these sayings of Christ.

The word 'treasure' refers to a rich store; what is laid up, or hoarded; a deposit in the bank or treasury. The assumption being that it is human nature to lay up a treasure. That is taken for granted. The idea of doing nothing with one's life but drift to death trusting in a system which purports to take over all one's responsibilities in perpetuity had not occurred in those realistic and common-sense times.

It is assumed that men will live their lives determined to have something to show for them. As a result of their own labour, and no one else's. The consequence of this, the thing shown in consequence of labour, the life-result, what one has worked for and laid up, is called 'treasure'. One set one's heart on accruing it and now one has got it. Results. No one else has a right to this treasure. The law has no right to it: the duty of the law is to protect a man's lawful treasure, not be made illegal by the authorities in order to steal what does not belong to them or any other body, so as to give to those without pride or self-respect.

Neither does one's death alter one's inalienable right to do what one will with one's own and dispose of it as one wishes without interference. 'Thou shalt not steal' is as binding on the governing as upon the governed. The fact of government does not give those in authority the right to violate law, wickedly create lawlessness, and then use the force of law to rob a man of his treasure on his death-bed.

Finally to add insult to injury by calling it 'duty'. Then to crown all that governmental lawlessness by giving the stolen fruits of careful husbandry and prudence to support the wastrel, the squanderer, the improvident when the fruits of *their* imprudence should come home to roost. What vile men — and women — are exalted in the place of their betters in a once-fair realm! 'The wicked walk on every side, when the vilest men are exalted.'

So then, it is not the spirited determination to amount to something, to achieve results, to show treasure at the end of one's life, that the Lord Jesus strictures. He expects that. That is the image of God: to create. That is true, independent, self-reliant human nature. That is the realisation of proper humanity. It is that, of course, that atheistic modern bureaucrats, haters-of-God and enemies of the truth, are attempting to quench. What an ambition in life: to kill responsibility and quench the spark of individualism in one's fellows! But Jesus commends what these antichrists hate. Where the warning and stricture of the Son of God comes is not upon that spirit in man, but upon what it is set.

Not earthly treasure. What does that amount to? Nothing. Something? But you cannot take it with you! You brought nothing into this world, and man, you'll take nothing out, either. But — unlike our modern soft-religious — *keep that spirit!*

Only set it upon treasure in heaven. That will be waiting for you. Just slip through the door at the end, a hand is waiting to support as you go, and there it is: 'reserved in heaven for you.' 'Where neither moth nor rust doth corrupt, and where thieves do not break through nor steal.' Well, figure it out for yourself.

One thing is sure, a man has one heart and it can only be set upon one thing. What one lives for. That is certain. 'Where your treasure is, there will your heart be also.'

Listen. Let us listen to our betters, yours and mine:

> Hence with earthly treasure,
> Thou art all my pleasure,
> Jesus all my choice.
> Hence thou empty glory,
> Nought to me thy story,
> Told with tempting voice;
> Pain, or loss, or shame, or cross,
> Shall not from my Saviour move me,
> Since he deigns to love me.
>
> Fare thee well that errest,
> Thou that earth preferrest,
> Thou wilt tempt in vain;
> Fare thee well, transgression,
> Hence abhorred possession,
> Come not forth again.
> Past your hour, O pride and power;
> Worldly life, thy bonds I sever,
> Fare thee well for ever.
>
> Hence all fears and sadness,
> For the Lord of gladness,
> Jesus, enters in.
> They who love the Father,
> Though the storms may gather,
> Still have peace within;
> Yea, whate'er I here must bear,
> Still in thee lies purest pleasure,
> Jesus, priceless treasure.

The next example of the unity of heart in pursuing heavenliness is that of the eye, and takes up verses twenty-two to twenty-three.

To understand this passage three mysteries must be solved. What is meant by the 'single' eye? What is meant by the 'evil' eye? What is meant by 'light' being 'darkness'?

What is meant by the single eye? First, the eye. The eye is said to be the 'light of the body'. This word 'light' is different from that used in the rest of the passage. It is a light, in the sense that a lamp is a light; it is not 'light' abstractly. The word has been translated Candle more times than it has been translated Light. So that we are to think of this as Lightgiver. The Lightgiver to the body is the eye: it lets the light in, it acts the part of a lamp. The meaning is clear: the intelligence is supplied through the eye. The eye is the way things are seen: all the light on things comes through that to the mind. And the mind controls the body. So, the light of the body is the eye.

As to the eye being 'single', this word has a variety of applications: liberal, with simplicity, bountiful: when used in connection with giving. Single, when used in connection with the eye. With the heart, variously the word may mean whole-hearted, guileless, singleness of heart. With the mind, open, frank, simple. With cloth — though this does not occur in the Bible — the Greek word has the connotation of 'without folds', without pleats. No shadows, no secrets, you see. Spread out in the open. Of substances, it refers to being without compound or mixture.

So that the single eye is a pure eye. It looks on things in a pure way, a heavenly way, a spiritual way. It feeds a mind with whatsoever things are true, whatsoever things are honest, whatsoever things are just, whatsoever things are pure, whatsoever things are lovely, whatsoever things are of good report. If — as intruding upon the view — it sees things bad, or evil, it sees them in the light of good and virtue, and sternly reprimands the vice. If, in passing, there should obtrude upon the gaze the works of darkness, the single eye but sheds light on their shady, worthless character and rebukes them. Whatsoever maketh manifest is light. However, the beams of this 'lamp' are fixed upon the Son of God, on the kingdom of heaven, on the blessed doctrine of his holy word. The single 'lamp' is settled upon things spiritual.

Therefore the 'evil' eye is an impure eye. It looks on things in an unclean way, an earthy way, a sensual way. It feeds a carnal mentality, an impure imagination, a hypocritical religion. It filters through thoughts of the heart which are only evil continually. To such, that is what their eye is for: to stimulate the dirty mind, to rouse the unclean passions, to gender lust and avarice, to seek human applause and worldly gain. This eye looks for money, for goods, for tricky ways of accruing them, for smart ways of outdoing the rest. It looks for others to be the same; it judges their corn by its bushel, it cannot believe good of anyone, it looks for the catch it is certain is there. This is an evil eye. A worldly eye.

All it ministers to the mind is darkness. That is all it believes in, looks for, and comes to see. Then, if *that* is what it lights up to the mind and body, if *that* is the kind of intelligence which makes up its 'light': whatever is its darkness like? If its light is so shadowy and shady: whatever is its dark like? Take heed that 'the light which is in thee be not darkness.'

In conclusion, you can see that there is no compromise. We have the choice set before us. All light. Or all dark. There are no shades. All or nothing. That is the teaching.

'God is light, and in him is no darkness at all.'

Finally — as regards these three illustrations to the totality and absolute unity of moral intention of heart — we have the case of the servant with two masters.

No man can serve two masters. Of course not, it is not in the nature of man. He will get fed up to the back teeth with being bossed two different ways at once. No sooner will he start this for one master, than he must begin something else for the other. As soon as he settles to that, then: Stop: go and do as you were told in the first place. It cannot be done.

Or take a single job. Do it this way. Fine. Along comes the other master. Whatever are you doing, man, don't do it like that. Do it like this. Then back comes the first. Impossible.

One will be reasonable, the other less reasonable. One will be likeable, the other less likeable. One will agree to one's own judgment of the way things should be done and the order of doing them, the other will prefer another way. One agrees with one's own precedents, the other does not. So what happens?

One of two things. Either one of the two masters will be hated for his persistent and impossible interference, and the other loved for his intelligent and reasonable agreement. Then the poor servant will make heavy weather of trying to serve both of them at once as best he can. Yet achieving satisfaction for neither. Or else the servant will take a stronger line with the two masters, and give up serving the one to a great extent, openly despising him, and turn to the other so as to hold to him. Then when the first master complains, the servant will openly scorn him, on the grounds that he has been commanded already. He holds to the one and despises the other.

Well what else can he do? After all, no man can serve two masters.

And ye cannot serve God and mammon.

One of two sets of alternatives. Either you hate mammon and love God. Or you love mammon and hate God.

Of course, there is the popular liberal-evangelical practice of loving mammon and pretending God has changed into something different which they can then love as well as loving mammon. But here we are talking of the truth. And the truth is, If you love mammon *of necessity* you hate God *as he really is*. Why?

Because God is absolutely set against your loving mammon, that's why.

The second set of alternatives is this: either you will hold to mammon and despise God. Or you will despise mammon and hold to God. One or the other. There is no, but no, absolutely no alternative.

And it is not, hold to God and despise Satan. Or, hold to Satan and despise God. It is not Satan that is in question here, but that behind which he effectively hides himself. That is, *mammon*. Or, worldliness.

And if a professed disciple holds to worldliness, Jesus says, *he despises God.* No matter what vociferous denials the would-be disciple might make, this is what the Son of God declares is the real truth of the matter.

And if a professing Christian loves the world, Jesus says, *he hates God.* No matter how — to justify himself — that 'Christian' changes the glory of the uncorruptible God into an image made like to corruptible man. Himself, for example. But it is all a vile lie, for the Lord of glory predicates the sound doctrine of the matter.

How could this apply to Christians or disciples? cries an indignant voice. 'Once a disciple always a disciple.' How these people stand the balanced apostolic presentation of the truth upon its head! They put their false-assurance schemes before the pilgrimage exhortations and solemn warnings of Christ and his ministers. If pressed, they pay lip-service to the latter, but immediately like a dog to its vomit return to the mess of the former.

I will answer them how this can apply to a disciple. In this way: And another of his disciples said unto him, Lord, suffer me first to go and bury my father. But Jesus said unto him, Follow me; and let the dead bury their dead.

Now, let them go and do likewise.

The Lord Jesus continues his dissertation upon godliness, in relation to the world and the things of the world, with a final, direct, and trenchant exhortation from verse twenty-five — 'Therefore I say unto you' — to the end of chapter six.

The operative expressions in this passage are the definite

'Take no thought,' and the gently ironical 'Why take ye thought?' Six times over the Greek word occurs in this latter part of Matthew chapter six, although we find it nowhere else in the 'Sermon on the Mount'.

This word translated 'taking thought' has been elsewhere rendered Care, or, To have care. It refers to worldly anxiety, to having the mind torn with worry, to being distracted, anxious over worldly things. It is this that is prohibited. Not only because it is foolish. Nor even simply because it is wrong. But beyond that, it is so deadly dangerous.

Observe. 'He also that received seed among the thorns is he that heareth the word; and the *care* of this world, and the deceitfulness of riches, choke the word, and he becometh unfruitful.' There it is: Care. And, consistent with our passage — godliness in relation to the world — it is, 'Care of this world'. We find the same word again in a variation of this quotation: 'And these are they which are sown among thorns; such as hear the word, and the *cares* of this world, and the deceitfulness of riches, and the lusts of other things entering in, choke the word, and it becometh unfruitful.'

Deadly dangerous. Consider the following passage also: 'And take heed to yourselves, lest at any time your hearts be overcharged with surfeiting, and drunkenness, and *cares* of this life, and so that day come upon you unawares.

'For as a snare shall it come on all them that dwell on the face of the whole earth.

'Watch ye therefore, and pray always, that ye may be accounted worthy to escape — mark that, *worthy* to escape — all these things that shall come to pass, and to stand before the Son of man.'

It is not merely that he who allows the indulgence of this sixfold anxiety falls short of the perfection demanded by 'Be ye therefore perfect, even as your Father which is in heaven is perfect.' It is worse than that. Worldly anxiety, allowed, indulged, and once become habitual, is a deadly danger.

'Therefore I say unto you, Take no thought for your life.' Here, verses twenty-five and twenty-six, Jesus is warning against anxiety in life. We are not to be anxious about life: worrying about the cost of living. How we shall meet the cost of food, drink, and the bills for clothing. Worrying about our children and anxious to push them on in their worldly career. This kind of worry and care is totally improper to a disciple, because it assumes that the Father is indifferent to his children.

Such an anxiety predicates a detached carelessness in God not merely as Creator to the creation, but specifically in the intimate relation of Father to his own children in Christ Jesus. This is a slur on the Creator, an insult to God, and a downright offence to the Father.

Certain questions follow. Which shall we put first: The life we live or the body in which it is lived? The care of the immortal soul or the clothing of the perishable body? The pursuit of the kingdom or the promotion of a career?

What of the birds of the air? Are they anxious for meat? Do they care for raiment? But are they not fed and clothed despite the absence of anxiety? After all, they are neither improvident nor idle. At the first blush of dawn they burst forth in song with all their might to hymn the Maker of heaven and earth. Do men? Do today's disciples?

But in a single pursuit of that which draws them, are the fowls — being without carefulness — not fed and covered?

Then will not the heavenly Father of his own dear children, occupied in the pursuit of things heavenly and spiritual and careless of worldly improvement, will he not, I say, himself care far more for them than he does the unintelligent creatures?

Of course he will. Then whence this fear and unbelief? From two sources. First, doubting that God actually created the heavens and the earth immediately and directly. The second is like unto it; doubting that God is actually involved in the immediate and direct providence of that creation at present.

This may be the blasphemy of the world. But why is it the unbelieving anxiety of the children of God?

How conspicuous is this anxiety about life amongst professing Christians! How desperately anxious are many parents for their children to gain the last vestige of advantage from the state educational ladder, even more so than the unbelievers. And this is not at all from a desire for pure learning; not even a question of human culture. No, it comes out of a desperation that with the best 'O' levels, or 'A' levels, or worldly degree, they should have the pick of the plum jobs. That is, the rungs are a way of their children ascending to the most prestigious and highly paid position. Meanwhile in the desperate scramble, the bare husks are left for God from the choicest years of youth.

I remember some years ago several young men and women in Glasgow were awakened under my ministry to seek first the kingdom of God and his righteousness. They found the location of their university and the demands upon their best energies and time unsuitable to what they saw the proper pursuit of true disciples. So they put first things first. What a storm! What a furore broke around my head! Persecuted was not in it! To their shame this came from the 'evangelical' leaders, particularly those had in great reputation; but many others, too.

However these people who hoped to frighten me from both following my Master and encouraging others to do likewise, soon found that they had picked upon the wrong man. We are of tougher stock than these blind guides shall ever bend, lead astray, or silence for one single second.

By way of postscript I would add that I have seen this excellent example of these children of Abraham followed by others as a result. They are all nothing worsened but rather made better for 'leaving all, and following him.' Even in worldly ways!

In verse twenty-seven another question is asked: Who can really alter his appearance? Many years ago my father, a prominent businessman of substance, was offered as a side-line the sole concession in Great Britain and Europe of an American mass-production cosmetic firm now a household name. Although a completely worldly man, without any profession of religion of any kind, and as hard-headed and far-sighted a businessman as one could find, still, he utterly disdained and was ashamed to be associated with such a new-fangled and ill-bred conception. So did the best of his generation, on purely manly grounds. How things have changed, and how much America is responsible for that change.

Yet with all their foundation garments, their cosmetics,

their dyes, wigs, surgery, creams, ointments, scents, sprays, lipsticks, eye-shadows, and other frantic attempts to stave off ugliness and old age: 'Which of you by taking thought can add one cubit unto his stature?'

What a stupid waste of time and money. But what a damnably dangerous risk of an immortal soul: to be called into eternity whilst painting the face in the mirror!

And why take ye thought for raiment? Consider the lilies of the field. They have no anxiety, but they have wonderful beauty. They clothe the grass of the field, and, saith Jesus, it is all God's doing. And how does God clothe the grass of the field? With mini-lilies one year, and maxi-daisies the next? Is this year's in-colour saffron, my dear, and next year's turquoise? Are rough textures and tweedies the thing this season, and by day the new bluebell look, whereas nightwear is as last year's black look? How about off-the-shoulder convolvulus for a really dashing preview of the coming fashion?

Of course with the new mini-lily fashion a great deal more of the bare stalk is visible than would have been thought temperate and modest since the foundation of the world, but, *darling,* with the new bright-hour all-American "Good News" fashion catalogue all those old fuddy-duddy ideas are out. Again, the head is uncovered this season, and once more every bulge and curve is emphasised. Girl flowers are wearing boy blooms as a real *must,* but what's with these old laws when we have the Revised Catalogue — but *everybody's* doing it, dear — to tell us black is white, law is freedom, and nature is grace.

For accessories, a sprinkling of gold, broided leaves, and costly array is essential to maintain the with-it trendy image, without which the horror of being out of fashion might become a dread reality. Every morning, a rope of dew-pearls is *de rigueur* for the up to date young and not so young new look. That's New Look, Revision House, Paternoster Way, Gomorrah.

Or, with God, do they come up the same every year?

Therefore take *no thought* saying What shall we eat? What shall we drink? Or, How shall we be clothed? Much less entertained. The Christian does not entertain worldly entertainment, neither will its instruments or devices be found in his house. He is a *slave*, not an idle lounger. His time is not 'Leisure' but the LORD'S. His holidays are not vanity but Holy days. We are not to waste precious time even thinking about these things.

'For after all these things do the Gentiles seek.' Clean to the contrary, the disciple seeks with every nerve on the stretch, the best hours of the day, the maximum freshness of his brain, and the greatest strength of his life. But what he seeks is the kingdom of heaven. And he does it with an undivided heart, a single mind, and with his gaze fixed upon the world to come. That is his career. It is called, The earthly pilgrimage.

As to the rest, our heavenly Father provides it. Sometimes scarcely; sometimes abundantly. Sometimes in poverty; sometimes in riches. Sometimes with meagreness; sometimes with plenty. But never short of what is essential; and never necessary to be sought by the disciple. The Christian must not waste time seeking earthly things. They are added to him without seeking. All the power of seeking must be set upon the kingdom of heaven.

340

'But seek ye first the kingdom of God, and his righteousness; and all these things shall be added unto you.'

But what about the future? What about a job? What about tomorrow? 'Take no thought for the morrow.' Try being a real Christian instead. 'For the morrow shall take thought for the things of itself. Sufficient unto the day is the evil thereof.'

MATTHEW CHAPTER SEVEN

¶ Judgment and the kingdom. Ch. 7:1-27

The first twenty verses of this chapter are taken up with Messiah's doctrine instructing the disciples in every aspect of judgment.

'Judge not.' Yet it is not judgment absolutely that is prohibited. Because the passage goes on to demand self-judgment. It then implies — once judgment is laid to the line, and righteousness to the plummet, of one's own inmost soul — that one will be clear-eyed enough to aid one's brother by the same rule which one has first applied to oneself. Therefore 'judge not', before that time and process.

'Judge not,' demands he who said 'I judge no man.' The one who 'came not to judge'. Still, it is he that promptly adds, 'Thou hypocrite!' Clearly then, one must not jump to over-simplified conclusions, but be instructed aright and fully. Otherwise we shall not learn of him who said 'I judge no man. And yet if I judge, my judgment is true.'

'Judge not,' is not the end of chapter seven, but the beginning. But we are the children's children of those who in their day made the first two words of the chapter the beginning and end of it, and more: the be-all and end-all of Christianity. If they threw away their eyes, then in what kind of a dark valley of the blind shall their grandchildren be found in their day?

'Judge not,' saith he. Then proceeds to tell how to cast out motes. How to judge men who are dogs and pigs. How to obtain pure and righteous discernment. How to apply it in judgment. How to discriminate the entrance of a profession of conversion, and never to separate it from the whole long way of life. How to judge between two entrances of profession, the two ways of life and death. How to separate the precious from the vile, the false prophet from the true. How? It is not by the false prophet's sermon matter, his evangelical talk or prominence. For that looks like a sheep. It is by a judgment so keen that it rolls back both fleece and skin. 'Judge not'? Not absolutely.

'Judge not.' So spake the Messiah; and then adds *'but'*. 'Judge not but judge,' John 7:24. That is it: judge not wrongly, but judge rightly. Matthew seven verses two to twenty expound how to do this. John seven twenty-four simply adds 'Judge not, but *judge righteous judgment.'*

Judge not those whom the Lord has saved who were before of a profligate and dissipated character. Judge not, as the elder brother judged, the repentant wastrel now brought home to his father's house. Judge not, as Simon the Pharisee judged, the penitent whore who washed the feet of Jesus with her tears and dried them with her hair. Judge not the erstwhile reckless and wild Mary Magdalene, out of whom had gone seven devils. But the born religious, the 'Christians' from their mother's breast, they judge by nature such as are converted from out of the world as adults. However, the latter are the present work of God. The former are the heirs of their parents.

I remember that when I was first converted my lot fell for a while between two different baptist churches. I was regarded with stand-offish suspicion by these people, apt to twitch their lace curtains with distaste at my approach to engage them in prayer. Yet, looking back, if there was a converted soul among them, then I must thank God for well-hidden grace. Because of my lawless and wild past, they viewed me askance. They could not really bring themselves to forgive me as God had done. I recall that the minister — nice enough in himself — a Spurgeon's College graduate who affected pulpit mannerisms and alliterative initials, would not at first baptise me.

I challenged him, 'It is because with my wild past you doubt that it will last!' He could not deny it. Speechless, he had the grace to blush. I went on 'In this Bible which I have just begun to read I see that those whom the Lord had saved were baptised straightway. Now, I believe, and believe me, you are going to baptise me forthwith.' Straightway I was baptised: though knowing what I now know about the treacherous doctrinal perfidy of the Baptist Union, I wish I had found somewhere clean. Not to mention authority from heaven.

Judge not. That is, judge not the faithful servant of the Lord who lifts up his voice like a trumpet, to show God's people their transgression and the house of Jacob their sins. Judge not him whom God hath appointed to reprove in the gate. But the scorner loveth not one that reproveth him. Fools and blind, it is for thy welfare! And such haughty scorning of the Lord's servants by those who put themselves above reproach shall not profit.

For the terrible one is brought to nought, and the scorner is consumed, and all that watch for iniquity — that is, to discover hoped-for iniquity in God's servant, the reprover — are cut off:

That make a man — that is God's servant, the reprover — an offender for a word, and lay a snare for him that reproveth in the gate, and turn aside the just for a thing of nought. No, judge not God's servant, for he is for thy salvation.

Judge not thy brother. But not absolutely. Because the language of the humble brother is on this wise: 'Let the righteous smite me; it shall be a kindness: and let him reprove me; it shall be an excellent oil, which shall not break my head.' But, he that reproveth a scorner getteth to himself shame: and he that rebuketh a wicked man getteth himself a blot.

The rule is this: Reprove not a scorner, lest he hate thee: rebuke a wise man, and he will love thee. Yet notwithstanding God has sent his prophets to reprove the scorners of the house of Jacob. 'How long, ye simple ones, will ye love simplicity? And the scorners delight in their scorning, and fools hate knowledge?' Yea, God hath sent his servants as reprovers unto Zion, crying, Wherefore hear the word of the LORD, ye scornful men, that rule this people which is in Jerusalem ... be ye not mockers, lest your bands be made strong: for I have heard from the Lord GOD of hosts a consumption, even determined upon the whole earth.

Judge not thy brother with petty criticisms, carping fault-finding, miserable murmurings. Judge not from the wrong motive of diverting thine own attention from thine own faults by accusing others. Judge not from the wrong motive of exalting thyself through belittling others. Judge not by dismissing those that sin, err, and transgress as irrevocably beyond salvation. Judge not by habitually censoring and correcting others and doing little or nothing yourself. Judge not by presupposing thyself so very correct and untouchable. Judge not others, but thyself first.

And speak not even right judgment upon others' conduct and spirituality, however much thou knowest it to be just, when thou thyself art young and inexperienced. If it is needful, God shall open thy young mouth. Remember Elihu. A genuine insight, a disinterested desire for the good of souls, is not in itself the title to reprove. Age, experience, a leading of the Spirit withal, are also required. Still 'these little ones' are sometimes made to cry out. Only, let God do it to thee.

So then, the judgment that is prohibited in this place is that of useless censoriousness, the criticism of others to no constructive purpose. But the judgment that is positively required in context is that which affects one's own path, and which must — absolutely must — be made if spiritual progress is to continue.

Disciples are not to indulge in the fretting, dividing, backbiting judging of those who are forever criticising other people — yet never themselves — and who never make any spiritual progress whatsoever. They are static. They sit and judge everyone else. They never take a step forward as a result of their judgment, the sole purpose of which is to run others down. Especially those who walk in the fear of the Lord. Such as these, the just in particular, the religious critics sit and judge. They occupy the seat of the scorner. Till they get out of that disastrous place, and judge it, together with the fellowship that goes with it, they never will make one move towards God.

What is absolutely essential for the disciple — and required in the context of Matthew seven — is the judgment which faces moral, spiritual, personal, congregational, doctrinal, ministerial, and ecclesiastical issues. It is not too much to say that this is the distinctive mark of the real Christian. Of course it is; it must be: because this is the manifestation of genuine righteousness. Not to criticise others — God forbid — but to judge issues put in one's path, that one may deal rightly with them so as to continue walking — together with those who do likewise — in a way which pleases the Lord. This is to judge righteous judgment.

The lack of it is the great hold-up today, upon which any spiritual outpouring is undoubtedly conditional. When the gospel is corrupted, fellowship compromised, and judgment has ceased, then reformation must precede revival.

There now follow certain good reasons for refraining from condemnatory judgment upon others. 'That ye be not judged', who do the judging. Here is another reason: the unkind, pitiless, and unmerciful judgment which the critic hurls at others from his scorner's chair, is that which shall be hurled at him in turn from the throne of heaven. Has he forgotten so soon? 'Blessed are the merciful: for they shall obtain mercy.'

Another good reason: such people who corrupt the essential faculty of discrimination — a faculty given that the righteous may judge aright — into a censorious contempt of sinners and others not of their party, such people, I say, have a log in their eye. How about getting that out first?

For this is the subject of verses one to five of chapter seven: self-judgment comes first. Not theoretic self-judgment to bring the intellect into line with doctrinal schemes. Real self-judgment about one's walk. One's state of heart. About the length of time spent regularly in private prayer. About the extent and duration of secret daily Bible reading. One's purity of conversation. One's rectitude of life. About the felt work of God upon and within one's soul. About union with the Lord Jesus, communion with the Father, and abiding in the Spirit. One's time. One's 'spare' time. About money. One's devotedness. One's fellowship.

Things like that. They come first. Then one can help others with their motes. 'Then will I teach transgressors thy ways.'

But even that must be discriminate. 'Give not that which is holy unto the dogs.' For you must learn what is holy by being holy. And you must judge who are dogs by being a sheep. 'Beware of dogs' saith the apostle Paul. And who are they? Why, legalists who cry up the law, but actually live lives which contradict it by their unholiness. They 'make a noise like a dog, and go round about the city.' But not into it, for, 'without are dogs.'

And pigs. 'Neither cast ye your pearls before swine.' So you must judge the value of pearls aright, which no pig ever did, though it grunted at your right judgment. And you must discern pigs clearly, much as they may squeal 'judge not, judge not' whilst you are doing so. Fear them not, but judge righteous judgment in the fear of God.

I will say how the righteous discern the swine. Then you may tell both the righteous and the swine, and what is more, tell them apart. Not so easy as it sounds, for this requires the passage of time.

The swine make a noise of liberty, but in fact they are the slaves of corruption. The swine escape the pollutions of the world, but afterwards return to their swill. The pig receives the knowledge of the Lord and Saviour Jesus Christ, but later takes that name to go back with it and become entangled and overcome of the world. The pig's beginning is fair, but its end is the worse for that. Swine know the way of righteousness, but subsequently pollute it in their mire. Pigs take the holy commandment delivered unto them, but having taken delivery they wallow upon it in their sty. However the profession is still there. Once a pig always a pig. Once swine, always swine.

For just as the dogs are locked out of the city, so the swine shall be choked in the deep. They will find that their false profession will do them no good.

Neither will unholy alliance with them — under the smoke-screen of 'we must not judge, brother' — do the sheep any good. Let the sheep flock together. And let the swine herd as they will elsewhere.

Give not that which is holy unto the dogs, neither cast

ye your pearls before swine. You will do them no good. You will lose the pearls in the trampled mire. And you yourself shall be rent open, and do well if you but escape with your life.

Verses seven to twelve do not appear to be concerned with the subject of judgment, and yet evidently such must be the case. The first six verses of the chapter speak of self-judgment leading to discrimination. And from the thirteenth verse onwards there is no doubt that discernment and judgment dominate the remainder of the 'Sermon on the Mount'.

The passage in question — Ask; Seek; Knock — appears as it were sandwiched between consistent layers of judgment, and the reader will ask, Why is it there? The answer must be, That in connection with righteous judgment, with spiritual discernment, with divine discrimination, the saints are encouraged to apply by faith for the certain answer of God's counsel. It is not, ask for anything: but, for this good thing. So necessary is it that the disciple obtains inspiration and direction in every case that he is invited to ask, to persist, and to rap upon the door of heaven, till the Urim and Thummim of unerring counsel appear to his soul.

This is a passage fairly bursting with encouragement. Bounty seems to split the seams of each laden text, spilling over with good things, so to lie thick upon the page as handfuls of purpose for the gleaning of faith.

So categorical! It shall. Ye shall. It shall. Not a cloud in the blue of heaven: who can doubt? No sooner ask: given. Even as sought: immediately found. As the knuckles rap: forthwith the door opens. 'And it shall come to pass, that before they call, I will answer; and while they are yet speaking, I will hear.'

So impartial! Every one. And he. And him. So generous! Asketh receiveth. Seeketh findeth. Knocketh openeth.

So inevitable! Find the man whose child, clinging to his father's legs, looks up with wide eyes all trusting, and cries Abba, bread. Find the man, I say, who gives a stone and dares to see the crushed disappointment of betrayed trust in the eyes of uncomprehending innocence.

Or a fish; to the son of his loins, the hope of his house, the blood of his blood, the bone of his bone: will he give a venomous serpent? What man?

We, fallen, evil, rotten as so often we have found our hearts to be, still we cannot. Oh, for shame, cannot, stoop to so despicable a betrayal of sweet unquestioning trust in our children. Rather die! If we, for all the sickening discoveries of bottomless perfidy we dare not explore but quickly hide, if we cannot deny such loving certainty of trust in the fresh young eyes of our lad: can God? Can our Father in heaven deny us? No, he cannot do it. It is not in him to deny us. Just not in him.

But how to walk, how to go, what to do, how know the right? That is it; the question of unerring judgment in every case, he will give it. The meek he will guide in judgment. No good thing will he withhold from them that walk uprightly. He will instruct us and teach us in the way which we shall go: he will guide us with his eye. If any man lack wisdom, let him ask of God, who giveth to all men liberally, and upbraideth not. He shall lead us into all truth. There is no question about this. It is at once categorical, impartial, generous and inevitable.

Only, as he does to you, do thou to thy fellows. As to that, whatsoever ye would that they should do to you, do that to them; for this is right judgment. Moreover, it is the law and the prophets. It is also the secret counsel of the indwelling Spirit of God.

We come now to the famous verses on the wide gate and broad way, contrasted with the strait and narrow. A matter for unerring judgment if ever there was one.

The gate to the narrow way is described in terms of that which produces character. It is known by character. But it is not a real gate. It is a spiritual description of a moral entrance. Therefore it is entered by character. When a man's soul is reduced to the right moral size and shape, he can get past. When the character is conformed by and to this kind of straitness, the gate has happened to us, and we are through.

It is not a gate of doctrine. It is a gate of the inward experience which alone warrants confidence that the doctrine applies to *me!* It is the gate of the work of the Spirit which gives *title* to the doctrine. Well, isn't it? Does it say, Enter ye in at the Justification gate? Or the Calvary gate? No it does not.

But you say, We must believe in justification, we must

trust on the work of Calvary. True. However multitudes, multitudes affirm that they do this, yet if they are honest with themselves they must admit that they have no more experience of the strait gate than they have of the North Pole. And yet far from desiring to be told this, they are infuriated. They do not believe that they are in danger, strait gate or no strait gate. Then they do not believe Messiah's doctrine.

They do not believe his words and teaching, but pare down the gospel to a 'simple believer' system. This is a pernicious excuse completely to dispose of the necessity for the work and evidences of the Holy Ghost, as well as dismiss both vast tracts of the New Testament and its exhortatory and warning tenor. No wonder what I say about the strait gate irritates them! Only it is not I, but the Lord.

It is a fact that the gate is described for our judgment — *your* judgment — to recognise from the description. And that description is not 'Forgiveness gate' or 'Believer gate', it is *strait* gate. Have you been through *that* one? Or do you prefer to follow man, and rest in the cushioning lies of the decayed evangelicalism softly falling since the end of the last century?

It is called a *strait* gate: this gives a man true title to the doctrine, just as it really validates one's believing. Neither our doctrine nor our believing validate *it*. Did they, the name of the gate would be Doctrine gate, or Believer's gate. But both those must be bottomed on this, tried by it, and searched out through it: *strait* gate. That is the judgment.

And it is not only a matter of judgment, but action. *Enter* ye in. And not only so, for Luke tells us the Master saith '*Strive* to enter in.' Don't think that you can slide, walk, ease or drift in: you cannot. In its nature, *this gate hurts.* Hence 'Many, I say unto you, will seek to enter in, and shall not be able.' Why? Because they cannot, and they will not, stand the pain.

This exhortation of the Lord Jesus to his disciples, 'Enter ye in at the strait gate,' is now reinforced by two pertinent motives, negative and positive, set in contrast the one to the other.

These motives are revealed respectively by the words 'For', and 'Because'. Enter ye in at the strait gate *for* this reason, verse thirteen. *Because* of the following fact, verse fourteen.

Enter ye disciples in at the strait gate, *for* it is so very easy to take the alternative. So many have done this and of course multitudes are doing it at present. Besides, all these are led by those who are famous and had in such reputation in the religious world, and it would seem right to follow the majority encouraged to safety by such reputable guides.

For example, the whole of Judaism — as an entity — was being led straight through the wide gate, right down the broad way, forthwith to plummet over the precipice and be pitched twisting and turning until they disappeared from sight into the bottomless pit. If so, then who on earth was leading them? Devils incarnate? No. The sons of Aaron. The chief priests. The Levites. The learned scholars. The profound exponents and exegetes. Masters in Israel. The elders of the people. The judges of Israel. The official preachers, prophets and teachers of the people. Scribes and Pharisees, Sadducees and doctors of the law. The council and Sanhedrin of Israel. They led the people. They led them both to deny the Messiah and reject the Holy Ghost. They led them to destruction. And the people went in thereat.

That is, save for a remnant according to the election of grace. Otherwise, the people blindly followed. No doubt saying of Peter and the apostles 'We must not follow a man.' No, they would follow the tried old paths of their fathers. But what if their fathers were wrong? There is a way which seemeth right unto a man, the end whereof is death. It is the majority way. The way of following majority leaders. 'Many there be which go in thereat.'

Generally speaking the wide gate and broad way have been represented as irreligious, contrasted with the religious strait gate and narrow way. Long faces, usually old women, with wagging fingers, have intoned against fretting youth, warning of the evils of drink, of gambling, of smoking, of the picture house, theatre, and the dance hall, of the big city, representing these to be the wide gate and broad way. A typical example of misapplying scripture to protect one's own personal interests by using veiled threats to resist the flight of the fledglings from the nest. Such methods never worked. More often than not their motive was really parental selfishness.

Instinctively youth sensed the low motive and anyway resented the lack of trust. Not that I would for one moment condone drink, gambling, smoking, dancing or picture-going. Any more than worldly 'sport'; or come to that, radio and television. The best of these is unnecessary, a waste of time and energy, interfering with the single-minded pursuit of heaven. The worst, actually prevents it. But it is no good calling such things the 'wide gate and broad way', because that is just not the meaning.

The wide gate and broad way is an *alternative religious way*, not at all the way of the world in contrast with religion.

Consider: Matthew 5:1 refers mostly to Israel and wholly to seekers. That in itself makes it a religious context. But far more so, for — out of religious Israel — the Messiah's 'disciples came unto him, and he opened his mouth and taught *them*.' They came voluntarily, wanting, needing, a more profound religion than that taught in Israel. It was to *them* that he said in consequence 'Enter *ye* in at the strait gate: for wide is the gate, and broad is the way, that leadeth to destruction, and many there be which go in thereat.'

There could be no possible question of the alternative to the disciples being the lusts and irreligion of the world. The danger was of soft and easy, or self-righteous and strict, false religion. That therefore is what is being designated 'wide and broad': the danger to the disciples.

Observe that two gates and two ways are contrasted. Now then, consider in the broader context of the whole Sermon on the Mount what has been contrasted elsewhere. Is it the lustful, wasteful irreligious Gentile world, set against the way of true religion? No it is not.

Chapter five. 'Your righteousness' is over against 'the righteousness of the scribes and Pharisees'. Three times 'Ye have heard that it was said by them of old time', is contrasted with 'But I say unto you'. Twice 'Ye have heard that it hath been said', with 'But I say unto you'.

Chapter six. The hypocrites do alms this way; but you do it that way. The hypocrites pray thus; but you pray so.

The hypocrite fasts in one manner; only you fast in another manner. Those who draw near with their mouth have their heart or their treasure on earth. But you who draw near with your heart have your treasure in heaven. The mouth professor is worldly; but the children of God are heavenly.

Coming to the narrower context of chapter seven, consider the contrasts: Judge not; but judge righteous judgment. They judge after the flesh; you ask, and shall be enabled to judge after the Spirit. Strait is the gate and narrow the way; but wide is the gate and broad is the way. False prophets are contrasted with true prophets. Good trees with corrupt in religion. It is not everyone that says to Christ 'Lord, Lord,' whom he owns, but in contrast only those to whom he himself owns Lordship. 'Whosoever heareth these sayings of mine and doeth them', is set over against those that 'hear these sayings of mine and do them not'.

Invariably two ways of religion — one safe and true, the other false and damnably dangerous — are set in contrast. Therefore the wide gate is the majority religious entrance, and it includes those who profess Messiah's words as well as those who advocate Moses', and plenty who mix the two together. Hence the broad way is not for a moment irreligious, because it is filled with the self-righteous still attempting to do what was said of old time, as well as prophets, judges, trees, fruits, 'Lord, Lord's,' casters-out-of-demons, and many who did — they thought — wonderful works for Jesus.

That is the wide gate and broad way. And it yawns still to this day. If one is religious, committed, has made one's decision, is a believer, then, without really strong resistance, one will be swept into it. Mighty strivings are needed, yea, are essential, before the strait gate may be attained.

The second, and positive, motive follows.

Because strait is the gate, and narrow is the way, which leadeth unto life, and few there be that find it.

How this way — the only authorised way: the divine way: the LORD'S way — of describing Christianity has fallen into disrepair and disrepute. It is utterly out of fashion. In place of the strait gate there rests a feather-bed easy-believism, cushioned with a let-go-and-let-God frivolity of the most shocking proportions. Over the past century a series of American mass-evangelists employing dollar-backed advertising and popular political meeting techniques evolved in the hustings have been here today and gone tomorrow, claiming vast figures in the interim. Going for the easy decision, the immediate result, this corruption clean contradicts these very words of the Lord Jesus, making a mockery of the persecuted simplicity of the apostles, and a travesty of the entrance into the kingdom.

Quite apart from the fact that the LORD describes a conversion, believing, or becoming a Christian as a Strait Gate, requiring earnest and long striving, there is also the designation of the Narrow Way. This is not described by Messiah as life. He says that it 'leadeth unto life'. And although without doubt life is found in it, still the LORD cuts off all presumption, all stopping short of Canaan, all easy-believism and audacious trifling by saying that it *leadeth* unto life'. And not surprisingly, few there be that find it.

The truth is, few even get faithful descriptions of it.

Observe then, and mark strictly, the lifelong path is *inseparable* from the entrance gate, in the description of Christianity given by way of warning from the Son of God. It is a question of judgment. Judge ye what I say.

The apostolic gospel not only converted men so that 'ye turned to God from idols to serve the living and true God' — which the 'strait gate' describes — but moreover that same gospel in the belief of it made them to be the church 'which is in God the Father and in the Lord Jesus Christ.' If the gospel of their salvation did not itself create them into the church of God it was false: but with the apostolic gospel in the early church it did so create them. The gospel formed the church. It was not something superfluous to it, an extraneous optional matter. Their conversion was the gate. The narrow way describes that congregation called the church of God which had entered that gate. Those who entered the strait gate were, *per se* upon the narrow way. That was what led to life. And that body of pilgrims seeking it was described as the church.

To separate *gate* from *way*, as American evangelism does, is damnable. As if 'your decision' could take the place of the strait gate! But then heartlessly to leave the decisionists floundering for themselves — telling them they have life for good already — making 'the church of your choice' answer to the narrow way, this is both deceitful and fiendish. When the apostle preached the strait gate, and by the grace of God converts were brought through it onto the narrow way, they became the church of God. They were not enticed to go to a church: they were the church. It was not a question of the 'church of their choice': they were the church of God's choice.

And moreover the apostle continually — mark that,

continually — yearned over them as a distinct congregation raised up in consequence of his preaching. He prayed for them, wept for them, earnestly exhorted them, trembled for them, shepherded them, stayed long time with them, revisited them, and wrote to them. He did not feed synagogues, state churches, denominations or sects with his converts, leaving nothing distinct behind. His preaching left the church itself behind. And when the apostle could not go himself he sent those under him in the ministry that the church might continue faithful to the end. There was no question of 'booking speakers'. Oh, it has all gone rotten. But yet the LORD shall mightily raise up his holy word and so grant us a little reviving again.

Now then hear this: hear Messiah's description of the true Christian religion.

It is described first as a 'strait gate'. That is the entrance. Therefore this answers to believing, being converted, turning, repenting, being saved, being regenerate or in any event becoming a Christian. In Messiah's words it is entering the strait gate.

The word translated 'strait' — στενός, *stenos* — is in this form used exclusively of the gate. However it belongs to a family of five words having exactly the same stem and differing only in the ending to give a different grammatical bearing. The root — and hence the essential meaning — remains the same. Let us consider the use of this root.

It is used of the children of Israel under sore bondage in Egypt when over the years their heart-rending sighs ascended to heaven, and, saith JEHOVAH, I have seen, I have seen the affliction of my people which is in Egypt, and I have heard their *groaning*, and am come down to deliver

them. Groaning. Στεναγμός, *stenagmos:* the experience of
the strait gate. The tragedy was that though they all groaned
with straitness, many did not continue in the narrow way
to Canaan, but fell in the wilderness. Didn't they?

This straitness does not go away with entrance. It stays
with us. For, Even we ourselves *groan* within ourselves; we
that are in this tabernacle do *groan;* still, our light affliction
is but for a moment — this present life — and works for us
a far more exceeding and eternal weight of glory. It is a
groaning, an affliction, all along the path: still, the joy that
is set before us lightens the pressure, and we press forward
all the faster.

The word in the Greek tongue literally means Narrow;
as, narrow-throated, narrow-shaped, narrow-chested. It
refers to straitened cries, to unnatural contraction of the
pupil, to hair so fast set in that one screams when it is
pulled out. It is used to describe hard pronunciation, of
one being in difficulties, of a narrow or small-minded
person. The word is employed to describe a narrow space,
a narrows, straits; and that is the primary meaning.

Metaphorically therefore it implies pressure sideways.
Scraping through a constriction so narrow that the ribs
bend and there is an agonising danger of getting stuck. The
place is so tight the arms must be thrust forward, the
chest groans, the shoulders creak, the hips are crushed,
claustrophobia sets up a panic; that is straitness.

And the real Christian starts this way and more or less, it
is always with him. 'In this we groan, being burdened.' Oh
yes, it is a strait gate: the spiritual pressure is past what the
flesh can comprehend or endure. 'Pressed out of measure.'
But the Comforter takes us through.

The way is described as 'narrow'. There are two grammatical forms of the New Testament Greek for this word, θλίβω, *thlibo* and θλῖψις, *thlipsis*, both having the same basic meaning and differing in no more than the part of speech. It means pressure downwards. The word has been used to convey crushing, oppression, compression, castration by crushing, affliction and reduction. To me, perhaps the most graphic picture of this word is that of the pressure of the wine press, distorting the grape out of shape until the skin can bear the crushing force no longer, and bursts to splatter out the precious juices. Pressure downwards.

That is what is characteristic of the narrow way. But it leads to life. It is not life, but it leads to life. All right, sensations of life are promised, felt, and given along the way. But the great tenor of the apostle and his apostles' preaching as to the pilgrim way is this: 'Let him that thinketh he standeth take heed lest he fall.' Let not him that putteth on the harness boast as he that taketh it off. All right, rejoice; but I counsel thee, as one not without favour from and fruit towards God: Rejoice with trembling. Not without it. We are not home yet.

This pressure, squeezing, affliction, is the lot of all who are upon the narrow way, and those who do not have it are not upon it. Pressure is the name of the way. It may not be the lot of Catholic, state, orthodox or denominational churches, but it is the lot of the true congregations of the Lord's people. Invariably. That is how you may tell them. They are upon the *pressure* way. They are to this day still 'the sect everywhere spoken against'. They are separate, outside the camp, and the bearing of Christ's reproach is no small burden. But they count it all joy and say, We were comforted in all our afflictions.

Consider the apostle. 'Bonds and afflictions abide me' he cries. He writes 'out of much affliction and anguish of heart'. He ministered 'in much patience and afflictions'. He 'filled up that which was behind of the afflictions of Christ'. But for their sakes he 'desired that they faint not at my tribulation'. Nay, he gloried in tribulation, was exceeding joyful in all his tribulation. Now these words, affliction, tribulation, are basically the same Greek as that for 'narrow'.

Consider the church. They 'received the word in much affliction'. They were exhorted 'that no man should be moved by these afflictions: for yourselves know that we are appointed thereunto'. The saints were told faithfully 'we should suffer tribulation even as it came to pass'. The apostle rejoiced at their steadfastness, these brethren who would not accept deliverance by choosing the popular easy way 'So that we ourselves glory in you in the churches of God for your patience and faith in all your persecutions and tribulations that ye endure'. And which church is this today? The Parish Church? The modern 'free' churches? The brethren assembly? Not likely. It is a church that has well-nigh disappeared but which yet God shall raise up again by his holy word to reappear and shine forth in all her separate, humble, lowly, heavenly and divine glory.

The narrow way. All the way. Nothing but pressure sideways, and pressure downwards. Men do it to us in this world; mostly religious and professing men. Church men. 'Evangelical' men. And God shall do it to these men in the next world: 'It is a righteous thing with God to recompense *tribulation* to them that *trouble* you.' That is, they trouble, pressurise, us throughout this world, and we must meekly bear it. But God will recompense, repay, the tribulation they gave to us in this world, by pressurising them in the

next. Only with our comforts, it seems a light affliction.
And this world is but for a moment. And they are but men.
However the next world is forever. And for them there are
no comforts. And their pressure, world without end, is
from God and not men. And it is not light, but an endless
heavy burden. So 'you who are troubled, *pressurised*, rest
with us, when the Lord Jesus shall be revealed from heaven
with his mighty angels, in flaming fire taking vengeance on
them that know not God, and that obey not the gospel of
our Lord Jesus Christ.'

As these men did to us in this life, so God will do to
them in the next life. So it is said: 'God will render to
every man according to his deeds: To them who by patient
continuance in well doing seek for glory and honour and
immortality, eternal life.' It was hard for them. Some have
had so little gospel light. Some much. But in common they
all looked to the world to come and utterly lived for it
answering to what gospel light they had. They all strove in
the fear of God and the light of Messiah to please him by
patient continuance in good works; good works in which
they put no trust, but rather hoped in his mercy. God will
reward them — by Christ Jesus — with eternal life.

'But unto them that are contentious, and do not obey
the truth' — though such people appoint themselves the
sole exponents of the truth, its publishers and custodians;
still, they do not *obey* the truth; only talk of it — 'but
obey unrighteousness.' That is what they obey whilst they
talk of the truth. Meanwhile they persecute those who do
obey it; that is, the humble and obedient few who seek for
glory and honour and immortality by patient continuance
in good works. Such as these, the talkers persecute.
Well, God will render them their portion in the world to
come.

363

'Indignation and wrath' world without end shall without fail be upon them. They persecuted those on the strait — στενός — and narrow — θλῖψις — way on earth. In hell God will reward them according to their deeds world without end. 'Tribulation — θλῖψις — and anguish — στενός — upon every soul of man that doeth evil, of the Jew first, and also of the Gentile.' It is not said without *talk*, but it says that without *holiness* no man shall see the Lord.

So then, those that neglected to apply the cross to their own lives; who carefully searched out a doctrinal scheme to avoid the entrance of the strait gate; those who despised patient continuance required upon the narrow way in this short life, fail utterly. They shall have that straitness and narrowness — which they shunned here below — whether they like it or not, in the next life. And have it world without end, and have it from God and not men. And have it far worse than could ever have been possible on earth. The mouth of the Lord hath spoken it. That is the judgment. 'Στενός and θλῖψις.'

Therefore my brethren, therefore, heed the Messiah:

'Enter ye in at the strait gate.'

Because of the agonising importance of determining between the two gates and their consequent ways in religion, there follows immediately the solemn warning:

'Beware of false prophets.'

These are the ones, in context, who shepherd multitudes through the wide gate, with bland assurances of everlasting safety. These are they who, with many a jolly jest, usher the unthinking multitude — that has already gone in through the wide gate — happily along the broad way that leadeth to destruction, assuring them the meanwhile of certain and eternal security.

Hence — because without such zealous advocates, such blind guides, not so many would go that way — hence, I say, the imperative 'Beware of false prophets.'

Now, it is obvious that the context demands the linking of this warning about false prophets with the danger of the wide gate and broad way; and seeing that it is certain that such false prophets advocate that wide gate and broad way; moreover given that the wide gate and broad way exist to this very moment — they are presently extant — then I ask, Who takes any notice of Messiah's warning now?

But, should we wake up and take notice, how shall we know these false prophets? First, from the very context, in that they do not repeat nor do they enforce these warnings of Messiah. If not, then they are not of Messiah's prophets. Who is of Christ, repeats and enforces his doctrine. Who is not, cries Peace, Peace, when there is no peace. Well saith Isaiah of them 'They are all dumb dogs, they cannot bark.' They give no warning, you see, no warning. They cannot and will not awaken the sleepers to danger: they cannot bark. No danger of hell? No danger of unholiness? No danger in a shallow profession? No danger of worldliness? No danger of turning back? Dumb dogs do not bark when danger comes. They continue to lick feet, fawning and cringing for another handout. Meanwhile the people perish. No trumpet is ever blown by false prophets.

That is the characteristic of the false prophets from

context. Christ gives warning, crying 'Beware!' These dogs grin dumbly, clowning and ingratiating themselves to be patted, whilst a wall of fire roars down upon the city of destruction.

Now however, Messiah actually describes these false prophets in the words of his doctrine, so that we may be able to judge them by his description. If we fail to do so, and are religious, we shall be taken in by them. Judgment of this right kind is essential if we are to be saved. 'Beware of false prophets' saith Christ, and forthwith describes them. 'We must not judge brother' say the false prophets, thereby condemning Christ for his description. And many there be which go in thereat. 'Nice' is not the criterion. Salvation is. And if you do not judge righteous judgment, you shall let salvation slip through your gullibility.

'They come to you in sheep's clothing.' Then there is no exterior difference between them and the sheep. As to all outward appearance they are just the same. The same exterior letter of scripture. The same external company of professing Christians. The same occupation as the true prophets. The same doctrine and confession as the real Christians. The same appearance of meekness and docility. A gentle, affected niceness. If an avoidance of certain truths, still, such human warmth, such devotional sentiment.

But they are utterly damnable, beguiling multitudes to hell with fair words by which they deceive the simple. Beware of false prophets, which come to you in sheep's clothing, saith Christ.

Yet how can they possibly be told apart, you ask? Apart from what, I inquire? Why, the sheep of course, you answer. Well, that is hard, but not impossible. However, where one can easily tell them apart is in the difference between them and the true prophets. The true prophet soon finds out the false, and in love to the souls of the people, roundly exposes and thunders against the impostor! Whereas the false prophet coyly smirks with what he hopes looks like a 'Christlike' spirit, gently murmering, We must not judge, brother; let us rather pray for the poor misguided critic. And how many silly sheep are taken in by this sort of cant, too.

As to telling the difference between false prophets in sheep's clothing, and the sheep themselves, however, it cannot be done by outward appearance, and therefore requires a discrimination concerning the cultivation of which all too many are rashly impatient. The difference can only be discerned inwardly. The distinction is in the interior. The discrimination lies in being able to tell what is spiritual from what is lupine. Despite all that appearance, *inwardly* they are ravening wolves.

They have the dead letter, but they have not the living Spirit. They have tables of stone but they have not fleshy tables of the heart. They have self-righteousness, fretting, and irritation in the flesh, but they have not righteousness, peace and joy in the Holy Ghost. They have the forms of baptism, breaking of bread, the Lord's supper, but they are not buried with Christ, have not eaten his flesh, neither do they drink his blood. They have an outward profession but they have not an inward union. They have the word but not the power. They have the theory but not the reality. They have the Bible but not the Saviour. They have Jehovah but not the Father. They have the tables of stone but not the engraving of the Spirit. They can point to Christian parents but can give no account of vital regeneration.

They are deadletter preachers. They bite and devour both sheep and one another. Sheep ache and waste under their dry ministry. They multiply books but neglect the Holy Bible. They talk oft one to another, but their closet is neglected and dusty. They can carp but not cry. Whisper but not weep. Slander but not supplicate. Preach but not pray. Show degrees but not calling. These are your inward wolves. They come to you in sheep's clothing.

And another way to tell them, saith Christ, is by their fruits. By their fruits ye shall know them. They look like sheep: but they do not beget lambs. They seem like sheep: but they slaver like wolves. They feel like sheep: but they howl with the pack. What comes out reveals what is really within. Moreover, this kind is seed-bearing within itself: it reproduces only after its own kind. What the false prophets reproduce is not the fleece that conceals, but the wolf that destroys. They beget none of the fruit of the Spirit within the heart. What they bring forth is the intellectual party-forming of the flesh which divides the flock.

I say, they appear to be sheep, but they beget no flock. Well, that is how you know them. Wolves bear no lambs. Grapes bear no briars. Figs bear no thistles. Sheep beget lambs. Vines beget grapes. Fig trees beget the fruit thereof. But wolves drop wolf cubs. Briars shoot out thorns. Thistles spread forth their own curse. Not by the appearance, but by their fruit ye shall know them.

It is the same with trees. If the tree is good the fruit is good. But if the tree is rotten the fruit is rotten. The tree bears what it is. It can bear no other. Though the rottenness be hid deep within, so far as to be hidden in the roots, though the exterior be fair, the fruit will show the secret evil. Conversely, a battered, wind-torn, weather-gnarled old tree, twisted and bent and knotted in the hard battle for life, yet, when the heart is sound, though the exterior be so scarred, the fruit is good.

More. Here an inevitability is discovered. A good tree cannot bring forth evil fruit. It is not possible. No more can a corrupt tree bring forth good fruit. Not ever. It was all determined in the planting. With time of fruitbearing, the case long settled, comes to light. From the planting the fruit is inevitable. Just so with the two kinds of prophets. You cannot change them: they are what they are. Then what is all this talk of staying in orchards of rotten trees to 'do good within'? Who are these people to set the words of Christ at nought? By their fruits, saith he, ye shall know them. And by them, their state is settled.

For the corrupt, the Last Judgment alone remains: every tree that bringeth not forth good fruit is hewn down and cast into the fire. That is the Gehenna of the lake of fire. There shall they burn forever.

But discerning disciples, exercising righteous judgment, are not to wait till that last day. If for lack of judgment or fear of judging they swallowed too much evil fruit, what would become of them? The wolves would take their sick souls. They are to judge and act for their own soul's salvation *now*. Straightway.

'Wherefore by their fruits ye shall know them,' verse twenty. That is for the disciples' judgment. Safe; he has told you before.

Now follows the LORD'S judgment, verses twenty-one to twenty-seven.

First of all, his discrimination of professing Christians and of the church in the day of judgment. He is of purer eyes than to accept the mere profession of his name, or claimed service of his gospel. His eyes, in fact, are as a flame of fire, and it is by these that his discrimination is determined. Not by the acceptance of what the church declares to be so, or by what its hierarchies, ministers, pastors or priests claim on his behalf.

'Not every one that saith unto me, Lord, Lord, shall enter into the kingdom of heaven.' Not by any means.

Nevertheless, every one that saith unto him, Lord, is at the very least a professing Christian and a nominal member of the church. Far more than this, whosoever saith Lord, Lord — twice over — is by implication much keener than the mere singular member.

Yet, I ask you, is it not true that the vast, vast majority trust in the simple profession of his name, provided only that it is endorsed by the acceptance of 'normal evangelical circles'? Given that some minister, or respected brother, knows someone who knows someone amongst the Keswick circle of speakers or Filey round of entertainers, then it is assumed that — with those whom they pronounce Christians — this closes the matter on earth just as much as any Catholic would blindly trust in a papal absolution. I say to you plainly, this sightless trusting in man on the part of blind evangelicalism is worse than any popery, and its blind guides more disgusting than any sacramental Catholic priest. Judge for yourself.

In that day, far more profound evidence will be required by the Son of God. The failure of the church constantly to preach this agonisingly important fact for so long a time — and this indictment includes many popular and even idolised preachers, dead and alive — is to me almost as vicious an error as Arianism. After all, if the deluded soul is lost in and for eternity, what will he care — in his everlasting torment — as to any distinction in the earthly instrument that caused his downfall? Indeed the more specious, the more damnable the advocates of error.

I say, Christ does not accept the mere profession of his name at the bar of his judgment-seat, no matter how acceptable that was supposed to have been on earth. Now, 'Lord' or 'Lord, Lord' count for nothing in and of themselves in heaven. Weightier evidence shall be required at that day. At the Judgment all the earthly verbal and dispensational juggling about the 'Bema' — ineffectually hoping to excuse themselves that 'great white throne' — will dissolve to nothing: the sheer quality of life will appear in glory, as to those who 'shall not come into condemnation, but are passed from death unto life'. In that day all the erstwhile bland assurances of ministers, missionaries, evangelists, elders, deacons, leaders, that 'all you have to do is ...', will count for less than nothing. *The soul stands alone.* His props dissolved in the fire. He must answer for himself without reference to others or their persuasions.

Starting awake at the trumpet's blast, lit by the icy glare of a throne impervious to excuses, the trembling soul is finally torn loose from the false comforters and their constantly administered opiates. How tawdry now that decadent religion obsessed to assure its adherents 'God loves you; everything will turn out all right.' But it is not all right. Blasted from such cosy delusions, forced to

371

face responsibilities previously shrugged off or hopefully
dismissed because 'everybody does', now the former
blandishments made in the Lord's name by speakers,
preachers, teachers, and the merry band of their fellow
travellers, besides the general persuasion of the 'evangelical'
majority, lie in broken shards about the feet. The great
assize tears away every veil, and the last vestige of pretence.

Hanging suspended between heaven and earth, fixed
by the inexorable light of eternity, poised between two
everlasting seas of timelessness on the right hand and on
the left: the soul, every soul, your soul, mine, shall be made
to stand absolutely alone, thus to render full account. Even
then, 'Many will say to me in that day, Lord, Lord.' They
knew him? Well, he never knew them.

Serried ranks shall rise aghast from the heaving cauldron
of the disintegrating creation, many in horror clutching the
fading memory of erstwhile clerical dignity. Pope after pope
shall cry 'Did we not pontificate in thy name?' Cardinal
after cardinal, prelate after prelate, priest after priest:
Lord! Lord! Archbishop after archbishop, bishop after
bishop, minister after minister, evangelist after evangelist,
worker after worker, Sunday-school teacher after Sunday-
school teacher: 'Lord!' after 'Lord!' All accompanied
against a continuous background of the awful and stricken
wail from those great multitudes who stupidly followed
and emptily trusted such blind guides, now at last come to
the endless discovery of who it was that really 'followed a
man'.

What wails arise; 'Lord, have we not prophesied in thy
name?' What of that? A lifetime of Christian prophecy will
in many, many cases be followed by an eternity of hellish
misery. Such preaching in his name! Such spellbinding

oratory! How the congregations hung upon every word, the galleries silent with the mighty effect. What gift, what prophecy; what a saint, what a follower of apostolic doctrine! Yes? Did they then prophesy in his name? Are they *so* sure? Multitudes were so sure and still are sure. But saith Christ '*Many* will say to me in that day, Lord, Lord, have we not prophesied in thy name? Then will I profess unto them, I never knew you.'

If these impostors were so obvious here below, then why the dreadful shock on high?

Many will object to his condemnation of them in that day, 'Lord, Lord, have we not in thy name cast out devils? And in thy name done many wonderful works?' The basis of such a complaint against his judgment is this: Since the Lord gave such miraculous testimony to their ministry on earth, such signs, wonders, providences attended them, what right has he to disown them in heaven? This right: 'The Father hath committed all judgment unto the Son.' The right of a court from which there is no appeal. The right of 'his bishoprick let another take.' The right of a Judge who cannot err. The right of 'none of them is lost but the son of perdition.' The right of the Almighty who turns to heaven or hell forever. And, pray, who are you that sayest unto him, What doest thou?

But I will tell you this: ever since the decease of the apostles, nothing is more dangerous in the history of the church than miracles, and never more so than in the last days. Claimed signs and miracles are to be regarded with the utmost suspicion. In my judgment they are best left and ignored. At the end of the age such 'miracles' — healings, wonders, manifestations, tongues, exorcisms, foretellings — are the mark of the beast. The term beast is simply a metaphor. It means a unified religious 'form' that becomes a new acceptable worldly and earthly copy of the old heavenly and spiritual faith. This deceives the whole world: 'Deceiving them that dwell on the earth by the means of those miracles which he had power to do.' Lord, Lord, have we not prophesied in thy name? And in thy name cast out devils? And in thy name done many wonderful works?

Works such as supposed 'tongues'? Such as claimed 'healings'? All these pentecostal or charismatic claims? You can keep them. I want my Bible; I want my closet; I want to fall on my face and fear God; I want the Lord to teach me his gospel; I want the interior power of saving faith with that word; I want to meet with plain godly serious brethren who do likewise out of their own spiritual exercises. Let the majority follow men if they will! 'All the world wondered after the beast.'

But, hearken unto me, ye children, saith the Spirit, and I will teach you the fear of the Lord.

Signs and wonders in the last days? These are the days when God sends 'strong delusion' on those that depart from the old gospel faith. I remember recently the head of what is supposed to be a great missionary society beside himself as he enthused to me of certain fantastic miracles he claimed were happening in the far east. I received this with total unenthusiasm. He pitied me. However the test in the Old Testament of who was God, or who was not God, under Elijah, was this: He was God who brought down fire from heaven. Well, look at the dangerous state in the last days: the 'beast' of pseudo-Christianity 'doeth great wonders, so that he maketh fire come down from heaven on the earth in the sight of men, and deceiveth them that dwell on the earth.' All right, it is a figure. But tell me, since it matches the test of who was God in the Old Testament, a figure of what?

And in all earnestness let me plainly ask you in turn, Think you that it is possible for you yourself to be deceived? And if I am asked also, I answer, Yes, O yes, I am utterly helpless and vulnerable: therefore I must have the solid certainty of his holy word alone, and a clear, tested, and tried witness of his interior teaching of it. As I write this at half past three in the morning, reader, alone in my closet with an open Bible, I tell you of a truth — for all my personal worthlessness — I would not declare these things had I not got them alone from my God for the purpose.

However, let me now come to the criteria for which the LORD does in fact look as veritable *sine qua non* in the day of judgment. There are two.

In view of the fact that this passage teaches that multitudes — perhaps the majority — of the religious are apparently deceived by their false standards and inaccurate suppositions, which, observe, the Son of God prophesies they will plead right up to and at the final day of judgment, how agonisingly important it is for us to grasp his own foretold criteria. Nothing, but nothing, is more important than this in the life of men or women.

And remark, if this be so of the religious, what of the occasional nominal 'C. of E.', or 'R. C.' or the 'worshippers' of 'other faiths' — as corrupt liars call it these days — or even worse, of the vast mass of irreligious and godless mankind? For if the righteous — that is, righteous in character; it is not what is imputed to them; it is what they, being justified, wrought out in themselves by the Spirit of

God: they *are* righteous — I say, if the righteous scarcely be saved, where shall the ungodly and the sinner appear?

How vital to our immortal destiny then, to observe these criteria told us beforehand by the Judge of all the earth. For the LORD shall judge his people. And, just here, he tells us by what rule.

The first criterion of Messiah's judgment is laid down: 'He that doeth the will of my Father which is in heaven.'

This is so agonisingly important, that it may, must, ever be before the face of all that hope to enter into the kingdom at the last day. Therefore I am bound to make this a separate heading:

☆ The first criterion of Messiah's judgment of his people.

'Not every one that saith unto me, Lord, Lord, shall enter into the kingdom of heaven; *but he that doeth the will of my Father which is in heaven.*'

That is the first and overwhelmingly significant criterion as to the judgment of Messiah concerning who are — as opposed to those who erroneously think themselves to be — his people. There is one other criterion, the morality of which springs from and hangs upon the first.

Therefore my duty here is to show precisely in what consists 'the will of my Father which is in heaven.' Having done this, immediately I must explain exactly how to do that will. Finally to exhort as many as I may possibly reach

— if it were possible, all mankind — actually to commence this grand essential and one thing needful, that they may not be found naked and disillusioned in that day.

The will of Christ's Father which is in heaven is not legal. It is not that he might be served according to law. Indeed, the Father never was and never could be known by or under the law, nor did the legal service ever become a reality in one single case, neither could the law open heaven. Therefore those who apply to law, 'moral' or otherwise, put their necks under an old yoke which 'neither our fathers nor we were able to bear'.

Consider: The name 'Father' was not revealed by law or under it. The law was given by Moses, but grace and truth came by Jesus Christ. That truth is this: '*I* will declare thy name unto my brethren.' And that name is as follows: Father.

Under law, moral, ceremonial, judicial, inwritten, inscribed, it maketh no odds, for there is no difference: law is law is law, and its parts *inevitably* connected and inextricably integrated. I say, under law, the name revealed was JEHOVAH and absolutely no other. The thing *seen* under that name was not the person revealed as JEHOVAH. The thing seen was a closed veil. The fact perceived was that JEHOVAH could never be seen. Moreover it was *on earth*. The Father is *in heaven*. Law can never open heaven.

And today, whenever men turn to look at the law, the veil falls: the earth comes in, and heaven is obscured. Even if they say — with complete inaccuracy — 'Father' to God, when in fact they are turning to him as JEHOVAH, the *fact* does not change. Once look at law, and the proper name is, JEHOVAH. What they will see in fact is sheer obscurity. And what they will learn is resentment, failure, wrath, weariness, sin, earthliness, and at the last either desperation or self-righteousness.

The Father is revealed by the Son alone. This revelation of the Father is utterly, but utterly, apart from law. The only thing about the law seen in Christ, is that in him we are delivered from the legal curse, the law itself, its speech, its commandments, and its entire system of morality. This deliverance is seen in a five-scarred broken and crucified body, dead and buried in the tomb. Cursed be he that undoes this truth, whosoever he be, though an angel from heaven or an apostle from the dead. CHRIST HATH DELIVERED US FROM THE LAW. That is the foundation of the gospel way. It also brings in the revelation of the Father. This is how the Father is seen, heaven opened, and his heavenly will made known: In the Son.

The viewer must see no tables of stone, he must see no man, save Jesus only. The handler must handle no engraved granite, no carved commandments, he must 'handle *me*, and see that it is I myself.' The hearer must hear no other director of morality, neither Moses nor Elias, for 'This is my beloved Son: hear *him*.'

This is what was from the beginning of the faith in the New Testament. This was he whom the apostles heard; which they have seen with their eyes, which they have looked upon, and their hands have handled, of the Word of life: JESUS ONLY. Is he not morality enough for thee? Inanimate law, however right, is dead: it is you yourself that must draw from your own life to keep it. That is what the legalist opts for. But whom the Son chooses, has the Word of life within. He becomes his life. Does the Son of God need human law to tell him how to live divinely?

'For the life was manifested, and we have seen it, and bear witness, and show unto you that eternal life, which was with the Father, and was manifested unto us.'

Then what is the will of Messiah's Father which is in heaven? To honour the Son. 'That all men should honour the Son, even as they honour the Father. He that honoureth not the Son honoureth not the Father which hath sent him.' And no man ever yet honoured the Son, with one eye on Moses. No man can honour the Son, who turns to the law in any shape or form. To honour the Son, he must become to you absolutely and totally exclusive. That is the first and great criterion for 'doing the will of my Father which is in heaven.'

For example, Matthew 12:46-50. Jesus' 'mother and brethren stood without,' while he preached his gospel to those within. They sent someone in with this message: 'Behold, thy mother and thy brethren stand without, desiring to speak with thee.' Oh, yes? That is how to dishonour the Son.

Consider. 'His mother and brethren' called for him while he preached the gospel. They laid claim on his duty to the law — 'Honour thy father and thy mother' — to stop what he was doing for the Father and come to them. They appealed to his sense of obligation on the basis of natural relationships. They put him in an inferior position, to use his resources publicly to serve those relationships first. 'Come to us.'

Well, what were they doing standing outside? If somebody says, perhaps they could not get in, I answer, then let them get there earlier like everybody else. In any event, if over-crowding was the problem, I notice that this did not stop the four men with the litter upon which was a certain paralytic. Besides, if the mother and brethren could not get in, then how did the man manage whom they sent with the message? In any event, who are they that think to command Christ and his work? Let them not stand without and send for him. At the least, let them sit down and wait till he comes out, if his doctrine within is too strong for them.

Now, what they did then was certainly not 'the will of my Father which is in heaven'. They honoured their own nature, and attempted to use the Son to stop everything and demonstrate that before the people. But this would have humiliated and dishonoured the Son. They attempted — by standing without — to demonstrate their superiority over their need to listen to him and to his gospel. 'Suffer me first,' saith old Nature, and splutters the law to prove it. 'But he answered and said unto him that told him, Who is my mother? and who are my brethren?'

You see then, how the 'mother and brethren' in this case attempted to use the law to be more than the Father, in their claims upon the Son. He was about his Father's business. But they attempted to use their natural relationships and his legal obligation to them to make that more important than either the Father or his gospel. They tried to put the gospel under what was in fact an inferior obligation, a legal rule. However, neither they, nor their fathers, ever kept the pure spiritual precept of the law. All they did was to observe its exterior form to inward selfish purpose. Galatians precisely. How to dishonour both the Son and his Father.

Thy mother and brethren stand without? But certain sit within for all that. They too are called brethren. They too have a Father. Tell me, reader, are you 'within' where Christ serves the Father in perfect Sonship with his brethren? Or are you without, attempting to call him to serve your natural interests under the guise of legal obligations? If you will permit, I counsel you to do the will of your Father which is in heaven, and forthwith enter within. The others? Well, they have feet too, you know. But your feet are yours alone, given to take steps for God irrespective of any other person. Get within. Then you shall be shut in the interior of your soul with the Father and the Son, absolutely subject; entirely enrapt.

'And he stretched forth his hand toward his disciples, and said, Behold my mother and my brethren!
'For whosoever shall do the will of my Father which is in heaven, the same is my brother, and sister, and mother.'

Observe how much is here, by which we may honour the Son. The mother of Jesus was there: hence his virgin birth; real humanity, and impeccable manhood, are honoured. His Father is declared: 'my Father' he saith. Then his everlasting divine relationship in deity as the eternal Son with the Father is honoured, and if honoured on earth, then in the incarnation. But he is one personality: then in one person dwell two natures, one eternal, essential and divine, his from everlasting; the other human, created, and assumed into union in point of time, forever to be united to his divine nature in one person. Without a sight of this, and total continuous and active worship in consequence, the will of the Father in heaven is not done on earth at all. For without it, let none think that they honour the Son. If they pretend to honour, it is their imagination that they honour, not the reality.

Consider that the will of the Father is there fulfilled in

manhood. Disciples sit at the Son's feet and hear his word. And if so, then redeemed by precious blood, purchased through redemption, and brought nigh by grace. To honour the atonement, this is to honour the Son. And they are called 'my brethren'. Then the Holy Spirit of sonship is there, by whom the holy brethren are sanctified to do the will of the Father of Jesus Christ and of their Father.

Intellectuals may or may not discuss from without. However, contrary to that pharisaical ilk, brethren unite within. If so, there is a separation unto a union with the Father and the Son in one Spirit. One body, one Spirit, called in one hope of their calling. One Lord, one faith, one baptism. One God and Father of all, above all, through all, and in all. Oneness. And in heaven. Not law for man on earth. Divinity for sons in heaven. Heaven in sonship and sonship in heaven: what a union! It is all out of heaven from God. 'Coming down from God out of heaven.' And it is all in the Son. To see it, and get within, to do it: this is 'the will of my Father which is in heaven.' So much for Matthew 12:46-50.

However, I read that by two witnesses every matter is established. Then I give one more example of 'the will of my Father which is in heaven.'

John 5:30-31. 'I can of mine own self do nothing: as I hear, I judge: and my judgment is just; because I seek not mine own will, but the will of the Father which hath sent me.' Now here is the very essence of sonship. How contrary to the essential nature of the law. The law says, This do and thou shalt live. The life-giving Son cries, I can of mine own self do nothing. And none of these sophistries about 'this do — that is, do the righteousness of the law — by the Spirit,' which is unmitigated rubbish. The Spirit is not given by or for law, nor does the law require it. It is righteousness from *you*, unaided, that the law demands; that is what it is all about.

To the contrary however, consider the Son. What a difference! The perfect Man. Not like us who are filled with sin. He is perfect from the womb, filled with the Spirit, spotless in his life, impeccable in his humanity; and yet withal that: 'I can of mine own self do nothing.' Now, *that* is the will of your Father which is in heaven.

Consider these words. 'As I hear.' It is not, As I read. As I hear. Mine ears, saith he, hast thou bored. It is the Spirit to whom he refers. He that hath an ear, let him hear what the Spirit saith. Seven times — a perfect number — Jesus is recorded as praying in Luke. He prayed alone, from the calm, tranquil interior of the inward man. No human voices. No worldly clamour. No earthly distraction. The Spirit could speak to him. Always. 'As I hear.' This is the will of the Father: to hear the Spirit.

'I judge.' Here it is righteousness that is seen as the will of the Father which is in heaven. The word of the gospel brought in and applied in principle by the Spirit. This is essential to the faith, and is that without which it cannot exist. Today, there is abhorrence of such righteous judgment. Worldly tolerance and universal indulgence rule the professing church. But these things totally negate the faith. They are utterly against the will of the Father. Saith the Son, 'I judge.'

'And my judgment is just.' How? Why? 'Because I seek not mine own will, but the will of the Father which hath sent me.' When judging, it is for this sole cause. There is no other reason. It is exclusively to please the Father. Then without such judgment, the Father cannot be pleased, nor his will done.

Observe the process: how the Son judges. First, I can do nothing. Second, I hear. Third, I judge. This the disciples must follow, if they are to 'do the will of their Father which is in heaven.' Then, fourthly, note the character of that judgment: it is just. It is a judgment at once divine, heavenly, and active upon earth. It is the quality of sonship.

Now, I tell you plainly, 'The Father seeketh such' — it is plural — 'to worship him.' Such are separated from the world. United together. Filled with the Spirit. Inwardly in heaven. Obedient to the gospel. In union with the Son. Joined to the Father. And appreciative of sonship.

And I tell you faithfully: in that day, he will own them as his disciples.

☆ The second criterion of Messiah's judgment of his people.

This appears in verse twenty-three and is concluded from inference. 'And then will I profess unto them;' that is, to all who emptily professed his name. 'I never knew you;' though undoubtedly they claimed the most personal and intimate knowledge of him. Now comes the relevant sentence:

'Depart from me, ye that work iniquity.'

This, at the great day of judgment when time and the present world shall be no more.

The conclusion is inescapable. Whilst the present world continues; during whatever time remains; so long as heaven and earth shall last; now then, let those that seek the everlasting kingdom of God and his Christ *reverse* to themselves the terms on which he turns out the hypocrites at the last day.

Since the Lord condemns many in that day: 'Depart from me, ye that work iniquity,' then it follows of necessary inference that he cautions multitudes at the present time: 'Depart from iniquity, ye that work for me.' This is his sentence of discrimination. And if so, then it is the second criterion of judgment to be found in this momentous passage.

Therefore, until that day both the Son in heaven, and the Spirit from heaven, cry aloud on earth to those that claim 'Lord, Lord.' 'Depart from iniquity, ye that profess the Name.' And this the scripture also confirms as the absolute rule of righteousness for all those that confess the faith. This applies to every Christian and the whole of the professing church. 'Let every one that nameth the name of Christ depart from iniquity,' II Timothy 2:19. That is his seal, and he shall stand by it and enforce it in the day of judgment. This takes precedence over every claim, and none shall escape the ruling sentence. It is the criterion.

'Depart from me, ye that work iniquity.' Although the first time it is by no means the last that this imperative — or words to the same effect — is found upon the lips of the Lord Jesus. For that matter, neither is the expression original to the gospels. It occurs at least three times in one form or another in the Psalms. And — other than as an imperative — as counsel or exhortation the expression occurs on numerous occasions. So from the beginning of the world to the end of it, from the brink of eternity to the nethermost edge of time, whatever people can say that they were not warned?

'Depart from me, all ye workers of iniquity,' cries David in his song of remembrance to the Chief Musician on Neginoth upon Sheminith. 'For the LORD hath heard the voice of my weeping.' David wept whilst his persecutors laughed. But at length the LORD arises to judge David. Then the son of Jesse finds that his tears are had in remembrance, and so is the hypocrites' laughter. Hence the sentence: Woe unto you that laugh now! for ye shall mourn and weep. Blessed are ye that weep now! for ye shall laugh. David is aware by the Spirit of this impending sentence and hence he cries: 'Depart from me.'

And neither the hypocrite's empty profession nor his spectacular gifts can alter the judgment by one whit. For the Lord had been with his poor saints in the vale of tears, and there had heard the derision that was heaped upon the afflicted. Therefore in that day he that sitteth in the heavens shall laugh: the LORD shall have these workers of iniquity in derision. Now, we must bear it, even though the persecutors constantly prate 'Lord, Lord.' But vengeance is mine, saith the Lord. And avenge he shall: 'Depart from me, all ye workers of iniquity.'

So saith Christ three times over: 'Depart from me, ye that work iniquity' peals out at the last judgment, when the LORD judges not the world but his people. Judgment must begin at the house of God. Lord, Lord, they cry. I never knew you, he responds.

Again he saith at the great assize: Depart from me, ye cursed, into everlasting fire, prepared for the devil and his angels. And so departs forever that vast horde of professing Christians who so traduced the meaning of faith that they reduced it to an empty formula and left the true saints of their day hungry, thirsty, lonely, destitute, sick and imprisoned. Now, for all their evangelical talk in which they trusted, 'these shall go away into everlasting punishment: but the *righteous* into life eternal.'

Once again he forewarns us of that immutable criterion: 'I tell you, I know you not whence ye are; depart from me, all ye workers of iniquity.'

The Spirit agrees with this doctrine, saying in the psalmist: Depart from me, ye evildoers: for I will keep the commandments of my God, Psalm 119:115. The psalmist longed for perfect obedience, saw in the law of God and his commandments that which was holy, just and good, and with his whole heart applied himself to serve the LORD, saying 'I hate vain thoughts: but thy law do I love.' Not that righteousness came by the law, it did not, but still the law expressed it. In the gospel the righteous requirement of the law is fulfilled in us who walk not after the flesh but after the Spirit, with our eyes on the Son, and our pleasure the Father's will. Although not under the law, still, we can truly say — who thus seek perfection in righteousness, and approve that which is excellent — O how I love thy law! Then it follows: Depart from me, ye lawless!

Clearly the importance of this matter is incalculable. It behoves the Minister of the Word faithfully to show what is meant by Iniquity. To expound precisely what is entailed in Departure from it. Finally to exhort the hearers to pursue that vital spiritual action which actually achieves the end desired. Fear the Lord, and depart from evil, counsels the wise man; and again, A wise man feareth, and departeth from evil: but the fool rageth, and is confident. Once more: By mercy and truth iniquity is purged: and by the fear of the Lord men depart from evil.

'Let every one that nameth the name of Christ depart from iniquity.'

But what is iniquity precisely, that one may know clearly that from which it is imperative to depart?

The word used in Matthew 7:23 is ἀνομία, *anomia*. It occurs some fifteen times in the New Testament, being translated variously Transgression of the Law, Iniquity, Unrighteousness, and Transgress the Law. *Anomia* is a compound word made up of the prefix ἀ — and the form of the Greek word for Law — νόμος. The great idea in the word is 'Law': but it is entirely qualified by the preceding letter. The prefix ἀ expresses want or absence. It is not a negative, or indicative of being against the idea expressed — in this case law — it indicates a void: law is just not there: it is entirely wanting.

Anomia is not at all 'the transgression of the law'. It is *lawlessness*. It is the contemptuous dismissal of the whole idea of law, bounds, or restraint. The notion of restriction or discipline is flaunted. Lawlessness. The rule of law is treated as non-existent: as if God had given no prescription for human conduct. Those who thus live, move and have their being with such an attitude are called 'workers of iniquity'. The word is nothing to do with what people profess to believe: it is a word entirely to do with how they live and what their moral attitude is in respect of divinely prescribed rules of conduct.

This lawless attitude may be found under the strictest

outward profession of law and legality: 'Woe unto you, scribes and Pharisees, hypocrites! for ye are like unto whited sepulchres, which indeed appear beautiful outward, but are within full of dead bones, and of all uncleanness. Even so ye also outwardly appear righteous unto men, but *within* ye are full of hypocrisy and 'iniquity': *anomia, lawlessness.'* So ye see that it is inward: a matter of the heart.

This lawless attitude may be there under the brightest profession of faith, confession of Christ, and persuasion of evangelicalism. 'Lord, Lord!' cry the lawless. At the day of judgment the Son of man shall send forth his angels, and they shall gather *out of his kingdom* all things that offend, and them which do 'iniquity': *anomia, lawlessness.* So then, they were in his kingdom. And — although the word is different the principle is the same — the imperative 'Let every one that nameth the name of Christ depart from iniquity,' implies the naming before the departing for the exhortation to have force. And so Paul warns the Corinthian church that the unrighteous — whatever their profession — shall not inherit the kingdom of God, I Corinthians 6:9.

Of course they will not! Our Saviour Jesus Christ gave himself for us that he might *redeem* us from all 'iniquity': *anomia, lawlessness.* He did not give himself for us that we might safely continue in iniquity: or even in some righteousness and some iniquity. He gave himself for us that he might redeem us from *all* iniquity. Therefore the only final proof that we are those for whom he gave himself, as we profess, is that we are also those whom he actually delivers with a full, present salvation. That is seen as the distinguishing mark of those for whom he died, Titus 2:14. Jesus Christ does not save his people *in* their sins. He saves his people *from* their sins.

So then, either law or gospel can exist as an exterior profession consistent with making void the law, or working lawlessness, as an interior state of heart. For all the outward forms, restraints, obligation, and strictures of religion one can yet remain lawless — without law — as to the inner man. Where law, in whatever form, is flaunted, the mental state is one of lawlessness. Now, that is sin. It is both wilful and responsible, even if the doer is found wilfully ignorant. Deliberately the sinner ignores, thrusts from him, to himself annihilates, God's holy law. It is flagrant. This is lawless. It is the essence of sin. *Anomia* is the condition and attitude of the sinner when sinning in relation to law: wilful contempt and deliberate ignorance. This is to do lawlessness. To be a 'worker of iniquity'.

How many continually abuse forgiveness, constantly misuse the gospel, as an excuse to set law or restraint at naught? How many? All the workers of iniquity. To them, law is not there, or if it were, they cannot abide hearing of it. To them there is no law, whatever Christ and his apostles may say. Thus they dismiss law in the sense that their mind and heart, their mentality, voids it. It is defied, dismissed, so as the worker of iniquity acts irrespective of its existence, or of conscience bearing witness to its rule: they make themselves without law. They do what they like. And both law and gospel condemn their iniquity. But the saints will have none of this, for the righteousness of the law is fulfilled in us who walk not after the flesh but after the Spirit. And wherefore? Because our Saviour Jesus Christ hath redeemed us from all iniquity.

So then, the best translation — the most literal — of *anomia* is Lawlessness. A careful summary of the New Testament usage of this word shows that it may (a) characterise an act (b) indicate a state (c) describe an attitude, or (d) signify a condition. But in every case, the shade of meaning is set against the consistent background of ignoring law as if it did not exist: making void the law. This is a characteristic of the last days. So many professing Christians, would-be preachers, legalists, evangelicals, do what *they* like: as if there *were* no Spirit of God to rule the church in Christ's absence!

It is this from which we are to depart. Those who will not part from this in the present life must part from Christ in the life to come. No matter what they believed or professed, no matter how they cry Lord, Lord: in that day he will say of a certainty, Depart from me, ye that work iniquity.

Then how vital and paramount a criterion it must be to reverse the judgment sentence each one to ourselves, so that instead of 'Depart from me' then, it is 'Depart from iniquity' now.

But precisely what is meant by 'Depart'?

From what, and how, should Christians depart, that the Lord shall not say to them in that day, 'Depart from me'?

They should depart from going on with the form of religion, the shell of the church, the profession of the creed, the words of evangelism, the empty confession of Christ, when God and his glory do not fill the House. Instead they should fall on their faces and cry out after God in the closet with brokenness of heart. Otherwise they become like Samson who 'wist not that the LORD was departed from him', and like Saul when it was said, 'The Spirit of the LORD departed from Saul.' And like the House of God when ICHABOD — The glory is departed — was written over its doors. Dead Christians and dead churches ought to take heed in their departing from the living God, for their carcasses shall surely fall in the wilderness of eternity except they repent. They may start up with indignation in the resurrection at finding themselves amongst the goats, crying 'Lord, Lord,' but he shall say, Depart from me, I know not whence ye are.

They should depart from the practice of sinning. Whosoever abideth in him sinneth not: whosoever sinneth hath not seen him, neither known him. The truth is, that whosoever is born of God doth not commit sin. If these people do commit sin, then of whom are they born? I will tell you: Little children, let no man deceive you: he that doeth righteousness is righteous, even as he is righteous. He that committeth sin is of the devil; for the devil sinneth from the beginning. In this the children of God are manifest, and the children of the devil: whosoever doeth not righteousness is not of God. But how the hirelings howl against the true ministers of righteousness for saying this! Then whose part are they taking? Let them beware: Depart from iniquity, or, Depart from me, saith the LORD.

They should depart from the world, worldliness, worldly fashion, and worldly entertainment. Many who start well in this matter afterwards end by doing the very opposite. They are like Demas, who 'having loved this present world is departed.' But saith the apostle, Love not the world, neither the things that are in the world. If any man love the world, the love of the Father is not in him. And then where are you? But many of these things are legitimate, say some? I say to you, *all* that is in the world, the lust of the flesh, the lust of the eyes, and the pride of life, is not of the Father, but is of the world. Hence the Spirit saith, and withal there sounds a voice from heaven saying, Come out of her, my people, that ye be not partakers of her sins, and that ye receive not of her plagues. Indeed, Depart from iniquity! Perfect holiness in the fear of God, lest it be said at the last, Depart from me, ye workers of iniquity.

They should separate, or depart, from unholy alliances. Be ye not unequally yoked together with unbelievers. And yet for example the Baptist Union is a united organisation of modernistic — or unbelieving; it is the same thing, they disbelieve fundamental truths — and believing ministers and congregations. With the preponderance on the side of the modernists. Is such an alliance safe? And the same thing is even more true of the evangelical Anglicans subsisting in an unholy clerical and ecclesiastical alliance with a far greater majority of neo-papists, modernists, liberals, opportunists, pseudo-political commentators, pleaders for vice and sodomy, and I know not what else. But what communion hath light with darkness? What fellowship hath righteousness with unrighteousness? And is this not true of Presbyterians, Methodists, and of many others? Wherefore — let ministers, congregations, and, if they will not, then individuals — come out from among them, and be separate, saith the Lord, and touch not the unclean; and I will receive you, and will be a Father to you. Otherwise, what risks do you take? Better to eat, drink and be merry, for tomorrow ye die. One or the other. This half-heartedness is inexplicable in the light of judgment criteria.

Christians should separate from erroneous, superficial, uncalled and unsent ministers and clergy. They are called vessels unto dishonour. To be joined to them or to sit under their ministry, is distinctly referred to as lawlessness against Christ. But shun profane and vain babblings: for they will increase unto more ungodliness. And their word will eat as doth a canker: of whom is Hymenæus and

Philetus — you who accuse us, see how Paul names them! — who concerning the truth have erred, saying that the resurrection is past already; and overthrow the faith of some. Nevertheless the foundation of God standeth sure, having this seal, The Lord knoweth them that are his. And, Let every one that nameth the name of Christ depart from iniquity.

What iniquity is this in context? That of Hymenæus and Philetus and all of that vile pulpit-grasping brood ever since. For, In a great house — such as the profession of Christianity has become — there are not only vessels of gold and silver, such as Paul and Timothy, but also of wood and earth, such as Alexander and Diotrephes. Well, let a man purge himself from these. Let him exercise the judgment that evangelicalism forbids! Then he himself shall be a vessel unto honour, sanctified, and meet for the master's use, and prepared unto every good work. Depart, then, depart the iniquity of an unsent, chaffy, superficial, wordy and erroneous ministry. Depart ye, depart ye, touch not the unclean thing, saith your God.

Christians should separate from false doctrine and dry creeds, uniting into the spiritual and apostolic doctrine of Christ. Christians should separate from man-imposed church government, or no church government at all, uniting into the apostles' fellowship and whatever may be the holy order raised up of the Spirit in any given locality. Christians should separate from lawless and unsanctified forms of worship, either that limited to men's imposition or the other kind degenerated into human dissolution. They should come together in the Holy Ghost, being led by those qualified and gifted to do so amongst the saints.

Christians should separate from corrupted ordinances

and sacramentalism, coming together to pray for God to raise up his holy word, send them preachers from Christ and from heaven, so to ordain all those ordinances suited to the church of the living God, the pillar and ground of the truth; having a proper distinction between male and female, young and old, one and another. For God is not the author of confusion, but of peace, as in all churches of the saints, saith the holy apostle in this his divine authority. Wherefore, beware of men, and hear Christ, the meanwhile watching narrowly for his true sent ministers and judging withal that ye may profit under the hand of the Lord.

Now let us hear the sum of the matter. Depart ye, depart ye, go ye out from thence, touch no unclean; go ye out of the midst of her; be ye clean, that bear the vessels of the LORD. In a word, Let every one that nameth the name of Christ depart from iniquity. They that do this, agree with the second criterion of the LORD'S judgment, and shall not see death, but have passed from death unto life. They shall never hear the words, Depart from me, ye workers of iniquity. What they will hear is this: Come, ye blessed of my Father, inherit the kingdom prepared for you from the foundation of the world.

Thus it is that beforehand — Matthew 7:21-23 — the LORD solemnly warns all who are ever to name his name; all who shall ever call him LORD; every generation of the entire professing church; the total number that shall ever be called Christians: I say, he warns all beforehand just what it is at the Last Day in the resurrection from the dead that he shall call into question and require as his criteria.

What consequences such a warning should call forth!

No wonder the final words of the LORD Jesus in this exposition of the doctrine of the Kingdom commence with 'Therefore', verse twenty-four. After so momentous a statement, the weightiness of the truth hangs pregnant with demand for the delivery of a consequent application: 'Therefore'.

Now at the last Messiah comes to the conclusion of his doctrine, Matthew 7:24-27

> Therefore whosoever heareth these sayings
> of mine, and doeth them, I will liken him
> unto a wise man, which built his house upon
> a rock:
> And the rain descended, and the floods came,
> and the winds blew, and beat upon that
> house; and it fell not: for it was founded
> upon a rock.
> And every one that heareth these sayings of
> mine, and doeth them not, shall be likened
> unto a foolish man, which built his house
> upon the sand:
> And the rain descended, and the floods came,
> and the winds blew, and beat upon that
> house; and it fell: and great was the fall of it.

As with the wise and foolish virgins making up the complete profession of the faith, so here the wise and foolish builders constitute the total number of hearers of the word of the Lord Jesus, and believers of the same. The difference lies in the doing. But who would think so, to hear the dumb dogs that cannot bark, the watchmen without a warning, the petty clerks who force themselves into the 'ministry' today? All they can do is prate 'once saved always saved' and lull the people to sleep by overturning the truth of the cross into a system of false security that effectively robs these last words of the Lord Jesus of any real consequence. Well, of that, none can accuse me. I have not handled the word of God deceitfully. In the fear and presence of God, I have told you the truth.

Here are two builders. The judgment of one is wise. The other is a fool. Nevertheless they have certain things in common. To the superficial onlooker, they have everything in common: except perhaps that the one whom the majority would pick out as the best does his work much, much quicker and with earlier results.

Otherwise, on the surface, they are exactly the same. But the difference between wisdom and folly in the ministry, the Christian, and the church does not appear on the surface. That is what fools neither admit nor look for. The difference between the two buildings lies entirely underground. Unseen. In secret. This takes discernment, but not so much that it is not pretty obvious once you really start to look for it. Look at the foundations. And then look further. *

Notice what is in common between the two buildings. Both men are builders. Both men dig down. Both men lay foundations. Both men build identical houses with just the same materials. Both men's houses stand complete and indistinguishable once the work is concluded; there is no visible difference. Both houses stand for some time. Both

* See 'Foundations Uncovered'. John Metcalfe Publishing Trust.

men's houses are then at length assaulted with the same storm from heaven, the same rain, the same floods, the same wind, the same beating of the same tempest. Alike the rain descended, the floods came, the winds blew, and the whole beat upon the two houses, which in common sheltered their respective inhabitants who had reared them up against just this commonly foreseen contingency.

Only now is the difference revealed, which only before the beginning was discriminated. One house stood the test of time and the rage of the storm because it was founded upon a rock. Here is wisdom. The other house was exposed by the test of time and the sandy bottom washed away as the building collapsed before the rage of the storm, bringing ruin down upon its inhabitants. This is folly.

What was the difference?

The foundations?

Not the foundations. There is no ground for supposing that they were not identical.

The difference lay in where and into what the foundations were dug. Not the foundations but where on earth they were going to be laid: that is, into what substance. This goes much deeper than foundations, and existed before they were laid. Before ever the work commences it is a question of choice as to where to build: Where the rock is? Or where the sand? There is no question as to which is easiest.

So maybe the attitude of the builder to laziness before commencing any work at all, made the difference. And perhaps lack of prudence and foresight. Or just risking things and trusting God that there would not be a storm of the severity needed to undo all his good work. Such builders feel themselves to be special, and that somehow the rules won't apply to them. They make their own rules, and expect God to conform: the word for this is *'anomia'*.

They were like it, really, right from the start. Their 'Christianity' never touched this treacherous, 'sandy', heart of theirs: it was laid on top of it. From the beginning they never provided a vessel for oil as well as a lamp with oil: no, oil in the lamp was good enough for them, brother, like everybody else; and there were plenty more like them to lend encouragement, too.

Such quick workers never prepared the ground before the Sower sowed the seed. The seed of the word is good enough for them, brother! What's with all this prior digging, uprooting, stone-lifting, rock-breaking, ploughing and harrowing *before* the Son of man sows the word? Nonsense, they cry.

Foundations are good enough, they tell us. Of course, we are reformed, we are *petit* Calvinists (not *too* much, you know), we have a foundation, that is enough. But pray, do you not think the ground rather soft? Is that of no consequence then? Just foundations, is it? Just doctrine? Just hearing? Just 'believing'? Then tell me what this means: 'His foundation is in the holy mountains,' Psalm 87:1. Is theirs? And, reader, is yours?

God's foundation is in the holy mountains. Here are four things. The mountains. Holiness. The rock of which the holy mountains are composed. Finally, the painful, slow, and arduous labour of breaking, chipping and digging into that rock so as eventually to lay the actual foundation itself. That, as a whole, is called *God's* foundation and the psalm goes on to describe it. This is that to which Christ directs us here:

'A wise man, which built his house
upon a rock.'

Rock; the substance of mountains. Holy mountains; ensuring that the work is of God and not man, deeply inward and not superficial, for God and not self. Foundations; what was laid at the beginning, before the building. And for the interpretation of that in this place, I refer the reader to the beatitudes, before the Sermon proper commenced. That is the experience of laying the foundation in the rock.

On the basis of that sound grounding, which answers to the beatitudes being wrought — heard and 'done' — within the soul at the very beginning, the unshakeable edifice is raised up. The principle is expanded therefore to include the whole Sermon on the Mount: 'Hearing these sayings of mine and doing them.'

It is not, I repeat not, a question of doctrine or creed. That is taken for granted. It is a question of what professed faith produces. Does it work by love and produce humble obedience actually resulting in the hearing and doing of these sayings of Jesus in the Sermon on the Mount? If not, it is spurious, and the soul lawless. Then, at the last it shall be said, 'And it fell: and great was the fall of it.'

Wherefore the Holy Ghost saith, Today if ye will hear his voice — not read his word merely, mind; many get no further than that: but this is inwardly in heart to hear the Spirit's voice — harden not your hearts. Observe the cause of this exhortation: Wherefore. Wherefore? Because multitudes that came out of Egypt, kept the passover, ate of the lamb, passed under the sprinkled blood, were baptised in the Red Sea, afterwards perished in the wilderness. Their carcasses fell. Because they heard not the word? By no means; for they did hear it. Why then? Because of unbelief they afterwards perished. They might well pick and choose in his word: but the living voice from heaven spoke the whole, and spake it pertinently. He could never be contained within their paltry and limited outward creed.

However, as the stiffnecked and uncircumcised in heart and ears resisted the Holy Ghost speaking in Stephen's day and crying to their hearts, so the children of Israel would not hear the living voice of the Son of God, though they professed the scriptures. And today, to this generation, it is said: Harden not *your* hearts! But it is a generation very like to the Jews of old. Nevertheless, the word of the Lord still sounds from heaven, the Spirit still speaks to the churches, and surely there is still a faithful remnant according to the election of grace who 'Hear these sayings of mine, and do them.' Of them it shall be said, 'And it fell not: for it was founded upon a rock.'

Now then, I call to you, beseeching you by Jesus Christ: Be ye doers of the word, and not hearers only, deceiving your own selves, as multitudes do this day. In the Name of him who hath sent me to declare and write this unto you, I cry, 'Awake thou that sleepest, and arise from the dead, and Christ shall give thee light!' And again he saith to this untoward and worldly generation, Repent ye! Awake to righteousness, and sin not; for some have not the knowledge of God, though doubtless they cry oft 'Lord, Lord.' Well, I tell you plainly, Except ye repent, ye shall all likewise perish, whosoever ye be: for God respecteth no man's person.

'Let every one that nameth the name of Christ depart from iniquity ...

'... but follow righteousness, faith, charity, peace, with them that call on the Lord out of a pure heart.' Amen.

Finally we have the reaction to Messiah's doctrine of the Kingdom. And whensoever Christ speaks from heaven by his sent ministers, to the end of time, the result will ever be the same:

> And it came to pass, when Jesus had ended
> these sayings, the people were astonished at
> his doctrine:
> For he taught them as one having authority,
> and not as the scribes.

● ● ●

CURRENT BOOKLIST

Obtainable from the publishers

TITLES:

NOAH AND THE FLOOD   *new series*   *£1.20*

"Mr. Metcalfe makes a skilful use of persuasive eloquence as he challenges the reality of one's profession of faith ... he gives a rousing call to a searching self-examination and evaluation of one's spiritual experience."

The Monthly Record of the Free Church of Scotland.

"In an age which claims to put the practical accent on Christian interpretation of scripture, it is refreshing to go back and look at the spiritual meaning in the Bible. We need some forceful reminder that refuge may be found in the Ark."

The Catholic Fireside.

"Noah and the Flood is an excellent exposition of the story of Noah found in Genesis chapters 6-9. No one reading this book can fail to be stirred by the author's challenging and heart-searching exposition."

Dr. A. J. Monty White.

"Many will appreciate the original thought and clarity of expression and the application to the individual today."

Dr. F. Tatford (Prophetic Witness).

Do read this timely book!

Published by the John Metcalfe Publishing Trust. Price £1.20 excluding post and packing.
From your local bookseller, the publisher or
Tylers Green Chapel,
Tylers Green,
Buckinghamshire

ISBN 0950251577 NEWLY PUBLISHED IN 1976

A TREMENDOUS MESSAGE

Noah and the Flood expounds with vital urgency the man and the message that heralded the end of the old world. The description of the flood itself is vividly realistic. The whole work has an unmistakable ring of authority, and speaks as "Thus saith the Lord".

DIVINE FOOTSTEPS

40p

Divine Footsteps traces the pathway of the feet of the Lord the Son of man from the very beginning in the prophetic figures of the true in the Old Testament through the reality in the New; doing so in a way of experimental spirituality. At the last a glimpse of the coming glory is beheld as his feet are viewed as standing at the latter day upon the earth.

"Originality of thought and approach is apparent."

The Expository Times.

THE RED HEIFER

new series 75p

This book has been edited from a powerful sermon preached by John Metcalfe in Tylers Green Chapel. The verbal directness makes the book very readable and simple to understand.

The Red Heifer was the name given to a sacrifice used by the children of Israel in the Old Testament — as recorded in Numbers chapter 19 — in which a heifer was slain and burned. Cedar wood, hyssop and scarlet were cast into the burning, and the ashes were mingled with running water and put in a vessel. It was kept for the children of Israel for a water of separation: it was a purification for sin.

In this unusual book the sacrifice is brought up to date and its relevance to the church today is shown.

THE WELLS OF SALVATION   *new series*   *£1.50*

The Wells of Salvation is written from a series of
seven powerful addresses preached at Tylers Green
Chapel. It is a forthright and experimental exposition
of Isaiah 12:3, 'Therefore with joy shall ye draw
water out of the wells of salvation.'

We quote:

John Metcalfe, acknowledged to be 'perhaps the most
gifted expositor and powerful preacher of our day'
nonetheless possesses a controversial challenge in his
ministry which presses home long-ignored issues in a
way 'which cannot be ignored'.

This is to be seen clearly in The Wells of Salvation,
in and of itself a unique and richly rewarding study
worthy of the reader's careful attention.

"Among truly great Christian works."

Methodist review.

"Outstanding."

The English Churchman.

"Impressive."

The Life of Faith.

TRACTS:

The Two Prayers of Elijah . . . .

'Tract for the Times' series:

1. The Gospel of God . . . .

2. The Strait Gate . . . .

3. Eternal Sonship and Taylor Brethren . . .

THE TWO PRAYERS OF ELIJAH   *10p*

This tract, first printed in 1972, was reprinted in 1975.
It shows the spiritual significance of the drought, the
cloudburst, and the two prayers of Elijah.

THE GOSPEL OF GOD   *stiff cover, 25p*
Tract for the Times 1

Beautifully designed, this tract positively describes the
gospel under the following headings: The Gospel is of God;
The Gospel is Entirely of God; The Gospel is Entire in
Itself; The Gospel is Preached; The Gospel Imparts Christ;
and, Nothing But the Gospel Imparts Christ. The last two
headings also expose the recent moves to undermine the
truth that Christ is conveyed simply through the gospel.

"It takes the discernment of an utterly fearless man like
John Metcalfe to tear the mask off the moves that are
taking place in the high circles of the church today. Here
are 48 pages of verbal dynamite exposing the way in which
the evangelical faith is being undermined by the statements
of the Anglican-Roman Catholic Commission in its
pronouncements concerning the meaning of the eucharist,
the priestly and sacrificial character of the ministry, and
papal authority."

From the comment of a Methodist minister.

THE STRAIT GATE   *stiff cover, 25p*
Tract for the Times 2

Exceptionally well made, this booklet consists of extracts
from 'The Messiah', compiled in such a way as to challenge
the shallowness of much of today's 'easy-believism', whilst
positively pointing to the strait gate.

STOP PRESS ANNOUNCEMENT

Eternal Sonship and Taylor Brethren
Tract for the Times No. 3
Price 25p

has now been published,

45 pages, with special stiff gloss finished cover featured in
this high quality series.

This booklet is highly recommended, particularly for those
perplexed by James Taylor's teaching against the eternal
sonship of Christ.

This teaching impugnes the doctrine of J.N. Darby and his
colleagues, denies the teaching of the Reformation, and
refuses the orthodox preaching of the person of Christ
throughout the ages. Besides this it recants upon the earlier
ministry of Taylor himself. Above all, James Taylor's latter
teaching against the eternal sonship of Christ contradicts
the faith once delivered to the saints, and defies the
apostles' doctrine, denying what has always been held
about the eternity of Father, Son and Holy Ghost.

In a day when the term 'believer' is used so lightly that the
vast majority think of it as barely related to *what* one
believes — although in fact what one believes gives the only
true title to the term 'believer' — this Tract for the Times
thoroughly searches out truth from error, the believer from
the infidel, the true Christ from the false, and leaves the
reader in no doubt whatsoever as to the issue.

'APOSTOLIC FOUNDATION
OF THE CHRISTIAN CHURCH':

FOUNDATIONS UNCOVERED   *30p*

Volume 1

Foundations Uncovered is a small book of some
37 pages. This is the Introduction to the major
series: 'The Apostolic Foundation of the Christian
Church'.

Rich in truth, the Introduction deals comprehensively
with the foundation of the apostolic faith under the
descriptive titles: The Word, The Doctrine, The
Truth, The Gospel, The Faith, The New Testament,
and The Foundation.

The contents of the book reveal: The Fact of the
Foundation; The Foundation Uncovered; What the
Foundation is not; How the Foundation is Described;
and, Being Built upon the Foundation.

Our reviewer states:

"This book comes with the freshness of a new
Reformation.

"In this Introduction, the author sets out the
exhaustive method of arriving at the knowledge of
the apostolic doctrine of the Christian faith.

"He outlines that objective body of truth which sets
forth the Son of God, and which is the only valid
foundation on which the church is built."

THE BIRTH OF JESUS CHRIST   *new series*   *95p*
Volume 2

"The author expresses with great clarity the truths revealed to him in his study of holy scripture at depth. We are presented here with a totally lofty view of the Incarnation.

"This is a fascinating and enlightening study. The author's examination of Biblical material is the reverent approach of someone who recognises the living quality of God's Word, and who waits to be instructed from it without pre-determining his own attitude.

"The very spirit of adoration and worship rings through these pages. In this new section of his work 'The Apostolic Foundation of the Christian Church', there is again indication that John Metcalfe is to be classed amongst the foremost expositors of our age; and although the value of his contribution to Christian thought may not yet be acclaimed, his writings have about them that quality of timelessness that makes me sure they will one day take their place among the heritage of truly great Christian works."

From a review by Rev. David Catterson.

"A book to be studied ... an outstanding contribution."

The English Churchman.

"Uncompromisingly faithful to scripture ... has much to offer which is worth serious consideration ... deeply moving."

The Expository Times.

"A thoroughly orthodox outlook ... impressive."

The Life of Faith.

THE MESSIAH

new series £2.45

Volume 3

"This is no ordinary book. It is extraordinary, judged by the standards of godly doctrine in any age, and especially so when compared to the comparative impoverishment of the modern pulpit and pen. I firmly believe that it will be treasured as a spiritual classic by people not yet born.

"It draws out the inwardness of the beatitudes in a truly experimental way. It faithfully warns of judgment to come; with alarming descriptions of the Great Day. Law and gospel are distinguished, yet both honoured. Outstanding are the passages dealing with the threefold temptation of Jesus; and the Baptist's threefold description of the Messiah's work. What glorious light breaks out of the saying, 'Suffer it to be so now: for thus it becometh us to fulfil all righteousness.'

"It bears throughout the stamp of true ministry, raised up of GOD, not in letter but touching the spirit, bearing life. It comes from one who has been on his face, eaten the roll, and spoken only after sitting down seven days, (Ezekiel ch. 3) and the LORD'S people, whether they will hear or whether they will forbear (for they are a rebellious people) yet shall know that there hath been a prophet among them."

David Hughes, B.Sc., M.B., Ch.B.

"Its author is clearly a great lover of the Bible."

Maurice Nassan S.J., Catholic Herald.

"Something of the fire of the ancient Hebrew prophet ... Metcalfe has spiritual and expository potentials of a high order."

The Life of Faith.

The Son of God and Seed of David

Vol. 4 in the work entitled
The Apostolic Foundation
of the Christian Church.

250 pages

Hand-made
in England.

£1.10

from your bookseller
or
the Publishing Trust at
Tylers Green Chapel, Tylers Green
Penn, Buckinghamshire, England

'DOCTRINE ON FIRE'

'The Son of God and Seed of David'
by John Metcalfe

A Review by Dr. David Hughes

As with the earlier volumes, the reader feels that this man has kept company with Christ and his holy apostles, and is sent directly to our age to expose the glaring disparity between modern Christianity and theirs, to root out and to pull down, to destroy and to throw down, thenceforward to build up and to plant.

The author, opening and alleging that Jesus Christ is and ever was THE SON OF GOD, brings proof after proof and furnishes scripture upon scripture, with overwhelming effect. Who can withstand this avalanche of undeniable evidence? This greatest of subjects, this most profound of all mysteries, is handled with reverence and outstanding perception.

From plumbing such depths, the book turns to the consideration of THE SEED OF DAVID. A wealth of divine enlightenment appears. Reaching to magnificence, we now behold David the man, David the heir, and David the king. This flows, page after page, seraphic and sublime. Passages soar in eloquence; heights are scaled as the truth is unfolded with piercing clarity.

Finally, as the majesty of Christ is revealed, a crescendo is reached and it appears just how near the last Day we are, as the fast-moving events of the twentieth century are prophetically and penetratingly analysed.

On laying down 'The Son of God and Seed of David' one reaches this inescapable conclusion: Here is doctrine on fire.

David Hughes, B.Sc., M.B., Ch.B.

ORDER FORM:

(see overleaf)

INCREASED PRICES

When first the Trust was raised up, we printed and bound all our own books, passing on to the public little more than the cost of paper and ink. Freely we had received, freely we gave.

Now it has pleased God so to bless this work that no longer are we able to meet the demands for our books by the small and laborious hand-processing with which we began the work.

Therefore, having sold out of most of our stocks, we are obliged to fulfil present and future orders by having our books made by the up-to-date methods of professional printers elsewhere, and hence the considerable price rise.

Our principles however remain the same: not only are these reprinted titles passed on to the public at less than cost, but all of us at the Trust give you our services without money and without price. As always, there are no royalties or publisher's costs relayed to the public by the John Metcalfe Publishing Trust.

Why not? Because we seek our own benefit? God knoweth, we seek not our own, not yours but you, that you may be blessed from God the Father by Jesus Christ our Lord, in the free knowledge of the gospel of the grace of God.

'Thanks be unto God for his unspeakable gift.'

ORDER FORM

			Quantity
Noah and the Flood £1.20	+	*21p*	☐
Divine Footsteps 40p	+	*14p*	☐
The Red Heifer 75p	+	*14p*	☐
The Wells of Salvation £1.50	+	*29p*	☐
The Two Prayers of Elijah 10p	+	*8p*	☐
The Gospel of God 25p	+	*11p*	☐
The Strait Gate 25p	+	*11p*	☐
Eternal Sonship and Taylor Brethren . . 25p	+	*11p*	☐
Foundations Uncovered 30p	+	*14p*	☐
The Birth of Jesus Christ 95p	+	*21p*	☐
The Messiah £2.45	+	*60p*	☐
The Son of God and Seed of David . £1.10	+	*37p*	☐

(Figures in italics show postage & packing) *

NAME AND ADDRESS (in block capitals)

_____

_____

_____

Enclose remittance with order.
Cheques payable to 'The Publishing Trust'.

* *Postage costs are correct at time of going to press, and apply to the U.K. only.*

cut here